Ethical Approaches to Physical Interventions

Volume II. Changing the agenda

Edited by David Allen

Consultant Clinical Pyschologist,
Abertawe Bro Morgannwg University NHS Trust and
Professor in the Clinical Psychology of Intellectual Disabilities
at the Welsh Centre for Learning Disabilities, Cardiff University

British Library Cataloguing in Publication Data

A CIP record for this book is available from the Public Library

© BILD Publications 2009

BILD Publications is the imprint of:
British Institute of Learning Disabilities
Campion House
Green Street
Kidderminster
Worcs
DY10 1JL

Telephone: 01562 723010
Fax: 01562 723029
E-mail: enquiries@bild.org.uk
Website: www.bild.org.uk

ISBN 978 1 905218 11 0

Printed in the UK by Latimer Trend and Company Ltd, Plymouth

BILD Publications are distributed by:
BookSource
50 Cambuslang Road
Cambuslang
Glasgow G32 8NB
Telephone: 0845 370 0067
Fax: 0845 370 0064

For a publications catalogue with details of all BILD books and journals telephone 01562 723010, e-mail enquiries@bild.org.uk or visit the BILD website www.bild.org.uk

The British Institute of Learning Disabilities is committed to improving the quality of life for people with a learning disability by involving them and their families in all aspects of our work, working with government and public bodies to achieve full citizenship, undertaking beneficial research and development projects and helping service providers to develop and share good practice.

CONTENTS

EDITOR

Professor David Allen

David Allen is Consultant Clinical Psychologist and Head of Specialist Services for Abertawe Bro Morgannwg University NHS Trust and Professor in the Clinical Psychology of Intellectual Disabilities at the Welsh Centre for Learning Disabilities, Cardiff University. He is a fellow of both the International Association for the Scientific Study of Intellectual Disabilities (IASSID) and the British Psychological Society. He is also co-chair of the Challenging Behaviour and Mental Health Special Interest Research Group of IASSID, Chair of the Challenging Behaviour and Mental Health Research Advisory Group of the Learning Disability and Autism Research Network for Wales, and a member of the Welsh Assembly Government's Learning Disability Advisory Implementation Group.

Special Projects Team
Unit 3
Cowbridge Court
58–62 Cowbridge Road West
Cardiff
CF5 5BS

CONTRIBUTORS

Dr Peter Baker

Peter Baker is a Consultant Clinical Psychologist working for Sussex Partnership NHS Foundation Trust with a clinical leadership role for challenging behaviour services. He is also an Honorary Senior Lecturer at the Tizard Centre, University of Kent.

Gambier House
West Hill Rd
St Leonards on Sea
E Sussex
TN38 0NG

Patrick Bradley

After training as a Registered Nurse for people with learning disabilities, Patrick Bradley began working in a community project that facilitated the family placement of adolescents with a learning disability. As a Community Learning Disability Charge Nurse, he worked predominantly with service users with challenging behaviour and profound multiple impairment until moving into nurse education in 1998. He studied for first and post-graduate degrees in Education and Applied Social Research at University of Stirling, where he is now a Teaching Fellow and Programme Lead for the Common Foundation Programme. His major interests lie in the area of therapeutic responses to aggression and violence, the nursing care of individuals who challenge services and the informal care of people with learning disabilities.

Department of Nursing and Midwifery
University of Stirling
Stirling
FK9 4LA

Professor Shoumitro Deb

Shoumitro Deb is a Clinical Professor of Neuropsychiatry and Intellectual Disability at the University of Birmingham, UK. He has developed national and international clinical guides on the assessment and treatment of mental health and the use of psychotropic medications for the management of problem behaviours in adults with intellectual disabilities. His other clinical and research interests include epilepsy in people with intellectual disability, dementia in people with Down's syndrome, and advanced neuroimaging for patients with traumatic brain injury and apathy symptoms.

University of Birmingham Department of Psychiatry
The National Centre for Mental Health – Birmingham
The Barberry
25 Vincent Drive
Birmingham
B15 2FG

Dr Sarah Hawkins

Sarah Hawkins is a Consultant Specialist Clinical Psychologist who has worked with people with learning disabilities and challenging behaviour for the past seven years. Working within a specialist behavioural team, she provides intensive support to service users presenting with a wide range of behaviours, conducting assessments and designing intervention packages to meet the needs of both individuals and their carers. In addition to her clinical work, Sarah spends two days per week undertaking research and service development work within the field.

Special Projects Team
Unit 3
Cowbridge Court
58–62 Cowbridge Road West
Cardiff
CF5 5BS

Alan Jefferson

Alan Jefferson is a qualified Social Worker who has been regulating care services in the North West of England for over 20 years. He is currently the Care Quality Commission's Director for the North West Region and has previously held similar roles in the Commission for Social Care Inspection and the National Care Standards Commission. He has been involved with BILD's physical interventions work since the mid-1990s and has chaired the organisation's Physical Interventions Accreditation Panel since the scheme was established.

Care Quality Commission
1 Tustin Court
Port Way
Preston
Lancashire
PR2 2YQ

Dr Edwin Jones

Edwin Jones currently works with the Special Projects Team at Abertawe Bro Morgannwg NHS Trust based in Cardiff, promoting positive behavioural support for people with intellectual disabilities and challenging behaviour. He is an Honorary Fellow at the University of Glamorgan. Prior to this he was a Senior Research Fellow at the Welsh Centre for Learning Disabilities. His main interests include positive behavioural support, active support, person-centred approaches, practice leadership, the Periodic Service Review, staff training, and advocacy.

Special Projects Team
Unit 3
Cowbridge Court
58–62 Cowbridge Road West
Cardiff
CF5 5BS

Neil Kaye

Neil Kaye is a Senior Nurse, responsible for co-ordinating the Positive Behaviour Management (PBM) Training Programme for Abertawe Bro Morgannwg University NHS Trust. The training programme is commissioned extensively throughout the United Kingdom. He has achieved BILD Accredited Status via the Physical Interventions Scheme on several occasions and was extensively involved in the pilot scheme for this initiative. He has also been instrumental in devising a suite of nationally recognised qualifications related to PBM and in developing specific training packages for families, children and young people.

Abertawe Bro Morgannwg University NHS Trust
Directorate of Learning Disability Services
Training and Development
Elm Court
Cowbridge Road
Bridgend
CF31 3SR

David Leadbetter

David Leadbetter is a former Social Work Practitioner and Trainer with a long-term research interest in behaviour management in human services. His organisation was recognised as achieving the best results in a number of national level reports on restraint safety. In addition to UK training, consultancy and agency policy development, he has been involved in a variety of research and national policy initiatives in the UK, Europe and the USA. He has published extensively and is a regular contributor to international conferences.

CALM Training Services Ltd.
Elmbank Mill
The Charrier
Menstrie
Clackmannanshire
FK11 7BU

Alan Martin

Alan has over 20 years' experience of working in services for people who have a learning disability across a range of public, private and voluntary organisations in a variety of roles, including inspection and regulation. Most recently, Alan worked for BILD as the Manager of the Physical Intervention Accreditation Scheme, before joining CALM Training Services in July 2008 as a Training and Development Officer.

CALM Training Services Ltd.
Elmbank Mill
The Charrier
Menstrie
Clackmannanshire
FK11 7BU

Dr Andrew McDonnell

Andrew is a Clinical Psychologist and a Director of the Studio III Group He worked formerly at Monyhull Hospital, Birmingham and has a particular interest in the design of community settings for people who challenge. He has extensive experience of working with service users with a learning disability and/or autistic spectrum disorders who self-harm.

32 Gay Street
Bath
BA1 2NT

Dr Gill Nethell

Gillian Nethell is a Clinical Psychologist working in a specialist tertiary service for adults with learning disabilities and complex behavioural needs in the South Wales area. She has worked in this field within the NHS for nearly ten years. Her interests include complex formulation of personality difficulties, anxiety-related problems and also staff factors relating to implementation of positive behavioural support.

Specialist Behavioural Team
Glynteg House
Station Terrace
Ely
Cardiff
CF5 4AA

Sharon Paley

Sharon has worked in the field of intellectual disabilities for 28 years, during which time she has gained experience of providing support to children, young people and adults. She has been employed by the British Institute of Learning Disabilities in several roles over the past ten years and is currently the Development Manager for Positive Behaviour Support at the Institute. She has also worked as an Independent Consultant.

British Institute of Learning Disabilities
Campion House
Green Street
Kidderminster
Worcs
DY10 1JL

Dr Brodie Paterson

A Practitioner, Teacher and Researcher with more than 30 years' experience in services for people with learning disabilities, Brodie Paterson has degrees in psychology, education, social policy and sociology. He is a Registered Mental Health and Learning Disability Nurse and was a member of the cross-government working party of violence. He is presently a member of the Security Management Service Expert reference group and the Steering Committee of the European Network of Trainers in the Management of Aggression and Violence.

Department of Nursing and Midwifery
University of Stirling
Stirling
FK9 4LA

Dr Mark Smith

Mark Smith is a Consultant Specialist Clinical Psychologist who works in a specialist behavioural team for adults with learning disabilities and complex behavioural needs in the South Wales area. He also works as part of the Special Projects Team, undertaking projects designed to enhance the quality of support provided to this service user group His interests in the learning disability field include staff resilience and coping, risk assessment and management, forensic issues, and issues of capacity and consent.

Special Projects Team
Unit 3
Cowbridge Court
58–62 Cowbridge Road West
Cardiff
CF5 5BS

Introduction

'Never tell everything at once'
(Ken Venturi)

The first volume of *Ethical Approaches to Physical Interventions* appeared, somewhat scarily from my point of view, almost seven years ago. At the end of 2007, I received an e-mail from Alan Martin, who was then working at the British Institute of Learning Disabilities (BILD), indicating that stocks of the book were running low and asking whether I would consider doing an updated version or, in Alan's kind words, prefer to 'consign it to the bin'.

Given that the original book had been well received, I was not overly enthused by the second suggestion. Before making a decision to produce a new publication, however, I wanted to carefully weigh up the pros and cons of producing another book on the same theme. The latter included the fact that there had been a plethora of publications and policy documents that had appeared in the intervening years, and just adding to that list was not an attractive proposition. I also felt that simply updating the original was not something that I wanted to do. A more practical consideration was that editing a volume of this type is rather like herding cats and even if, as was true in this case, the cats in question are incredibly willing, friendly and talented, it is still a major undertaking and therefore not a decision to be taken lightly.

There were four important drivers that helped me decide to proceed. First of all, the topic of physical intervention was still a hugely important one, as evidenced by the fact that the abuse of such interventions still featured all too regularly in national scandals, such as the recent ones in Cornwall and Sutton and Merton, and that people with intellectual disabilities and other individuals with complex needs were still dying in the UK as a result of the use of inappropriate restraint. This constituted fairly clear evidence that, despite the undoubted high profile of BILD's activities in this area, they had still failed to permeate certain sections of the care sector supporting this user group, and that there was still a job to be done. Second, although the scope of the original book was fairly wide, there were a number of important topics that it failed to cover. The use of seclusion, mechanical restraint and as-required medication stood out in this sense. Third, there were a number of topics which, several years down the line, merited fresh scrutiny or which represented a new innovation in relation to physical intervention. The BILD Accreditation Scheme and the evidence base for the effectiveness of training in physical intervention were good examples of the former, while the drive to develop a tool to assess the risks associated with individual physical interventions was a prime example of the latter. Finally, a personal concern (but one that I know is shared by many practitioners) was that the agenda around the care and support provided to people with intellectual ability and challenging behaviour appeared to have become overly focused on and preoccupied with the issue of physical intervention. There was, therefore, a need to begin to create a bridge between where the physical interventions agenda is at present and what the agenda needs to be in the future. Together, these considerations pointed to the need to produce a second volume, rather than an updated version of the original book.

This book is therefore a response to these drivers, and it is divided into three overarching themes that together address each of the topics outlined above. The first major section deals with training in physical intervention and comprises of four chapters. In the first, Andy McDonnell conducts a new review of the evidence base for the effectiveness of this training. Given the profile of such training and the financial investment that it attracts, his conclusions make for very sobering reading and reinforce the scandalous lack of research evidence behind what is clearly a major industry. Alan Jefferson then reflects on the experience of chairing BILD's Physical Intervention Training Accreditation panel since its inception in 2002. The accreditation scheme remains the only one of its kind in the UK, and the chapter offers much food for thought as it assesses the strengths and frailties of the current model. One of these frailties is perhaps the scheme's failure to consider the actual interventions taught by organisations that apply to it. To a large extent, this is a function of the lack of an appropriate tool against which such interventions can be assessed. The next chapter, by Alan Martin and colleagues, is therefore particularly timely, describing as it does the first steps in the construction of exactly such a tool. The final contribution in this section, by Sarah Hawkins, David Allen and Neil Kaye, looks at a significant area of omission in relation to physical intervention training – the provision of training to parents. The chapter explores and dismisses some of the myths and dynamics behind the fact that while most paid carers are likely to receive some training in the management of challenging behaviours, it is frequently assumed that family carers cannot or should not.

The next major section addresses the general theme of controversial topics in behaviour management. Edwin Jones and David Allen discuss the use of mechanical restraint in relation to self-injury – a particularly important topic, given that to date the focus of the physical intervention initiative has been almost exclusively on personal restraint and the management of aggression. The chapter provides some guidance on the best practice principles around the use of mechanical restraint, but points out the concern that there has been little innovation in this area over a quarter of a century. Shoumitro Deb then addresses the controversial topic of emergency medication for managing challenging behaviour, an intervention that is a common alternative or adjunct to the use of physical intervention, or which may require the use of physical intervention for its implementation. The following chapter by Sharon Paley deals with equally controversial topics: the use of seclusion and time out. She explores some common misunderstanding around the use of these approaches, adds to concerns that seclusion 'by other names' may be a common occurrence in services, and discusses suggestions for the modernisation of this practice. Together, these chapters also highlight a specific weakness in the physical intervention agenda. Improving practice in relation to restraint and other physical strategies is hugely important, but such strategies are simply *one* type of response to out-of-control behaviour. To achieve genuine improvements in practice, all possible reactive strategies (physical interventions, seclusion and emergency medication) need to be critically examined and subject to extremely clear policy and monitoring. Finally in this section, Brodie Paterson and Patrick Bradley present an updated account of fatalities that have occurred in restraint within UK adult care services. Their analysis of common causal factors and implications for practice, and balanced discussion of the relative risk associated with different restraint positions, is essential reading.

The focus in the UK on physical intervention via the initiatives of BILD and others has been invaluable in terms of driving up standards in this critical but, ultimately, rather circumscribed area of practice. The final section addresses the paradigm shift that is required to move the field forward from a position where the focus on physical intervention arguably reinforces a purely reactive approach to challenging behaviour, and towards a more proactive, preventative approach. David Allen offers further background on this perspective and provides an account of one organisation's journey between these two poles. Positive behavioural support, which includes reactive management as a central component, but which majors on primary and secondary prevention, is proposed as the obvious model for achieving this change. The two chapters which follow then go on describe the principal primary prevention strategies of positive behavioural support in greater detail. Peter Baker firstly discusses the use of antecedent behavioural strategies for challenging behaviour, and then Gill Nethell and Mark Smith illustrate how teaching new skills to service users can be a critical preventative intervention. Although the information that these chapters contain will be known to psychologists and others who work within behaviour analytic frameworks, it will not be familiar territory to the majority of practitioners who make up the physical intervention training industry in the UK, those who commission their services, and a significant number of those who receive them. This alone justifies their inclusion here. A particular strength of the chapters also lies in the fact that they emphasise the use of these primary prevention strategies with the very behaviours that most typically are associated with the use of physical intervention. Finally, David Leadbetter discusses issues and practices around restraint reduction. As he points out, this is an area that has received significant attention in North America but very little in the UK. In a sense, the primary concern in the USA has been 'restrain less', whereas in the UK, it has been 'restrain better'. These are clearly complementary rather than mutually exclusive objectives, but Leadbetter's contribution points to another clear weakness in the UK position on physical intervention use. Summing-up the whole of this section, this chapter highlights the fact that successful strategies for restraint reduction have almost nothing to do with improving our approaches to physical intervention, but are instead essentially concerned with putting in place or improving the basic building blocks of high-quality services for people with complex behavioural needs.

The future challenges for UK practice in general and BILD in particular are clear. There are aspects of the physical intervention agenda that still need to be urgently addressed. There is a clear job to be done in developing the Accreditation Scheme so that it assesses physical skills taught by applying organisations, and not just their training processes and broader adherence to the Code of Practice. This requires more work on the risk tool and could, potentially, result in *fewer* accredited organisations – which may not be a bad thing. Having promoted and led a 'restrain better' initiative, BILD now needs to champion a 'restraint reduction' initiative, at the centre of which will be positive behavioural support. This will be a significant task that requires a major change of direction in what remains a very provider-led market, and one that arguably lacks the critical skills to drive this new direction forward. Guidance on physical intervention needs to broadened to encompass restrictive reactive strategies in general, and specifically to encompass emergency medication and use of seclusion. Finally, BILD should play a role in promoting and supporting new research that begins to address the evidence-free and opinion-dominated practice model that pervades this whole industry. If those challenges can be met, then BILD's contribution to improving the quality of life of people with intellectual disabilities who challenge services will comfortably exceed its already remarkable achievements in this field to date.

David Allen

SECTION 1:
Training in Physical Intervention

Chapter 1
<hr>

The Effectiveness of Training in Physical Intervention

Andrew McDonnell

> 'Contrariwise,' continued Tweedledee, 'if it was so, it might be, and
> if it were so, it would be; but as it isn't, it ain't. That's logic!'
> (Lewis Carroll, 1832–1898, *Through the Looking Glass*)

Introduction

Large numbers of staff in the UK receive training in physical interventions on a
regular basis. While the underlying assumption would appear to be that this
training is beneficial, this assumption may not necessarily be based on sound
empirical data. By definition, physical interventions pose immediate risks
(Leadbetter, 2002) and may also elevate the risk of abuse to high-risk individuals
with intellectual disabilities (Baker and Allen, 2001). The purpose of this
chapter is to review the current research into the effectiveness of staff training in
physical interventions. General research surrounding staff training in services for
people with intellectual disabilities will first be examined, and then some key
issues surrounding physical interventions outlined. Finally, a review of staff
training in physical interventions will be examined and recommendations made
for future research.

Staff training in behavioural skills: What do we know?

Training is an important strategy in the transmission of skills to front-line staff
(Smith and Cumella, 1996) and staff training in behavioural skills has been a
well-documented area of research (Cullen, 1992; Milne, 1986; Mittler, 1987;
Reid and Parsons, 2002).

Early studies in institutional settings in the UK reported clear effects of service
culture and context on the implementation and delivery of behavioural
programmes (Moores and Grant, 1976). In a classic study, Woods and Cullen
(1983) examined a number of behaviour programmes conducted by staff in an
institutional setting; at follow-up, the most empirically valid programme (room
management) had been discontinued by staff and the least successful programme

(toilet training) was still being maintained by staff. This study demonstrates that the motivation and maintenance of staff behaviour is a far from simple matter. Thus, staff training may not be sufficient to directly alter staff behaviour *per se*. Baker (1998), for example, used a multiple-baseline design to examine the effects of three video-based training packages (training in basic support, health and safety and values training). Staff observations were conducted with six staff in two residential houses for people with a learning disability. He found effects for simple target behaviours (hand washing, glove usage and frequency of positive interaction); however, the more complex target behaviour (frequency of valued activities in the community) was not altered by training.

Generalisation of skills from training environments is clearly a critical element of behaviourally based training (Stokes and Baer, 1977), but staff training studies do not always produce good evidence of the transference of skills from one setting to another. For example, Smith et al (1992) reported data on the acquisition and generalisation of skills of a five-day workshop in behavioural theory and intervention techniques for 31 residential staff in the USA. They reported evidence of the acquisition of skills post-training, but found no evidence of transfer of these skills to the care settings concerned. An earlier study of behavioural interventions training reported similar acquisition skills data, but little evidence of generalisation of skills to group homes (Schinke and Wong, 1977).

Despite the findings mentioned above, there is some evidence that training interventions can produce changes in staff behaviour. Positive results were reported by Jones et al (2001), for example, who evaluated the impact of an active support-training package which was designed to increase residential participation levels. Using a pre-post, follow-up design, they reported findings of a two-day training course conducted for 303 staff in 38 residential facilities. Behavioural observations were conducted prior to training and one month after training delivery, and the results showed a 35 per cent increase in planned activity after training. There were no significant changes in reported levels of challenging behaviour, however.

Staff feedback and monitoring are important components of successful training and there is a considerable literature on the role of supervisor feedback in increasing staff performance in a variety of care settings (Hewitt et al, 2004; Parsons et al, 2003). Parsons and Reid (1995) used classroom-based instruction, on-the-job observation and feedback, and trained ten supervisors who would then implement teaching programmes themselves. Training improved supervisors' teaching skills but was insufficient to improve the quality of feedback they provided to direct-service staff regarding the staff members' teaching skills. Subsequently, both classroom-based instruction and on-the-job observation and feedback that targeted supervisors' feedback skills were provided. Following training in provision of feedback, all supervisors met the criteria for providing feedback to their staff.

The context of teaching has also been viewed as important. Classroom-based teaching approaches are in some cases being superseded by *in-vivo* training.

Real-time training (Hardcastle, 2000) involves training staff in service environments with appropriate feedback from supervisors. This considerably reduces some of the generalisation difficulties created by more traditional classroom instruction. Cullen (1987) argued that staff training is a complex process since the number of potential establishing operations is extremely large. Establishing operations are antecedent events which are related to behavioural responses and include motivational and environmental factors (McGill, 1999).

Organisational factors can clearly influence the outcome of training. Staff turnover, for example, will incrementally dilute its effectiveness. It has also been argued that staff who most require training often avoid training courses (Campbell, 2007). Baker and Feil (2000), in their survey of 44 services, found that successful staff training was associated with staff structures, which included procedures involved in recruiting staff, building teamwork and maintaining performance. Feedback mechanisms for staff can also influence training. Effective training involves both classroom-based and 'on the job' elements (Van Oorsouw, Embregts, Bosman and Jahoda, in press). Providing corrective feedback to staff in these situations is an important element in skill development, but recent evidence appears to indicate that staff in organisations rarely appear to have any systematic feedback on their actions (Mansell and Elliott, 2001).

In conclusion, staff training is viewed as necessary, but not sufficient, to alter staff behaviour (Cullen, 1992). There exists a complex interaction between training and organisational variables. Training can be expensive to deliver and it can be difficult to get individuals to acquire and generalise skills. Post-training monitoring and feedback are important factors in the maintenance of effective training. In many cases, staff receive training but are rarely monitored afterwards. This type of approach has been referred to as the 'train and hope' model (Milne, 1986). This research has clear implications for evaluating staff training in physical intervention.

Physical interventions: key issues

The term 'physical intervention' has been widely adopted in the UK to describe physical management strategies for out-of-control behaviours that pose risks to service users and others. Although restraint is generally viewed as aversive, physical restraint in itself is not an aversive or non-aversive procedure. Studies have shown that restraint can act as a positive reinforcer in some instances (Favell, McGimsey and Jones, 1978). It may also suppress an aggressive behaviour and be a form of *punishment*.

Despite the influences of positive behaviour support approaches (Carr et al, 1999), physical restraint is still used extensively in services for people with an intellectual disability. A study of crisis procedures in Minnesota found that physical restraint, especially manual restraint, was the most commonly used management procedure in community settings (Nord, Wieseler and Hanson, 1991). Emerson et al (2000), in a survey of 500 people in the United Kingdom and Ireland labelled with challenging behaviour, reported 23 per cent of the sample had experienced physical restraint. A similar survey of disability services in Canada reported that 13.3 per cent of a sample of 625 service users had physical restraint as a component of their intervention plan (Feldman et al, 2004).

Baker and Allen (2001) highlighted that high-risk service users may be at risk of abuse from staff using physical interventions. A survey in secure mental health facilities conducted in the UK produced a worrying pattern of injury on training courses, with 27 per cent of nursing staff reporting that they received injuries whilst participating on training courses in the management of aggression (Lee et al, 2003). Seven per cent of these staff required medical attention. In sum, the processes which lead to staff and service user injuries when implementing physical interventions are still poorly understood.

Leadbetter (2002) distinguished between injury caused by the employment of an ad-hoc or unsafe technique by an untrained member of staff and a similar injury caused by a technique which has been directly taught to staff as part of an approved training programme. This challenges the assumption that staff training in training environments is inherently safe. There are documented cases where deaths have been associated with the use of physical restraint in the USA (Weiss, 1998). In the UK, a recent survey reported twelve cases of death associated with physical restraint between 1979 and 2000 (Patterson et al, 2003) (see also Paterson and Bradley, this volume). It is important to note that there is limited evidence on the relative safety of specific physical interventions (Leadbetter, 2002). In a survey of 338 UK Psychiatric Nurses about their experiences of restraint usage, 13 per cent of the sample reported injury to service users when applying physical restraint (Lee et al, 2003). The authors reported that these injuries were minor, although no data were provided to support this point. No comparable survey has been conducted in intellectual disabilities services. Hill and Spreat (1987) reported that 30 per cent of staff injuries in a university-operated residential facility for people with intellectual disabilities were due to the use of physical restraint.

In the UK there has been a debate about the use of pain in managing aggressive behaviour (Leadbetter, 2002). The control and restraint system which was developed to manage violence in prison populations does involve techniques which include the application of pain (Allen, Doyle and Kaye, 2002; Tarbuck, 1992; Topping-Morris, 1995). The BILD Code of Practice for the use of physical interventions does not appear to advocate the use of physical techniques which inflict pain (BILD, 2006). It states that 'morally and ethically BILD is opposed to the use of touching, guiding or holding techniques that might, or are known to, cause pain or discomfort, or techniques that are designed to use pain as an effective component to gain compliance, and believes the presumption must be that they are not to be taught' (p 16). Despite these reservations, the use of pain as a method of control still has its advocates. Anecdotal evidence would appear to indicate that such methods are less commonly used in services for people with intellectual disabilities. A national consultation exercise in the UK found considerable support for not teaching techniques which inflict pain on individuals (Harris, 2002).

The effectiveness of physical interventions training

There have been a number of reviews of the staff training literature. Beech and Leather (2006), in a general review of training models, concluded that 'although aggression management training is widely available it is often inappropriate for the needs of different staff groups' (p 41). Allen (2001) reviewed studies, both published and unpublished, from a variety of care settings and concluded that the research was at best crude. What, therefore, is our current knowledge about the effectiveness of staff training in physical interventions? The remainder of this chapter will present a brief review of the staff training literature in services for people with intellectual disabilities and/or autism.

Method

For this review, the Web of Science search engine was used. The literature search consisted of three main databases: Cochrane database of systemic reviews (2001 to March 2008), Medline (1966 to March 2008) and Social Science Citation Index (1956 to March 2008). Keywords for the search included the following: aggression, violence training, mental retardation, learning disability, mental handicap, elderly, care staff, education, psychiatry, mental health staff training, disruptive behaviour and psychiatric. Staff training was used as the major keyword in all comparisons.

Websites of twelve training organisations approved to deliver training in UK services for people with a learning disability (up until March 2008) were examined for evidence of published research. All training papers selected for the review had their reference sections examined in an attempt to discover any articles that may have been missed in the electronic searches. This process produced no new research. The earlier review by Allen (2001) was used as a comparator, and inter-rater reliabilities were calculated for the major categories shown in the tables below. The author and a second researcher examined the original papers to check that the data had been transcribed accurately.

Results

Fourteen studies were included in the final review. *Table 1* represents the outcomes of all of these studies. Only three studies appeared to meet a minimum standard of experimental design of having either a control group or contrast group (Allen and Tynan, 2000; McDonnell et al, 2008; Patterson et al, 1992). In addition, a multiple-baseline design was adopted in one small scale study (Van Den Pol et al, 1983). Time series data without control groups were reported in two cases (Allen et al, 1997; McDonnell and Reeves, 1996). In both cases, reductions in physical intervention usage was reported. An increase in physical intervention usage post-training was reported in one study (Baker and Bissmire, 2000).

Allen et al (1997) did report reductions in staff and service user injury data. The relationship between injury rates (to both staff and service users) and training in physical interventions is often proposed by proponents of training. As stated above, Hill and Spreat (1987) reported that 30 per cent of staff injuries in a residential facility for people with intellectual disabilities were due to the use of physical restraint. Injuries to staff were much more likely to occur during emergency physical restraint, whereas planned, mechanical restraint appeared to be much safer. These data would indicate that the assumption of benefits in terms of injury rates requires more empirical evidence, especially given that physical restraint has also been associated with deaths in childcare and adult facilities both in the USA (Morrison et al, 2002; Nunno et al, 2006) and in the UK (Patterson et al, 2003).

Table 1: Outcomes of physical interventions training research.

Author	Design and setting	Duration of course and title	Description and reliability of measures	Outcome data
Allen, McDonald and Dunn et al (1997)	Time series design (n = 7 service users). Six bedded unit for adults with learning disabilities and challenging behaviours. Combination of descriptive and parametric statistics.	Preventing and Responding to Aggressive Behaviour.* Two–three day course (one day theory, one–two days physical interventions)	Aberrant Behaviour Checklist (Aman and Singh, 1986). Rates of Physical Restraint usage. Rates of seclusion usage. Medication as required usage. Staff and service user injuries. No reliability data reported.	Reduction in overall rates of behaviour; reduction in physical restraints and emergency medication; 'decommissioning' of seclusion; and reduction in staff and service user injuries.
Allen and Tynan (2000)	Quasi-experimental design (between subjects element: trained versus untrained staff; within subjects element: untrained group, which then received training) n = 109. 51 exposed to training, 58 not exposed in community services with people with learning disabilities. Non-parametric statistics used.	Preventing and Responding to Aggressive Behaviour.* Two–three day course (one day theory, one–two days physical interventions)	Ten-item confidence measure (Thackrey, 1987), (Cronbach's Alpha = 0.88) A 20-item reactive strategy questionnaire (Cronbach's Alpha = 0.64)	Trained group was significantly more confident than untrained group Trained group scored higher on reactive strategy questionnaire. Both measures statistically increased when untrained group received training.

* Now known as Positive Behaviour Management.

Author	Design and setting	Duration of course and title	Description and reliability of measures	Outcome data
Baker and Bissmire (2000)	Pre/post within subjects design with a two-month follow-up period (n = 17). Staff received training in a ten-bedded unit for adults with learning disabilities and challenging behaviour. Non-parametric statistics used.	Two-day training course using the SCIP system.	Course evaluation questionnaire (seven items). Analysis of challenging behaviour in service setting five months prior to training commencing and two months following training completion. No reliability data for either measure.	Slight reduction in untoward incidents after training. Proportion of incidents requiring physical intervention increased post-training. Staff reported increases in confidence in both handling behavioural crisis and preventing challenging behaviour. Staff reported being more confident in the support provided by their organisation.
Edwards (1999a)	Retrospective study, interviews with nursing staff (n = 11) in a service for people with learning disabilities about their use of control and restraint methods. A qualitative study.	Duration of course not specified. Control and restraint training.	Semi-structured interviews. No reliability data provided.	Staff reported improved team working and communication after training. Some staff reported feeling safer, and that people had been restrained less often.
Edwards (1999b)	Retrospective study, interviews with nursing staff (n = 11) in a service for people with learning disabilities about the effects of gender on the use of control and restraint methods. A qualitative study.	Duration of course not specified. Control and restraint training.	Semi-structured interviews. No reliability data provided.	Female staff reported they were less dependent on male staff after training. Male staff reported as being more confident in allowing females to participate in physical restraint after they had received training.

Author	Design and setting	Duration of course and title	Description and reliability of measures	Outcome data
Green and Wray (1999)	Descriptive case study on an 11 year old boy with Prader-Willi Syndrome and challenging behaviour. Parents received training.	Unspecified duration and course title. Breakaway skills taught to parents and monitoring of the skills occurred after training.	No reliability is reported.	Child maintained at home after one year. Parent reported more confidence with managing violence.
Kaye and Allen (2002)	Time-series examined the frequency and use of physical interventions over a nine-month time frame. 42 physical interventions taught to staff (n = 17) on an eight-bedded admission unit for people with a learning disability.	Descriptive statistics used. Preventing and Responding to Aggressive Behaviour.* Duration not stated.	Paper is qualitative. Aberrant Behaviour Checklist (ABC). Frequency and use of physical interventions. Reliability data provided for the ABC. No reliability provided for the physical interventions.	Fifteen types of physical interventions were used out of the 42. 90% of the interventions involved 'evasive or breakaway procedures'. 4% 'removal procedures' 6% 'physical restraint'. No differences in ABC scores in client population.
McDonnell (1997)	Pre/post design with staff (n = 21) who work in a service for people with learning disabilities. Parametric statistics used.	Three-day training course in the management of challenging behaviour (Studio III System).	20-item violent incident knowledge test (Cronbach's Alpha = 0.50). 15-item confidence scale (Cronbach's Alpha = 0.92). Video restraint role-play test (inter-rater reliability 94%).	Increases in knowledge and confidence scores post-training. Role-play test reported an inverse correlation between age and performance.
McDonnell and Reeves (1996)	Time-series design (compared incident data three years prior to training with two years post-training). Staff (n = unspecified) in a locked hospital	Three-day training course in the Management of Challenging Behaviour (Studio III System).	Rates of seclusion and physical restraint usage. No reliability data provided.	Reduction in seclusion usage post-training. Slight reduction in the use of physical restraint post-training.

* Now known as Positive Behaviour Management.

Author	Design and setting	Duration of course and title	Description and reliability of measures	Outcome data
McDonnell and Reeves (1996) (contd)	ward for people with learning disabilities and challenging behaviours. Descriptive statistics reported.			
McDonnell, Sturmey, Oliver, Cunningham, Hayes, Galvin, Walshe and Cunningham (2008)	Quasi-experimental design.	Three-day training course in the Management of Challenging Behaviour (Studio III System).	The staff support and satisfaction questionnaire (Harris and Rose, 2002; test–retest reliability 82%). Shortened ways of coping scale (Hatton and Emerson, 1995; internal reliability 76%). Thoughts about challenging behaviour questionnaire (Dagnan, 2007; internal consistency rating 85%). The challenging behaviour confidence scale (McDonnell, 1997; internal consistency ratings 95%). The checklist of challenging behaviour (Harris, Humphreys and Thompson, 1994). No reliability data.	Significantly increased staff confidence, but not other measures of staff belief, support or coping. No evidence of a reduction in client challenging behaviours. Significant post-training differences between the experimental and contrast group, with the experimental group having higher scores than the contrast group for role clarity, coping resource, risk factors, supportive people and staff support.
Paterson, Turnbull, and Aitken (1992)	Pre/post within subjects design. Two groups of staff (n = 12, n = 13 of nursing staff with learning disabilities and psychiatry backgrounds).	Ten-day training course in control and restraint.	Sixteen-item knowledge questionnaire (test–retest reliability 83%). General health questionnaire (Goldberg, 1972).	Significant improvement in physical competence in de-escalation, disengagement and control and restraint.

Author	Design and setting	Duration of course and title	Description and reliability of measures	Outcome data
Paterson, Turnbull, and Aitken (1992) (contd)	Non-parametric statistics used.		Job satisfaction questionnaire (test–retest reliability 74%). Role conflict and ambiguity scale (no reliability data). De-escalation video role-plays (inter-rater reliability ranging from 0.82–0.89). Disengagement role-plays (inter-rater reliability from 0.75–1.0), control and restraint role-play (inter-rater reliability from 0.73–1.0).	Significant decrease in stress and measure of role ambiguity. No increase in job satisfaction questionnaire. Knowledge increased significantly post-training.
Perkins and Leadbetter (2002)	Within subjects design with a six-month follow-up (n = 12). Staff (n = 14) trained in a school for children with severe and complex learning disabilities. Descriptive statistics reported.	Two-day training course in CALM system.	Staff knowledge test (no reliability data). School logbook data (no reliability data). Staff stress measure, assessed by a semi-structure interview at six months (n = 11); no reliability data.	Reported increases in de-escalation skills at six-month follow-up. 82% of participants indicated an increase in confidence. Major incidents did not decrease significantly pre- and post-training. Authors discussed problems of implementation when delivering training to partial elements of staff teams.
Shinnick and McDonnell (2005)	Single case study.	Training in low arousal methods and physical disengagement skills.	Interview follow-up eight months after training completed.	Family reported increased confidence at follow up.

Author	Design and setting	Duration of course and title	Description and reliability of measures	Outcome data
Van Den Pol, Reed and Fuqua (1983)	Multiple baseline design, examining three safety related skills (fire safety, emergency procedures after a person has had a seizure and physical self defence). Study took place in an 87-bedded residential service for people with a learning disability. Total n = 13: four trainees, three maintenance condition trainees, four trainers and two control trainees. 23-month follow-up of staff who had received training (telephone interviews). Descriptive statistics reported.	Three 30-minute workshops in emergency procedures.	Role-play assessments of self defence procedures rated by two independent raters (average inter-rater reliability 90%). Assessments took place on an unannounced basis. Five-item self-report questionnaire (no reliability). Telephone follow-up of (n = not specified).	Trainers demonstrated competency levels post-training in self defence skills. Control trainees showed no increase in any skill acquisition. None of the trainee staff were still employed at follow-up One trainee reported using physical intervention in the workplace.

Increases in confidence are reported in several studies. Two retrospective interview studies reported increases in staff confidence (Edwards, 1999a, b). In addition, a school-based study in Scotland reported increases based on staff feedback (Perkins and Leadbetter, 2002). Three studies which have employed psychometric-based measures of confidence reported increases (Allen and Tynan, 2000; McDonnell, 1997; McDonnell et al, 2008). This confidence effect would appear reasonably robust, although there is no consistent measure used across all of these studies.

Table 2 examines the content of these training courses. The description of physical interventions used on the training courses was very difficult to determine from the written articles. No visual representations were provided in the papers. This creates problems with identifying key elements of an independent variable and presents major challenges to researchers when evaluating training courses. One of the studies (McDonnell, 1997) did attempt to present a detailed description of some of the methods taught on a training course.

Table 2: The content of physical interventions training.

Author	Course content	Description of physical interventions	Description of teaching methods
Allen, McDonald, Dunn and Doyle (1997)	Understanding aggressive incidents; primary prevention; secondary prevention; reactive strategies, including. physical interventions; and post-incident support for clients and care givers.	Unclear in article, referred to unpublished training manual – Doyle et al (1996).	Classroom instruction, role-play and repeated practice of physical interventions.
Allen and Tynan (2000)	Training program specified in earlier paper (Allen et al, 1997).	Yes – need to refer to Allen et al (1997).	Classroom instruction, role-play and repeated practice of physical interventions.
Baker and Bissmire (2000)	Specified lectures covering: understanding challenging behaviours; service values; prevention; early intervention; health and safety; and legal framework. 25% of course devoted to demonstration and practice of physical interventions.	None specified.	Lectures and demonstrations.
Edwards (1999a)	Staff training appeared to cover physical skills (to safely restrain a person using a three-person team) and disengagement/ breakaway techniques.	Control and restraint training, mentioned breakaway skills and 'three-person team'.	Not specified.
Edwards (1999b)	Not specified.	Not specified.	Not specified.
Green and Wray (1999)	N/A.	Break away techniques – unspecified in paper.	N/A.
Kaye and Allen (2002)	Course duration and content not clearly specified in this paper.	42 physical interventions consisting of 27 moves covering evasive or self-protecting techniques. Nine techniques for removing distressed service users. Six restrictive restraint holds.	Classroom instruction, role-play and repeated practice of physical interventions.

Author	Course content	Description of physical interventions	Description of teaching methods
McDonnell (1997)	Course content specified in McDonnell (1997). Three-day course: *Day 1*: Understanding the law; causes of challenging behaviours; defusion of challenging behaviours; use of inter-personal skills; and strategies for managing difficult behaviours. *Day 2:* Non-violent methods of managing violent behaviour (including hair pulling, biting, scratching, grabbing wrists, grabbing and tearing of clothing and airway protection). *Day 3*: A 'chair method' of physical restraint.	Non-violent methods of managing violent behaviour (including hair pulling, biting, scratching, grabbing wrists, grabbing and tearing of clothing and airway protection). A 'chair method' of physical restraint.	Role-play and lecture based.
McDonnell and Reeves (1996)	Course content specified in McDonnell (1997). Three-day course: *Day 1*: Understanding the law; causes of challenging behaviour; defusion of challenging behaviour; use of inter-personal skills; and strategies for managing difficult behaviours. *Day 2*: Non-violent methods of managing violent behaviour (including hair pulling, biting, scratching, grabbing wrists, grabbing and tearing of clothing and airway protection). *Day 3*: A 'chair method' of physical restraint.	Non-violent methods of managing violent behaviour (including hair pulling, biting, scratching, grabbing wrists, grabbing and tearing of clothing and airway protection). A 'chair method' of physical restraint.	Lecture based and role-play.

Author	Course content	Description of physical interventions	Description of teaching methods
McDonnell, Sturmey, Oliver, Cunningham, Hayes, Galvin, Walshe and Cunningham (2008)	Course content specified in McDonnell (1997). Three-day course: **Day 1**: Understanding the law; causes of challenging behaviour; defusion of challenging behaviour; use of inter-personal skills; and strategies for managing difficult behaviours. **Day 2:** Non-violent methods of managing violent behaviour (including hair pulling, biting, scratching, grabbing wrists, grabbing and tearing of clothing and airway protection). **Day 3**: A 'chair method' of physical restraint.	Non-violent methods of managing violent behaviour (including hair pulling, biting, scratching, grabbing wrists, grabbing and tearing of clothing and airway protection). A 'chair method' of physical restraint.	Lecture based and role-play.
Paterson, Turnbull and Aitken (1992)	Covering theoretical and legal issues surrounding violence, instruction in verbal and non-verbal skills to prevent violence; breakaway/disengagement skills; instruction and techniques in control and restraint (physical restraint).	One hundred separate break away skills. For measurement ten were observed/used. Control and restraint: physical restraint not specified.	Lectures, video recordings and role-plays.
Perkins and Leadbetter (2002)	This includes a five-level system of physical interventions training based on non-aversive principles.	Not clearly specified in paper – reports use of 'a figure of four hold'.	Not specified.
Shinnick and McDonnell (2003)	Training included both physical and non-physical methods of disengagement.	Physical disengagement methods not clearly specified.	Role-play and didactic teaching.
Van Den Pol, Reed and Fuqua (1983)	Three 30-minute workshops. Staff taught how to train new staff. In addition staff taught how to conduct the emergency procedure.	Yes – blocking punches; blocking kicks; releasing clothing grab; using a 'thumb pry'; release of a body part grab; and using a chair for protection.	Workshop format used with modelling procedures and role-play.

Training and teaching methods were also variable. Ten studies specified that teaching took place in classroom – or lecture room – based formats. Nine training courses used 'role-play' methods. The length and duration of training courses varied from 90 minutes (Van den Pol et al, 1983) to ten days (Paterson et al, 1992). Description of methods and the methods of teaching are important in establishing the core elements of training. Two case studies (Green and Wray, 1999; Shinnick and McDonnell, 2003) reported training for parents. Training for parents that includes restrictive physical interventions would appear to be an important research area. Allen et al (2006), in a survey of parents, reported relatively high rates of usage of physical interventions. This study clearly demonstrates a need for research into application and effectiveness of training for this population (see also Hawkins, Allen and Kaye, this volume).

In summary, the evidence base consists of a limited number of mostly flawed studies. The next section will examine what can be done to improve the quality and quantity of this research.

Evaluating physical intervention training studies

There are many problems with evaluating physical intervention staff training studies. Conducting research in 'real-world' settings is fraught with difficulties of experimental control. Market forces may also limit training research. There are a large number of independent and statutory training providers competing in a training marketplace. In these circumstances, there exists a potential for bias in the interpretation of studies. All of the studies reported in this review do not appear to have been conducted independently and therefore should be viewed with a certain degree of scepticism. Reporting negative outcomes would also appear to be a rarity. To its credit, one study reported a negative outcome in terms of increases in physical interventions post-training (Baker and Bissmire, 2000). Despite these reservations, good evaluative research is difficult but not impossible to achieve.

Evaluating any staff training programme requires an analysis of multiple components. Training courses in physical interventions often contain theoretical and physical elements. Even if there are positive effects reported from a training study, it is difficult to state with any certainty which components of that training are the most important. Advice about de-escalation strategies would appear to be a component of many training courses. Future researchers need to focus on the effects of de-escalation training in isolation.

Collecting accurate data about the usage of physical interventions in a variety of workplaces may be difficult. There is limited anecdotal evidence that incidents in general may be underreported (Lion et al, 1981). The author would question to what extent incidents involving physical intervention are underreported. At present there is little hard evidence to substantiate such a claim that there is systemic underreporting across services. Information about the usage of physical interventions may be difficult to interpret as the use of physical interventions after staff training may be relatively low (Deveau and McGill, 2007; Kaye and Allen, 2002). Judging the practical significance of reduction of physical interventions after training is therefore not a straightforward task.

The notion that physical intervention skills are used and retained after training also appears to be based on very limited evidence. Kaye and Allen (2002) reported a follow-up evaluation of 42 physical skills (including breakaways) taught to staff in a intellectual disabilities hospital admissions service. Fifteen types of physical interventions had been used by staff at nine-month follow-up Ninety per cent of the physical interventions consisted of breakaway skills. In a study of breakaway training in a medium secure unit in the UK, 47 staff were tested using role-play simulations to assess their recollection of these skills. Sixty per cent of the staff tested managed to break away. Forty per cent were unable to break away from the simulated assault (Rogers et al, 2006). These limited studies do appear to question the effectiveness and practicality of such training (Rogers et al, 2007). Recalling physical interventions may be very context dependent. It could be argued that the moment training ceases, forgetting begins to occur (Leadbetter, 2007). While it is assumed that there must be an inverse relationship between the quantity of physical interventions taught and the retention and usage of those skills, there is a need for systematic studies in this area. The use of research from the areas of sport science may add clearer insights into this relationship (Leadbetter, 2008).

Confidence in relation to staff training would appear to be a key variable (Allen and Tynan, 2000; Edwards, 1999 a, b; McDonnell et al, 2008; Perkins and Leadbetter, 2002). Checklist self-report scales such as those developed by Thackrey (1987) and McDonnell (1997) could be used as a standardised measure of training outcome. Furthermore, an examination of constructs which may be associated with staff confidence, such as anxiety or fear, staff work satisfaction or risk-taking behaviour would be useful. The most recent study in this area (McDonnell et al, 2008) would appear to indicate that confidence may well be a separate construct. Another useful area of research would therefore be to investigate the effects of increased confidence after staff training and its impact on staff behaviour. Given the claims made for the utility of physical interventions training, it would be useful to examine whether training in de-escalation methods only could achieve similar confidence effects. Would training in non-challenging behaviour settings have similar confidence effects?

Many of the issues surrounding effectiveness of staff training in physical interventions are not going to be solved overnight. The literature review conducted in this chapter presents a very poor dataset. Also, there are issues of evaluation which may be more short-term in nature. Allen (2001) argued that, in the absence of effectiveness data, social validity measures may have increased importance. The social validity of interventions includes a number of factors such as the social importance and appropriateness of goals, procedures and outcomes (Wolf, 1978). A comparison of three methods of restraint (face down, face up and seated) has yielded consistent findings that seated holds were preferred by individuals with intellectual disabilities (Cunningham et al, 2002). Social validity is a construct with high face validity. In sum, it could be argued that in the absence of compelling research data to suggest that either approach is more effective, a construct such as social validity will be just as important in the selection of interventions (Allen, 2001).

The design of future studies requires greater scrutiny. Only four studies in the review contained rudimentary elements of experimental control. This means that the design of staff training studies which implies that evaluating training programmes in physical interventions presents significant practical difficulties for researchers. Robust research is by its very nature time-consuming and costly. Randomised controlled trials are considered to be a 'gold standard' in research, but using this approach in a 'market economy' presents real challenges to researchers. In addition, true randomisation is difficult to achieve as it would be hard to conceal effectively the nature of the training programmes in any study.

Other methodologies do exist which may help bridge the gap between pure and applied research. Multiple baseline designs are possible to implement in these instances. Killick and Allen (2005) evaluated a training programme in a children's service using such a design. The use of waiting list control groups can be relatively simple to employ in situations where demand for training is not perceived to be urgent. There are, however, obvious ethical concerns in having waiting list control groups in 'high risk' situations.

Direct observation of staff behaviour pre- and post-training is an essential component in assessing generalisation of skills. The author could find no staff training studies that contained a direct observation element. This lack of direct observation is a fundamental weakness in this literature. Injuries to staff and service users would appear to be an obvious basic measure that should be contained in all future reported studies. This should also include injuries reported during training courses.

Generalisation of skills from training to the work environment is not reported directly in any of the studies. One early behavioural study did attempt training within the work setting (Van den Pol, 1983), and this practice should be a minimum requirement. In the behavioural literature, generalisation of skills is a critical component of any intervention (Stokes and Baer, 1977). Intuitively there appears to be a good argument for training to take place within the working environment where the physical interventions are likely to be employed. Shinnick and McDonnell (2003) trained a family within their own home and practised skills in this setting. It does appear problematic to train staff in skills in environments that do not reflect the everyday settings. Training environments are often large and open. In some cases, matted areas are used to practise physical interventions which are obviously not present in the workplace. In these circumstances, the risk of injury when using these skills may be elevated.

Organisational culture and leadership is clearly a variable which is not evaluated in the studies reported in this review. Some evidence has demonstrated management monitoring of use of physical interventions can lead to reductions in physical intervention use (Sturmey and McGlynn, 2002). Norway has recently implemented legal instruments regulating the use of 'coercive' procedures for people with intellectual disabilities. These have reportedly led to considerable reductions in the use of restrictive interventions for people with intellectual disabilities (Roed and Syse, 2002). A recent study in the UK reported that better service quality outcomes for people with a learning disability appeared to be more commonplace in services with a more positive organisational culture (Gillett and Stenfert-Kroese, 2003). There is even some limited evidence that certain organisational cultures may actually increase service user vulnerability to abuse (White et al, 2003).

Deveau and McGill (2007) identified gaps in policy and delivery of organisational responses to physical interventions and suggested that the effects of direct staff training *per se* may well be limited. The recent enquiry into services for people with intellectual disability in Cornwall identified that the only consistent training given to staff was the local physical interventions training system (Healthcare Commission, 2006). We should not be surprised that, if training is not placed in an appropriate context, staff will use physical interventions as a first rather than a last resort (Deveau and McDonnell, 2008).

General conclusions

This chapter has highlighted the deficiencies in training outcome research in physical interventions for services for people with intellectual disabilities and/or autism. Relatively simple use of standardised measures, better detailed description of training (especially physical interventions) and the use of waiting list controls or multiple baseline designs could significantly improve the quality of the research.

Training in physical interventions does not occur in a vacuum. To some, training evaluation may be viewed as 'reductionist' in nature (Leadbetter, 2007). Organisational culture and structure has an influence on the effectiveness of staff training in physical interventions (Deveau and McDonnell, 2008). The effects of organisational culture are obviously important.

There is a danger with formulating difficulties in terms of organisational variables as this can detract from direct training issues. An obvious area is the debate about the specific risks of individual methods of restraint. The use of prone restraint holds is perhaps the most controversial of these areas. A ban of these methods has been called for by some individuals (McDonnell, 2007), whilst others have argued that a ban would be counterproductive (Paterson, 2007). With regard to intellectual disability services, a sector-specific ban may be possible (Leadbetter, 2007). Evaluation of specific methods in terms of safety is an obvious important step in relation to these issues. In addition, evaluating the effectiveness of specific teaching methods such as role play is also required.

Independent evaluation of training programmes would also appear to be an essential and urgent requirement, as currently training effectiveness appears to be evaluated solely by training providers. Would this situation be accepted in other areas of practice? Training in physical interventions in the UK and elsewhere could therefore at present be viewed as a large-scale uncontrolled experiment (Paterson, 2007). In addition, as a minimum standard it would appear sensible, when evaluating the effectiveness of physical interventions training, to evaluate only published peer-reviewed training studies rather than unpublished or in-house studies.

In summary, what do we know about the effectiveness of physical interventions training? At present, a worldwide training industry is based primarily on anecdotal evidence and fourteen studies, only four of which show reasonable design quality. An evidence-based approach represents the only way forward. To achieve this, we need to move from the logic of Tweedledee to hard facts and independent evaluation.

References

Allen, D (2001) *Training Carers in Physical Interventions: Research Towards Evidence Based Practice*. Kidderminster: BILD Publications.

Allen, D, Doyle, T and Kaye, N (2002) Plenty of gain, but no pain: A systems wide initiative. In D Allen (Ed) *Ethical approaches to physical interventions*. Kidderminster: BILD Publications.

Allen, D, Hawkins, S and Cooper, V (2006) Parents' use of physical interventions in the management of their children's severe challenging behaviour. *Journal of Applied Research in Intellectual Disabilities*, 19, 356–363.

Allen, D, McDonald, L, Dunn, C and Doyle, T (1997) Changing care staff approaches to the preventions and management of aggressive behaviour in a residential treatment unit for persons with mental retardation and challenging behaviour. *Research In Developmental Disabilities*, 18, 101–112.

Allen, D and Tynan, H (2000) Responding to aggressive behaviour: Impact of training on staff members knowledge and confidence. *Mental Retardation*, 38, 97–104.

Baker, D J (1998) Effects of video based staff training with manager led exercises in residential support. *Mental Retardation*, 36, 198–204.

Baker, D J and Feil, E G (2000) A self evaluation by agencies providing residential support regarding capacity to support persons with disabilities and challenging behaviors. *International Journal of Disability, Development and Education*, 47, 171–181.

Baker, P and Allen, D (2001) Physical abuse and physical interventions in learning disabilities: an element of risk? *Journal of Adult Protection*, 3, 25–32.

Baker, P and Bissmire, D (2000) A pilot study of the use of physical intervention in the crisis management of people with intellectual disabilities who present challenging behaviour. *Journal of Applied Research in Intellectual Disabilities*, 13, 38–45.

Beech, B and Leather, P (2006) Workplace violence in the health care sector: A review of staff training and integration of training evaluation models. *Aggression and Violent Behavior*, 11, 27–43.

BILD (2006) *BILD Code of Practice for the use of physical interventions. A guide for trainers and commissioners of training*. Second Edition. Kidderminster: BILD Publications.

Campbell, M (2007) Staff training and Challenging Behaviour: Who needs it? *Journal of Intellectual Disabilities*, 11, 2, 143–156.

Carr, J E, Austin, J L, Britton, L N, Kellum, K K and Bailey, J S (1999). An assessment of social validity trends in applied behavior analysis. *Behavioral Interventions*, 14, 223–231.

Carroll, L (1871). *Through the Looking Glass.* London: Macmillan.

Cullen, C (1987) Nurse training and institutional constraints. In J Hogg and P Mittler (Eds) *Staff training in mental handicap* Beckenham: Croom Helm.

Cullen, C (1992) Staff training and management for intellectual disability services. *International Review of Research in Mental Retardation*, 18, 225–245.

Cunningham, J, McDonnell, A A and Easton, S (2002) Social validation data on three methods of physical restraint: Views of consumers, staff and students. *Research in Developmental Disabilities*, 21, 85–92.

Deveau, R and McGill, P (2007) *As the last resort: reducing the use of restrictive physical interventions.* Canterbury: Tizard Centre, University of Kent.

Deveau, R and McDonnell, A A (2008) As a last resort? Reducing the use of restrictive physical interventions using an organisational approach. (*Submitted to the British Journal of Learning Disabilities*).

Edwards, R (1999a) Physical restraint and gender: Whose role is it anyway? *Learning Disability Practice*, 2, 3, 12–15.

Edwards, R (1999b) The laying on of hands: nursing staff talk about physical restraint. *Journal of Learning Disabilities for Nursing, Health and Social Care*, 3, 3, 136–143.

Emerson, E, Robertson, J, Gregory, N, Hatton, C, Kessissoglou, S, Hallam, A and Hillery, J (2000) The treatment and management of challenging behaviours in residential settings. *Journal of Applied Research in Intellectual Disabilities*, 13, 197–215.

Favell, J E, McGimsey, J F and Jones, M L (1978) The use of physical restraint in the treatment of self injury and as positive reinforcement. *Journal of Applied Behavior Analysis*, 11, 225–241.

Feldman, M A, Atkinson, L, Foti-Gervais, L and Condillac, R (2004) Formal versus informal interventions for challenging behaviour in persons with intellectual disabilities. *Journal of Intellectual Disability Research*, 48, 60–68.

Gillett, E and Stenfert Kroese, B (2003) Investigating organizational cultures: A comparison of a 'high' and a 'low' performing residential unit for people with intellectual disabilities. *Journal of Applied Research in Intellectual Disabilities*, 16, 279–284.

Green, T and Wray, J (1999) Enabling carers to access specialist training in break away techniques: A case study. *Journal of Learning Disabilities for Nursing Health and Social Care*, 3, 34–38.

Hardcastle, M (2000) Real time training for mental health staff working in an in-patient setting. *The International Journal of Psychiatric Nursing Research*, 6, 650–656.

Harris, J (2002) Training *on physical interventions: making sense of the market.* In D Allen (Ed) *Ethical approaches to physical interventions. Responding to challenging behaviour in people with intellectual disabilities.* Kidderminster: BILD Publications.

Healthcare Commission (2006) *Joint investigation into the provision of services for people with learning disabilities at Cornwall Partnership NHS Trust.* London: Commission for Healthcare Audit and Inspection.

Hewitt, A S, Larson, S A, Lakin, K C, Sauer, J, O'Neill, S and Sedlezky, L (2004) Role and essential competencies of the frontline supervisors of direct support professionals in community services. *Mental Retardation*, 42, 122–35.

Hill, J and Spreat, S (1987). Staff injury rates associated with the implementation of contingent restraint. *Mental Retardation*, 25, 3, 141–145.

Jones, E, Felce, D, Lowe, K, Bowley, C, Pagler, J, Gallagher, B and Roper, A (2001) Evaluation of the dissemination of active support training in staffed community residences. *American Journal on Mental Retardation*, 106, 4, 344–358.

Kaye, N and Allen, D (2002) Over the top? Reducing staff training in physical interventions. *British Journal of Learning disabilities*, 30, 3, 129–132.

Killick, S and Allen, D (2005) Training staff in an adolescent inpatient psychiatric unit in positive approaches to managing aggressive and harmful behaviour: Does it improve confidence and knowledge? *Child Care in Practice*, 11, 3, 323–339.

Leadbetter, D (2002) *Good practice in physical interventions*. In D Allen (Ed) *Ethical approaches to physical interventions. Responding to challenging behaviour in people with intellectual disabilities*. Kidderminster: BILD Publications.

Leadbetter, D (2007) Millfields charter: finding the middle ground. *Learning Disability Practice*, 10, 34–37.

Leadbetter, D (2008). *Personal Communication*.

Lee, S, Gray, R, Gournay, K, Wright, S, Parr, A M and Sayer, J (2003) Views of nursing staff on the use of physical restraint. *Journal of Psychiatric and Mental Health Nursing*, 10, 425–430.

Lion, J R, Snyder, W and Merrill, G L (1981). Under-reporting of assaults on staff in state hospitals. *Hospital and Community Psychiatry*, 32, 497–498.

Mansell, J and Elliott, T (2001) Prediction of consequences for their work in residential settings. *American Journal on Mental Retardation*, 106, 434–447.

McDonnell, A (1997) Training care staff to manage challenging behaviour: An evaluation of a three-day course. *British Journal of Developmental Disabilities*, 43, 2, 156–161.

McDonnell, A A (2007) Why I am in favour of the Millfields Charter. *Learning Disability Practice*, 10, 26–29.

McDonnell, A A and Reeves, S (1996) Phasing out seclusion through staff training and support. *Nursing Times*, 92, 43–44.

McDonnell, A and Sturmey, P (1993) *Managing violent and aggressive behaviours of people with learning difficulties*. In R S P Jones and C Eayrs (Eds) *Challenging behaviours and mental handicap: A psychological perspective*. Kidderminster: BILD Publications.

McDonnell, A A, Sturmey, P, Oliver, C, Cunningham, J, Hayes, S, Galvin, M, Walshe, C and Cunningham, C (2008) The effects of staff training on staff confidence and challenging behavior in services for people with autism spectrum disorders. *Research in Autism Spectrum Disorders*, 58, 1–9.

McGill, P (1999) Establishing operations: implications for the assessment, treatment and prevention of problem behavior. *Journal of Applied Behavior Analysis*, 32, 393–418

Milne, D (1986) *Training Nurses as Behaviour Therapists*. London: Croom Helm.

Mittler, P (1987) Staff development: Changing needs and service contexts in Britain. In J Hogg and P Mittler (Eds) *Staff training in mental handicap* Beckenham: Croom Helm.

Moores, B and Grant, G W B (1976) On the nature and incidence of staff patient interactions in hospitals for the mentally handicapped. *International Journal of Nursing Studies*, 13, 69–81.

Morrison, L, Duryea, P B, Moore, C and Nathanson-Shinn, A (2002) *The lethal hazard of prone restraint: Positional asphyxiation*. Oakland, CA: Protection and Advocacy Inc.

Nord, G, Wieseler, N A and Hanson, R H (1991) Aversive procedures: The Minnesota experience. *Behavioral and Residential Treatment*, 6, 197–205.

Nunno, M, Holden, M and Tollar, A (2006). Learning from Tragedy: A survey of child and adolescent restraint facilities. *Child Abuse and Neglect: The International Journal*, 30, 1333–1342.

Parsons, M B and Reid, D H (1995). Training residential supervisors to provide feedback for maintaining staff teaching skills with people who have severe disabilities. *Journal of Applied Behaviour Analysis*, 28, 317–322.

Parsons, M B, Reid, D H and Crow, R E (2003). Best and worst ways to motivate staff in community agencies: A brief survey of supervisors. *Mental Retardation*, 41, 96–102.

Paterson, B (2007) Millfields charter: drawing the wrong conclusions. *Learning Disability Practice*, 10, 30–33.

Patterson, B A, Bradley, P, Stark, C, Saddler, D, Leadbetter, D and Allen, D (2003). Deaths associated with restraint use in health and social care in the UK. The results of a preliminary survey. *Journal of Psychiatric and Mental Health Nursing*, 10, 3–15.

Patterson, B A, Turnbull, J and Aitken, I (1992). An evaluation of a training course in the short term management of violence. *Nurse Education Today*, 12, 368–375.

Perkins, J and Leadbetter, D (2002) An evaluation of aggression management training in a special educational setting. *Emotional and Behavioural Difficulties*, 6, 1, 19–34.

Reid, D H and Parsons, M B (2002) *Working with staff to overcome challenging behaviour among people who have severe learning disabilities: a guide for getting support plans carried out..* Morganton, NC: Habilitative Management Consultants.

Roed, O L and Syse, A (2002) Physical interventions and aversive techniques in relation to people with learning disabilities in Norway. *The Journal of Adult Protection*, 4, 1, 25–32.

Rogers, P, Ghroum, P, Benson, R, Forward, L and Gournay, K (2006). Is breakaway training effective? An audit of one medium secure unit. *Journal of Forensic Psychiatry and Psychology*, 17, 4, 593–602.

Rogers, P, Miller, G, Paterson, B, Bonnett, C, Turner, P, Brett, S, Flynn, K and Noak, J (2007) Is breakaway training effective? Examining the evidence and the reality. *Journal of Mental Health Training, Education and Practice*, 2, 2, 5–12.

Schinke, S P and Wong, S E (1977). Evaluation of staff training in group homes for retarded persons. *American Journal of Mental Deficiency*, 82, 130–136

Shinnick, A and McDonnell, A A (2003) Training family members in behaviour management methods. *Learning Disability Practice*, 6, 2, 16–20.

Smith, B and Cumella, S (1996) Training for staff caring for people with a learning disability. *British Journal of Learning Disabilities*, 24, 20–25.

Smith, T, Parker, T, Taubman, M and Lovaas, O I (1992) Transfer of staff training from workshops to group homes. A failure to generalize across settings. *Research in Developmental Disabilities*, 13, 55–71.

Stokes, T F and Baer, D M (1977) An implicit technology of generalisation. *Journal of Applied Behavior Analysis*, 10, 349–367.

Sturmey, P and McGlynn, A P (2002) Restraint Reduction. In D Allen (Ed) *Ethical approaches to physical interventions. Responding to challenging behaviour in people with intellectual disabilities.* Kidderminster: BILD Publications.

Tarbuck, P (1992) Use and abuse of control and restraint. *Nursing Standard*, 6, 30–32.

Thackrey, M (1987) Clinician confidence in coping with patient aggression: assessment and enhancement. *Professional Psychiatry: Research and Practice*, 18, 57–60.

Topping-Morris, B (1995) Breaking the lock. *Nursing Standard*, 9, 55.

Van Den Pol, R A, Reed, D H and Fuqua, R W (1983) Peer training of safety related skills to institutional staff: Benefits for trainers and trainees. *Journal of Applied Behavior Analysis*, 16, 139–156.

Van Oorsouw, W M W J, Embregts, P J C M, Bosman, A M T and Jahoda, A (in press). Training staff serving clients with intellectual disabilities: A meta-analysis of aspects determining effectiveness. *Research in Developmental Disabilities.*

Weiss, E M (1998) *Deadly restraint: A Hartford Courant investigative report.*

White, C, Holland, E, Marsland, D and Oakes, P (2003) The identification of environments and cultures that promote abuse of people with intellectual disabilities: A review of the literature. *Journal of Applied Research in Intellectual Disabilities*, 16, 1–9.

Wolf, M M (1978) Social validity: The case for subjective measurement or how applied behavior analysis if finding its heart. *Journal of Applied Behavior Analysis*, 11, 203–214.

Woods, P and Cullen, C (1983) Determinants of staff behaviour in long-term care. *Behavioural Psychotherapy*, 11, 4–18.

Chapter 2

Reflections on Accreditation

Alan Jefferson

Throughout the 1990s there was a growing acceptance that the behavioural challenges presented by a small number of people who use services may mean that responses which use some form of physical intervention are appropriate and unavoidable. The British Institute of Learning Disabilities (BILD) has been in the forefront of work to identify safeguards to ensure that people with challenging behaviour and those they come in contact with (including staff members) are safeguarded. The BILD Physical Interventions Accreditation Scheme (PIAS) is one part of those safeguards, but to properly evaluate the contribution it has made it is necessary to embed it within the wider context of work done by BILD and other individuals and organisations to support the appropriate use of physical interventions.

In 1996, BILD published *Physical Interventions – A Policy Framework* (Harris et al, 1996) to assist organisations working with adults and children with learning disabilities and/or autism to develop clear and effective policies and practices for the use of physical interventions (an updated second edition was published in 2008). This publication emphasised the important part that risk assessment plays in identifying potential risks and adverse outcomes for individuals, estimating their likely consequences and finding ways to avoid unreasonable risk. It acknowledged that the use of physical interventions inevitably involves some level of risk, but that any techniques that present unreasonable risks to people who use services, staff or members of the public should not be used. There was recognition of the crucial importance of the level of expertise of the people who implement a technique, arguing that the level of risk is raised if members of staff are poorly trained. The publication promoted a broad training approach that encompasses the context and values framework within which services must apply physical interventions, and is not merely restricted to teaching the techniques themselves. Chapter 10 of the Framework recommended that:

- Staff who may be required to use physical interventions should receive regular training on knowledge, skills and values

- Training should be provided by an instructor with appropriate experience and qualifications

- Staff should only employ physical interventions which they have been trained to use

- Staff deployment should be organised to ensure that appropriately trained staff are available to respond to any incident that requires a physical intervention

Today, this approach seems very familiar and non-contentious, but it is important to remember that this was not always the case a decade or so ago, when it was not unusual for training to concentrate almost wholly on the teaching of techniques.

In the 1990s there was little consensus among trainers about appropriate intervention techniques and curriculum content. As a relative outsider, coming from the field of social care regulation, it seemed to me that a partisan approach with significant interpersonal rivalries characterised the territory. In 2001, BILD set out to improve consensus and further develop a framework of good practice by producing and publishing The BILD Code of Practice for Trainers in the Use of Physical Interventions (the Code) (BILD, 2001). The Code was developed after extensive consultation that involved a wide range of stakeholders and with reference to some key organisations, such as government departments and professional bodies. This broad-based approach has been instrumental in supporting the widespread acceptance of the Code. BILD hoped it would become an important point of reference for both service providers who commission training and the people responsible for the delivery of training, helping them to determine:

- What kind of training is appropriate for particular groups of service users and staff?

- How training on physical interventions should be integrated with other training on the management of challenging behaviour?

- How many staff should be included in a training session?

- How much training is required for staff working in different settings with different service users?

- How much importance should be attached to refresher training?

BILD also hoped that the Code would improve agreement between trainers about the way in which training should be commissioned and delivered. It was anticipated that it would lead to closer collaboration and discussion between service providers and the trainers they employ, and that this would, in turn, lead to more effective monitoring of training and to a raising of standards. BILD anticipated that the practical benefits from adherence to the Code would be:

- increases in the skills and confidence of individual members of staff

- a reduction in the incidence of injury

- less reliance on the use of physical interventions to manage challenging behaviour

Initially trainers and training organisations were invited to formally adopt the Code and comply with it whenever training was delivered. BILD maintained a database of the trainers that signed up to the Code and agreed to make this information publicly available so that service providers could use it when selecting trainers. Trainers were also encouraged to endorse the Code in their publicity material. The limitation of this approach was that monitoring depended on the people who used the trainers notifying BILD if they were dissatisfied. Effectively there was little to prevent a training organisation from formally adopting the Code but never actually applying it in the training that it offered.

Recognising these limitations, the Department of Health (DoH) and the then Department of Education and Employment (DfEE) encouraged BILD to establish a scheme for the accreditation of those trainers in physical interventions who implement and are able to demonstrate adherence to the standards of the Code. The Physical Interventions Accreditation Scheme (PIAS) was established in 2002.

An accreditation scheme involves a recognised body assessing and acknowledging that an individual or organisation meets pre-determined and published standards. Although generally a voluntary process, accreditation is more rigorous than the mere formal adoption of the standards because it involves evaluation, and usually periodic re-evaluation, of compliance with the standards. Accreditation can be a peer-review process, or it can be carried out by an external organisation. In the latter case, there are usually associated costs. The extent to which an accreditation scheme is given formal endorsement by influential external bodies is a determinant of its success. Accreditation can maintain and improve quality, stimulate collaboration between those who are accredited, and strengthen public confidence in the accredited product.

Successful accreditation programmes have a number of essential operating requirements:

- They must be underpinned by relevant achievable performance standards

- They must have objective and transparent information gathering and decision making processes

- The people who contribute to or make the judgements must be, and be regarded by the applicants as, knowledgeable and credible

- Finally, if they are to contribute to the continuous improvement of quality standards, they must offer opportunities for the accredited organisations or individuals to receive education and support

I believe that the BILD PIAS performs well against these criteria, but I will go on to identify areas where further improvement is possible.

At an early stage, the PIAS was given a high level of legitimacy by the references to it and to the Code contained in the Government's July 2002 publication *Guidance for Restrictive Physical Interventions* (DfES/DoH, 2002). References in the National Minimum Standards for Care Homes for Younger Adults (NMS)

(DoH, 2001) to physical intervention being used 'only as a last resort by trained staff in accordance with Department of Health guidance ...' (NMS 23.5) enhanced this legitimacy. It can be argued that this strong government endorsement should have led to a greater take-up of the scheme than has actually been the case, and the reasons for the level of take-up will be explored below.

For an applicant organisation, the BILD accreditation process begins with it agreeing to formally adopt the Code. The Code provides the relevant and achievable performance standards that have been identified as an essential component of an accreditation scheme. The standards contained in the Code quickly acquired widespread acceptance and were further strengthened by a second edition in 2006 (BILD 2006) that was again developed after extensive consultation. However, it is necessary to acknowledge that there are some organisations that consider the revisions were too accommodating and that they weakened the firm direction of the initial Code. One of the most successful aspects of the PIAS is the range of organisations that, notwithstanding different approaches and traditions, have proved willing to subscribe to the Code. I believe that this has contributed significantly to greater cohesion within the sector, though I acknowledge that there is a view that some of the accredited organisations are not as committed as they ought to be to implementing the Code. What is undoubtedly the case is that the Code and the PIAS have widened and stimulated debate among people and organisations that previously regarded themselves as having little in common and, to that extent, it has helped to improve and change practice.

The PIAS is clear that it will only accredit organisations to provide training for services that work with adults or children with learning disabilities and/or autistic spectrum disorder and/or emotional and behavioural difficulties. This is a two-edged sword. On the one hand, it clearly sets out the area of expertise of the accreditation scheme and this is helpful for coherence. On the other hand, it creates difficulties for training organisations that have a wider brief who find themselves in a situation where some of their work is accredited but other aspects are not. Though difficult, this is probably unavoidable. Although some of the actual physical interventions techniques that are taught by accredited organisations may be transferable to settings like Accident and Emergency Departments in hospitals, prisons and nightclubs, the underpinning philosophy and values base of the BILD scheme will be much less so. The PIAS is very clear that it is accrediting a total system and not just the teaching of techniques.

Once an interest has been expressed in accreditation and the Code has been adopted, applicants are invited to attend an induction workshop The workshop provides relevant documentation, advice about the accreditation process, the assessment visit that is part of the assessment process and the timescales for dealing with an accreditation application. It also gives an opportunity to meet with other training organisations considering making an application.

The application has three main elements: a written submission by the applicant, often referred to as the 'portfolio'; a visit by a BILD assessor to observe the delivery of training by the applicant, and a meeting with the PIAS panel, during which the applicant will make a presentation and answer questions from panel members. The panel will then make a decision based on all the evidence available to it. This will be a pass or fail decision, because the scheme does not make provision for any conditional registration. Whatever the panel decision is, the organisation will be provided with comprehensive feedback to enable further improvement and development. There is an appeals process that enables panel decisions to be challenged.

Essentially, the PIAS process fulfils the criterion of being objective and transparent. The scheme handbook provides detailed and comprehensive advice about the production of the written submission. The assessment criteria, both for the observation visit and for the panel decision-making, are set out in detail so applicants have a clear idea of what is expected of them. That said, there are some areas of difficulty. Observations are sometimes of one or two days of a longer training course. Inevitably, and understandably, not everything is covered during the period of the observation visit and, in these circumstances, the assessor has to make assumptions about the extent to which the rest of the requirements of the Code will be covered during periods of training that are not being observed. This does not result in an entirely even-handed approach because, if the length of the course is consistent with the observation, a much more complete assessment is possible. A second area of difficulty relates to the quality of the written submissions from applicants. Notwithstanding clear written advice and oversight from the PIAS manager, some submissions have been difficult to follow and have meant that the applicant has not given the best possible account of the training offered. In the early period of the PIAS scheme, this latter problem was exacerbated by a decision that panel members, other than the chair, would not see the submission until the day of the panel in order to ensure the integrity of the 'intellectual property' contained in the submissions. It simply was not possible to do justice to the extent of the documentation submitted by some applicants in this short timescale, and a subsequent decision to circulate the full submission to all panel members a few days in advance of the panel meeting has overcome this difficulty.

The panel decision is made by assessing the information provided in the oral presentation, the written submission and the report of the panel visit against the requirements of the Code and the scheme handbook. At the beginning of panel meetings, it is made clear to the members of the panel that these are the only criteria on which a decision can be based, and efforts to ensure that this is the case have generally been successful. There have been no complaints that information provided for the purposes of an accreditation decision has been used by any panel member for any other purposes.

The PIAS has also benefited from having knowledgeable and credible people to carry out the observation visits, and individual panel members have brought a wide range of experience and technical knowledge. The credibility of the panel has not been challenged. That said, the panel sometimes contains a majority of people who have a direct involvement in training. This can have two disadvantages: it may raise applicants' concerns that their training materials are being shared with potential commercial rivals; and it may also lead to panel members wanting to evaluate applications against their own views and experiences rather than against the formal criteria set out in the scheme. A particular example of this is the extent to which panel discussions can become bogged down by debates about the appropriateness of particular interventions that are taught by applicants. It is advantageous that the panel chair and vice-chair are not trainers or involved in the day-to-day delivery of services, because they recognise that they do not have much to contribute to debates about particular physical interventions, and this helps them to bring the discussion back to matters that are contained in the formal criteria.

As well as supporting them throughout the application process, BILD provides accredited trainers with a range of development opportunities to support the implementation of the Code. These include: a two-day annual behaviour support conference; events held throughout the country to promote the use of risk management in challenging behaviour and physical interventions; and continuing professional development workshops. One of the positive outcomes from the scheme has been evidence that it has led to collaborative working and research between accredited organisations, some of which would have been unlikely to work together at earlier periods in their history.

The absence of a conditional accreditation option in the PIAS ensures that organisations cannot operate for substantial periods of time without fully complying with the scheme criteria. There is provision, and a transparent process, for accreditation to be withdrawn if it can be demonstrated that: there has been significant malpractice; if there has been training that has breached the Code or has been a significant or contributory factor to the inappropriate management of violence or aggression; or if there have been other substantial breaches of the requirements of accreditation. Accreditation is granted for a period of three years, after which it has to be renewed. The re-accreditation process involves the articulation and assessment of developments, additions and changes within the programmes delivered. The criteria for re-accreditation are becoming increasingly rigorous, and this is contributing to the development of the quality of physical interventions training. Overall, the PIAS makes good use of all the available opportunities to make accreditation effective.

At the time of writing, 23 organisations are accredited within the PIAS, and this includes many of the most active and influential ones. The coverage is sufficient to ensure that training commissioners have a range of accredited trainers to choose from. However, there are still a considerable number of trainers who have not chosen to apply for accreditation and there is evidence that many of these continue to be used regularly. In some respects, this is disappointing, particularly bearing in mind the Government's strong endorsement of the scheme. It is necessary to ask why this is? In part, it is simply a reflection of the impact of any accreditation scheme. Whenever participation is voluntary and organisations are able to operate without being accredited, there will be some that choose not to join the scheme. The PIAS has a pricing structure of fees to be paid by an organisation seeking accreditation that includes small fees for adopting the code of practice and attending an induction workshop, and fees ranging from £3,500 + VAT to £7,500 + VAT (depending on the size of the organisation) for the three-year accreditation period. These are not insubstantial amounts, and an organisation would have to be convinced of the benefits of accreditation in order to pay them. Inevitably, the costs of accreditation are reflected in higher charges. Unfortunately, not all commissioners of training are yet convinced that the minimal extra costs of employing and accredited organisation represent best value. Neither are some convinced of the advantages of locating the training within the values base of a diversionary approach to managing challenging behaviour. There is some evidence of services providers opting for a one-day course that just teaches techniques rather than a longer course that puts the use of techniques in a good practice context, purely on the basis that a one-day course costs less. Commissioners of training have been provided with a framework within which they can evaluate the legal and professional framework of practice, but they cannot be made to use it. However, it is undoubtedly the case that the scheme has highlighted the need to put the use of physical interventions into a much wider framework of behavioural support, and there is evidence that many commissioning organisations are much more readily commissioning training on this basis. It is also encouraging that a substantial number of tenders for training do include a requirement for trainers to be accredited.

A further issue is that, for much of the time the PIAS has been in operation, there have been rumours that an alternative scheme sponsored by the National Institute for Mental Health in England (NIMHE) is to be established. NIMHE is an organisation that has closer links with the Government and it is understandable that some organisations have preferred to wait to see whether another accreditation scheme was developed. At the time of writing, there is no sign of any alternative accreditation scheme, and the further development of the BILD scheme would be enhanced if the Government were to re-state its support for the PIAS. BILD, too, could do more to raise awareness of the scheme, particularly among organisations that commission physical interventions training, especially in educational settings.

The PIAS is no different from any other accreditation scheme insofar as it has no powers to prevent the continuing operation of an organisation that has applied for accreditation but has not been able to demonstrate that it is able to meet the criteria for approval. An accreditation scheme, particularly one that includes the majority of the organisations in the particular field, may provide a stimulus for further improvement, but this is as far as it can go; the rest is up to the people in the marketplace. A number of organisations have failed to gain accreditation at their first submission, and most have worked hard to improve their practice and have been successful at a subsequent presentation to the panel. This is good evidence of the PIAS making a direct contribution to the improvement of the quality of the training that is being offered. Beyond this, there is little that accreditation can do to prevent an organisation that does not meet the standards from continuing to operate. Achieving this would require a statutory registration scheme that included sanctions against anyone who operated without registration.

The PIAS has made a valuable contribution to improving practice in the use of physical interventions. However, there are a number of areas where further progress is possible and desirable.

For a number of years, BILD provided clear and challenging professional leadership for this area of practice. In recent years, its leadership has been less strong. Changes such as the introduction of the Mental Capacity Act and the Deprivation of Liberty Safeguards legislation create new challenges for the support of people with challenging behaviour, and there is a need for leadership to be reasserted and re-focused.

Further work needs to be done on the scope and boundaries of the accreditation scheme. There is increasing awareness of and concern about the use of physical interventions with older people (CSCI 2007), particularly those suffering from dementia, and the boundaries between challenging behaviour and mental illness are not well covered by the PIAS as it is currently set up. Reference has already been made to the confusion that exists for organisations that do not have the full range of their activities covered by their accreditation. A limiting factor to the extension of the scheme is the extent to which the value base that underpins the Code can be extended to encompass different service user groups. BILD's terms of reference would be another factor to be taken into account.

As well as considering the types of people who can be covered by the scheme, there is also a need to review the settings that it covers. Much of the challenging behaviour that people exhibit in care services also occurs in family settings. However, the vast majority of training is done with paid care staff and not with family members (see Chapter 4, this volume). Family members want low-cost training that is available locally and at a convenient time. It is necessary to ask how their needs can be supported by and promoted through the accreditation scheme. The recent developments in direct payments and individual budgets mean that people are increasingly directly employing personal assistants to look after them rather than making use of existing care services. How will these people learn to use physical interventions safely and appropriately? What can the PIAS do to respond to the needs of personal assistants?

Although every effort has been made to avoid challenges (and overall, the efforts have worked well) the scheme remains vulnerable to allegations that there are potential conflicts of interest among many of the people who conduct the visits of observation and make up the panel. These are individuals who, themselves, provide physical interventions training and who are, in a number of instances, involved with organisations that are already accredited. Though everyone on the panel operates with the utmost integrity, the fact remains that these panel members are sometimes, in effect, passing judgement on their competitors. There would be advantages in having a scheme that does not include representatives of accredited organisations or people who have an active engagement in the teaching of physical interventions. Increasingly the skills that are needed and are used by the panel are linked to the assessment of evidence against performance standards. BILD could usefully widen the sources targeted for the recruitment of panel members.

There is a risk, and already some evidence, that increasing the rigour of the scheme adds to costs. Quite rightly, BILD expects that accredited organisations will be better able to demonstrate compliance with the Code when they come back to the panel for re-accreditation. Recent revisions of the scheme will see a greater emphasis on the comprehensiveness of the observation visits and there are cost implications attached to this. It has already been noted that the cost of accreditation may inhibit the coverage of the PIAS, and so increasing costs to sustain a more rigorous process may have a deterrent effect on further take-up of the scheme. This is an area that needs to be carefully monitored.

Thus far the PIAS has been reluctant to become involved in the review of the appropriateness or otherwise of individual techniques of physical intervention. This is an area that is fraught with difficulty. It can be argued that the whole idea of 'approving' particular techniques is incompatible with the notion, central to the Code, that responses to challenging behaviour should be individualised and geared to the minimum level of intervention that is consistent with the person's best interests at a point in time. The notion that an approved technique can only be used in carefully risk-assessed circumstances is relatively sophisticated and there is a danger that, in the heat of the moment, practitioners will use the 'approved' technique without bothering to undertake an assessment of whether it is necessary to use it. On the other hand, there is evidence that some techniques – particularly prone holds – can be extremely dangerous, and there is legitimate pressure on the PIAS to prohibit them being taught by accredited organisations and individuals. There are two possible approaches: to have a list of approved techniques (which would be a mammoth task, given the number of variations that exist) or to have a list of techniques that are not approved. The latter appears to be the most practicable approach, but the danger is that all the techniques that are not on the 'banned' list become regarded, by default, as 'approved', and this would be a dangerous situation for the PIAS to put itself in. BILD is currently undertaking work to devise an assessment process for individual techniques (see Chapter 3, this volume). This is a radical departure that will take the scheme into controversial territory that previously, Government departments have shown great reluctance to enter (though Wales is an exception). By beginning to look at how the safety of techniques can be evaluated, BILD is responding to strong pressures from 'the market' and this is a positive move. However, this is an area where there are some very polarised positions, and there is a risk that some of the consensus that the Code and the PIAS have managed to achieve will be damaged by disagreements about what is acceptable. If BILD is able to achieve any significant levels of consensus on this topic, it will have achieved a great deal and will have undoubtedly re-asserted its leadership role in physical interventions policy and practice. One desirable outcome from this work would be the production of a consistent model for assessing the risks inherent in particular techniques and clear guidance about the professional backgrounds and qualifications of the people who would be competent to make decisions using the model.

A final issue that needs to be considered arises from the comparative absence of research evidence to demonstrate that good quality training in the use of physical interventions actually has beneficial results. The evidence from the small number of studies that have been carried out does not strongly support the assertion that trained staff will correctly apply the right technique in a 'heat of the moment' intervention to deal with challenging behaviour. This may be because the real-life use of a technique is very different from the controlled circumstances in which it is taught and practised. It may, however, be that the research has, thus far, concentrated too much on the application of the techniques and not enough on whether the emphasis on teaching techniques in the context of a wider diversionary strategy has reduced the frequency of their use. Given the uncertainty of the effectiveness of the teaching of physical interventions, it would seem wise if BILD's work to further develop the PIAS is underpinned by it conducting or commissioning work on the impact of the scheme on day-to-day practice. It does not seem wise to continue to devote resources to refining the PIAS if it cannot be clearly demonstrated that it has a positive impact on practice.

The PIAS was a timely contribution to improving the quality of physical interventions training and practice and, as such, has been a positive development. There is some scope for further refinement of the scheme and this potential has not always been acted upon quickly enough. However, an accreditation scheme will never, in itself, be sufficient to guarantee high quality practice or that unsuitable providers are prevented from operating. Stronger statutory sanctions would be needed to achieve this, and this is an area that the UK Government needs to give further thought to.

References

Harris, J, Allen, D, Cornick, M, Jefferson, A and Mills, R (1996) *Physical Interventions a Policy Framework*. Kidderminster: BILD Publications.

Harris, J, Cornick, M, Jefferson, A and Mills, R (1996) *Physical Interventions a Policy Framework. Second Edition*. Kidderminster: BILD Publications.

BILD (2001) *Code of Practice for Trainers in the Use of Physical Interventions*. Kidderminster: BILD Publications.

Department of Health and Department of Education and Employment (2002) *Guidance for Restrictive Physical Interventions – How to provide safe services for people with Learning Disabilities and Autistic Spectrum Disorder*. London: Department of Health.

Department of Health (2001) *Care Homes for Younger Adults National Minimum Standards*. London: The Stationery Office.

BILD (2006) *BILD Code of Practice for the use of physical interventions (second edition*. Kidderminster: BILD Publications.

Commission for Social Care Inspection (2007) *Rights Risks and Restraints*. London: CSCI.

Chapter 3

Evaluating the Risks associated with Physical Interventions

Alan Martin, Andrew McDonnell, David Leadbetter and
Brodie Paterson

Introduction

The evaluation of physical intervention techniques is clearly a controversial issue. As successive national reports have recognised (eg Deveau and McGill, 2007; Hart and Howell, 2004), the present unregulated market economy of training provision and the poor quality of the research literature has meant that commissioners of restraint training are often heavily influenced by the marketing activities of commercial training companies promoting proprietary brands of training which are often unsupported by valid research evidence of their effectiveness. Indeed, the available data suggests that many such training models may increase risks – a conclusion with profound implications for safety and legal liability (see Leadbetter, this volume). Hence the quality of the debate on restraint safety in the UK to date has been primarily conducted in terms of asking, 'Whether system X is better than system Y?' or 'Should technique A or B be banned?'

In the absence of sound empiricism, 'expert' opinion prevails. Although a vital element of the discourse, the concept of 'expert' in this field raises complications in terms of who qualifies for this designation. Systematic studies have concluded that the term 'expert' is often misapplied (eg Bell and Stark 1998). At present there are few barriers to any aspiring trainer, regardless of background, understanding, or personal values, setting themselves up to deliver physical restraint training to health, education and care services. Indeed, opposition to initiatives such as the British Institute of Learning Disabilities' (BILD) physical intervention accreditation scheme attempting to raise the standard of practice and to ensure a professional care sector value base has been raised from a number of groups (eg www.nfps.info/BILDaccreditation.htm).

Although the recommendation in the recent Government report (Smallridge and Williamson, 2008) for a mandatory accreditation scheme is to be welcomed, an effective, properly funded, multi-sectoral scheme may be many years away. The absence of robust, valid outcome and biomechanical data on restraint safety has been a pivotal obstacle to the development of effective accreditation and regulation schemes in both the UK and USA. The construction of a reliable and valid evaluation tool is therefore a critical step and one that would provide the basis for further initiatives aimed at securing a policy and practice agenda based on evidence rather than rhetoric.

The evaluation of physical interventions described in this chapter owes its origins to the work originally conducted by BILD and which resulted in advice about policy development (Harris et al, 1996, 2008) and a Code of Practice for training organisations who teach the use of physical interventions (BILD, 2001, 2006). Alongside this, the publication of guidance produced jointly by the Department of Health and Department for Education and Skills (2002) provided the impetus for the development of a national accreditation scheme for training organisations teaching physical interventions in services for people with intellectual disabilities, people with autistic spectrum disorders and children and young people with emotional and behavioural difficulties.

The risk assessment of specific physical intervention methods was considered by many to be a natural extension of this work. A formal proposal that attempted to develop a risk assessment process for physical interventions was tabled by members of BILD in 2005. The key aim of this was to develop a 'traffic light' index of the relative risks of specific methods. During the initial consultation, it was determined that the scale of the task was extremely large and that the key focus should instead be to develop a generic risk assessment tool that could be applied to any physical intervention.

Having been invited to consult on the development of a Code of Practice for Managing Children and Young People's Behaviour in the Secure Estate (2006), BILD approached the Youth Justice Board for England and Wales (YJB) and was successful in securing financial support to further this work.

This chapter describes the construction of the tool and its application to five physical interventions in two separate studies, together with a third study that sought the views of service users on the same interventions. The full report on this work can be downloaded at www.BILD.org.uk.[1]

The initial development of the measure

The risk assessment tool was developed over a consultation period of six months by a panel of three members with an additional member acting as an outside reviewer. The panel members all:

- had extensive experience of violence management and restraint training

- held formal instructor qualifications in more than one training system

[1] The panel would wish to extend their thanks to those without whose assistance this project would not have been completed: Professor David Allen for his support, mentorship and encouragement; Justine Barksby for her work on the service user consultation; staff at YJB for their commitment to the project; and BILD for their ongoing commitment to promote safe practice in the use of restrictive physical interventions.

- had published outcome research on the effectiveness of staff training in peer reviewed journals

In addition to professional qualifications encompassing social work, intellectual disability nursing, clinical psychology, teaching, mental health nursing and clinical sociology, two of the panel also held high-level martial arts qualifications. The diverse professional backgrounds of panel members allowed individual members to contribute different perspectives which stretched and challenged the thinking of the group This allowed for a synthesis of views through discussion.

The panel members were initially asked to independently identify key questions that in their view were relevant to the assessment of risk of physical interventions. They then examined the items generated, both in terms of their construct validity and their specific wording. Finally, individual items were clustered into related categories. In all, there were seven iterations of the draft tool, the final version (see *Table 1* below) of which consisted of 39 items arranged into four sub-headings of safety, trainability, risks to service users and effectiveness.

The Juster Purchase Probability Scale (Colton and Covert, 2007) was used to assess each individual item other than those marked with an asterisk (the latter being categorical ratings). This scale was originally developed by market researchers and contains an 11-point scale with anchors ranging from 'No chance or almost no chance' to 'Certain, practically certain'. Probabilistic judgements are a central component of this measure. It was decided to adopt this scale as it contained a wide range of potential responses and, therefore, the measure would in theory be sensitive to different levels of risk posed by different interventions. Higher scores on individual items and higher scores on the total scale therefore indicated higher levels of risk.

In completing the tool, respondents are required to make four assumptions:

- Staff are of average fitness

- Staff have no predisposing injuries

- Trainers are teaching the techniques to a high technical standard

- The individual who experiences the physical intervention is generally in good health

Testing the scale

Collation of sample techniques

A selection of physical intervention techniques upon which the scale could be tested was generated by asking training organisations accredited through the BILD scheme to submit material from their training manuals for inclusion within the project. Positive responses were received from six organisations, one of which was not actually accredited by BILD; the authors are indebted to these

(Text continues on page 44)

Table 1: Final version of risk assessment tool.

Dimension	General definition	Item	Additional definitions
Safety	A technique is deemed safe when it is applied to an actively resistant/hostile service user and can be repeatedly used on a regular basis without moderate/serious injury to staff or service users.	1. Repeated regular (daily/weekly) use of this technique on a training course (Passive/no resistance from participants) is likely to cause injury to staff.	Minor injuries involve reddening skin swelling bruising which is not visible after 24 hours. Moderate injuries Bruising and minor lacerations which may require immediate first aid. Serious injuries includes breaking of bones, tissue damage requiring external medical treatment and fatality.
		2. Repeated regular (daily/weekly) use of this technique in a real world setting (with service user resistance) is likely to cause injury to staff.	As above.
		3. Repeated regular (daily/weekly) use of this technique in a real world setting (with service user resistance) is likely to cause injury to a service user.	As above.
		4. Use of this technique in a real-world setting (with service user resistance) is likely to restrict respiration (breathing).	A method may be deemed to compromise breathing if its application restricts movement of the ribcage, diaphragm and accessory muscles of respiration or airway.
		5. This technique uses a locking movement.	Any technique which when applied to a joint (eg head, arm, wrist, digit, knee, leg) uses flexion to extend the joint to maximum in one direction and does not allow the individual to move the joint without the staff member releasing pressure.
		6. There is a likelihood that the deliberate infliction of pain by staff is the active mechanism of control with this technique.	Pain compliance occurs when an average person who experience this technique repeatedly verbalise that they are experiencing pain and request its immediate removal'.
		7. Resistance by the service user will result in them experiencing pain.	

Trainability	Trainability relates to the ease of teaching of the method.	8. The safe application of this technique on a regular (daily/weekly) basis requires an expert skill level from staff.			An expert level of skill requires a high level of physical coordination and consistency of application of technique.	
		9. The safe application of this technique on a regular (daily/weekly) basis requires a high level of staff fitness.				
		10. Assuming 20 minutes teaching time to a group of 12, a trainee would be able to competently demonstrate the technique on at least three repeated test trials in a controlled environment?				
		11. This method would require intensive practice involving a minimum of 50+ repetitions to achieve competence within a controlled training environment.				
		12. This method would require a high level of practice (monthly) by staff to maintain competency.			Practice more than five repetitions of the method in the preceding month.	
		13. This technique requires an expert level of bi-lateral hand eye /co-ordination?				
		14. Would this technique be equally effective (as described) for children (under 18) and adults (18+)?				
Client risk factors	Any physical characteristic of the service user which may increase risk of harm when applying the method.	15. Medical obesity (a BMI of 30 or greater) in the subject, particularly excess abdominal adiposity, would increase the level of risk associated with this technique for the subject.				
		16. Anorexia (a BMI of less than 17.5) in the subject would increase the level of risk associated with this technique for the subject.				
		17. A physical disability in the subject would increase the level of risk associated with this technique for the subject.				

Dimension	General definition	Item	Additional definitions
		22. In the event of technique requiring more than one staff member. The technique requires: A high level of pre-rehearsed co-ordination between staff, requiring regular practice and communication.	
		23. This method has overtly sexualised elements.	A technique may be interpreted as overtly sexualised if it involves either direct physical contact or close proximity (within six inches to or on the genitalia, breasts or buttocks).
		24. The use of this technique on a regular (daily/weekly occurrence) basis would result in a traumatic triggering event.	A traumatic triggering event is characterised by the following symptoms of reliving the event, avoiding situations that remind you of the event, feeling numb and feeling hyper-aroused.
		25. The use of this technique on a regular (daily/weekly occurrence) basis could evoke previous traumatic experience.	
		26. This technique may have sexuality issues.	A sexuality issue occurs if the sexuality of the staff applying the method or the service user experiencing the method mediates the effect of the technique.
		27. A lay individual witnessing this method would make a formal complaint.	
		28. A lay individual (member of the public) witnessing this technique being used in a public area in response to 'low consequence behaviour(s)' would make a formal complaint.	Low consequence behaviour (ie low probability of injury to staff or service user if the behaviour is not restricted.
		29. A lay individual (member of the public) witnessing this technique being used in a public area in response to 'high consequence behaviour(s)' would make a formal complaint.	High consequence behaviour (ie high probability of injury to staff, service user or others present if the behaviour is not restricted.

	30. This technique would require more than an average space (a normal 12 x 12 feet or 4 x 4 metre room) to carry out safely.									
	31. The absence of a matted training area to practice this technique would increase the risks of an injury during training.									
	32. The application of this technique on a hard surface (wooden, ceramic or stone floor) would increase the risk of injury to staff and/or subject.									
	33. The application of this technique on a carpeted area would increase the risk of injury to staff and/or subject.									
	34. This technique would require at least five hours training for an individual to be able to safely instruct others to competence in this single procedure									
	35. This technique complies with the guidance on the use of physical interventions (ie National Institute of Clinical Excellence; Holding Safely; DoH and DfES; BILD Code of Practice; European Council 2004; Welsh Assembly Government).									
	36. Use of this method would comply with the principles of good practice in Moving and Handling									
Effectiveness A technique is deemed effective if it can be consistently applied and demonstrated to work on at least 80% of occasions irrespective of care context.	37. This method is likely to be effective when applied to a young child (Under 12).									
	38. This method is likely to be effective when applied to a teenager (12–18 years).									
	39. This method is likely to be effective when applied to an older person (65 years +).									

organisations for their support in the project. Of concern, however, was the fact that 18 of the accredited organisations chose not to submit techniques.

Each participating organisation was required to submit the written descriptions of the application of each technique submitted, along with at least three photographs/images of the application of the technique in practice. Physical interventions were then categorised into:

- physical disengagement techniques (including methods designed to disengage from hair-pulling, biting, hitting with an open hand)

- escort methods (including both one- and two-person escorts)

- physical restraint methods (including prone holds, supine holds and seated restraint)

The panel having considered the criteria for selection and then removing techniques which were duplicated amongst the six systems, a pool of 77 techniques remained. Thirty-eight procedures were designed for disengagement, 12 for escort moves and 27 restraint. The techniques were placed in sealed envelopes by BILD staff and number-coded into the above three general categories. This ensured that the methods themselves could not be attributed to any specific training system and that the organisations who submitted information to the project remained anonymous throughout.

Five representative techniques were selected from this pool for scrutiny via three different processes: by the panel members, via a web-based study, and by a group of service users. The five techniques in question were:

1. An escort technique in which two staff lift and carry the service user. This is an escalation from a standing hold and is described as a response to the service user dropping their body weight, hooking furniture/fixtures with the foot, and obstructing negotiation through doorways.

2. A restraint technique designed for one staff member to respond to self-injury in a service user who is lying on the floor. The description of the technique allows for an escalation in an additional member of staff to assist by holding the service user's legs.

3. A restraint which involves two members of staff approaching the service user from the front and taking them to the floor. The service user travels backwards to the floor.

4. A restraint technique designed to be used by one member of staff on a young person. The technique involves holding the service user from behind and using the wall as support to take the person to a sitting position.

5. A physical disengagement technique that involved the deliberate infliction of pain. The technique was described as being appropriate for use by staff to effect separation when a service user has grabbed hold of another service user or member of staff.

Assessments by panel members

All methods were reviewed by the panel using the same procedure. This was as follows:

- A visual representation of the method was presented to the panel

- A written description of the method was then read aloud to all panel members. This was repeated until the panel members agreed that they understood the method

- Panel members demonstrated the methods on each other with reference to both the visual representation and the written description. Each panel member undertook the roles of both staff and service users in turn

- Panel members were encouraged to discuss the methods openly in terms of how it made them feel and the technical issues involved in applying the technique

- Panel members each independently scored the method and their individual results were recorded

- After discussion of their individual scores panel members attempted to agree a consensus score (It was agreed at the outset that this agreement may not be attainable in all cases)

- Comments for each question were then collectively agreed by panel members

- A general overall set of comments were included for all of the methods

The value of all members demonstrating physical interventions on each other was a critical component in the deliberative process. In particular, this experiential component of the methodology appeared to help judgements of risk and fragility.

When applying the tool, the panel was able to fairly easily identify the potential vulnerabilities in each of the techniques and, whilst some techniques would clearly be described as being of low intrusiveness, even these techniques had the potential for things to go wrong and safety of both service user and staff member to be compromised.

As stated above, the different professional backgrounds of panel members allowed individual members to contribute varying perspectives that stretched and challenged the thinking of the group However, what was apparent from an observational perspective was the fact that all panel members, irrespective of background, professional experience and initial response to the process, were willing to debate and, through this process, show a willingness to be persuaded by reasoned argument and, at times, lively debate in order to develop a synthesis of views.

The reliability of individual panel member ratings on each technique were analysed using the following classifications. An item was classified as agreed if all three panel members rated the item within one scale point. An item was rated as partially agreed if two panel members rated the item within one point. An item was rated having no agreement if none of the panel members ratings were within one scale point of each other.

Across all five techniques, items were then further classified as having good inter-rater agreement if there were three or more 'agreed' ratings across the five techniques, and poor agreement if there was one or more cases of 'no agreement' across the five techniques. Any other combination of scores was regarded as evidence of partial agreement.

On the basis of the latter, 12 items had good inter-rater agreement (items 3, 4, 8, 9, 10, 11, 15,16, 18, 21, 26 and 28), 14 items had partial agreement (2, 6, 7, 12, 13, 14, 17, 19, 20, 31, 32, 34, 38 and 39), and eleven items had poor agreement (1, 5, 22, 23, 24, 25, 27, 29, 33, 36 and 37). Thus, 67 per cent of items showed good to partial agreement and 33 per cent poor agreement. Encouragingly, the items with good to partial agreement are fairly evenly distributed across all elements of the tool. The items with poorer reliability clustered around, although were not exclusively concerned with, some of the potentially more subjective psychological impact of physical intervention use (eg sexualised elements, triggering/re-triggering of trauma).

The panels' total score on their consensus ratings of the five techniques are shown in *Table 2* below:

Table 2: Panel consensus ratings.

Item	Total score	Ranking (1 = highest risk; 5 = lowest risk)
Technique 1	172	5
Technique 2	235	2
Technique 3	259	1
Technique 4	233	3
Technique 5	230	4

These results suggested that the tool was reasonably sensitive to differences in potential risk associated with particular techniques. The range between the highest and lowest risk procedures was 87 points, and it was possible to rank order the techniques from highest to lowest risk. Perhaps predictably, the intervention involving taking a service user to the floor was assessed as posing the highest risk; more surprisingly, the pain compliance procedure was ranked fairly low. The ratings for some techniques were numerically close, however, suggesting that differences in risk assessment may be fine in a number of instances and that the scale may need weight certain ratings in order to fully capture their importance. The ability of the tool to discriminate risk amongst apparently similar procedures will be an important future study goal.

Web-based study

A second test of the tool involved an electronic web-based study on the same techniques. The study was conducted over the internet via a web page on the BILD site that provided visual representations of the five sample physical intervention techniques evaluated by the panel; the images of the techniques were anonymised by using BILD staff to model the procedures concerned instead of using the originals supplied by the training organisations.

Participants were asked to complete two questionnaires. The first was a copy of the assessment tool which, when completed, could be submitted electronically to BILD. The second was designed to provide an opportunity for participants to provide anonymous comments about the assessment tool. They were able to rate the questions in terms of the most/least relevant and provide suggestions for modification of questions, or additional questions which may be of use.

Invited participants included all organisations currently accredited by BILD, professionals associated with the BILD Physical Interventions Accreditation Scheme, and individuals who have published articles in peer reviewed journals over the last five years. Access was also provided to the NHS Counter Fraud and Security Management Service, whose remit includes the management of violence and aggression in health services. It was their intention to circulate details of the study to local security management specialists based in hospitals and Primary Care Trusts. Additional invitees included the expert medical panel established by the Youth Justice Board to provide advice on the use of restraint in secure children's services.

The final study sample involved 67 respondents (45 males, 22 females). Sixty-four were physical interventions trainers with an average of 9.7 years of experience (sd = 8.70). Their mean age was 44.2 years (sd = 9.5). Ninety-five per cent of respondents were from BILD accredited organisations.

Details of the scores using the risk assessment tool are presented in *Table 3* below.

Table 3: Total mean scores and standard deviations for web-based study.

Technique	Number of responses	Mean	Standard deviation	Ranking (1 = highest risk; 5 = lowest risk)
1	23	206.5	39.9	3
2	10	213.3	39.8	2
3	10	235.6	49.5	1
4	12	202.8	49.9	4
5	12	188.8	59.3	5

The mean scores from the web-based study were more narrowly distributed than the panel scores, but again discriminated between techniques. While the participants agreed with the results of the panel study in terms of the rank ordering of techniques two and three, there was no agreement on the ranking of the remaining techniques. Importantly, as with the panel study, the technique that involved taking the service user to the floor was identified as being the intervention of highest risk; once again, however, the pain compliance procedure had a low ranking.

There was significant variance in the rating of the individual techniques between different participants as indicated by the sizeable standard deviations for each score, suggesting that the reliability of the tool may be poorer here than in the panel study.

Twenty respondents also submitted a response to the second questionnaire, which attempted to seek information from respondents as to their view of which questions where the most/least useful. The highest ranked most relevant questions items were, in order of highest to lowest, questions 4 (cited by 19 respondents in total), 3 (15), 21 (10), 12 (7), 6 (6) and 7 (6). These items covered techniques' impact on respiration, likelihood of causing pain, fragility and high-practice requirements. The least favoured items were 27 (cited by 7 respondents), 28 (6), 29 (5), 25 (5) and 16 (5); these items covered the likelihood of members of the public lodging complaints further to witnessing the use of the technique, the likelihood of the technique inducing trauma, and the safety of using the technique with an anorexic service user. It was clear that there was more agreement on favoured rather than on the non-favoured items. Interestingly, but perhaps not surprisingly, the most favoured items were amongst the items with highest reliability in the panel study, whereas the least favoured items were amongst those with lowest reliability.

The respondents also made a number of suggestions on how the tool could be improved. These included:

- The inclusion of a comments section
- Reducing the length of the tool
- Reducing repetition
- Improving clarity on specific items

Service user study

The web study had enabled the project team to ascertain the views of professionals in the field. An additional final stage sought to obtain the views of service users about the five sample interventions. Because of the complexity of the assessment tool, a qualitative approach was employed for this study.

A convenience sample of people with intellectual disabilities known to one of the authors was constructed. Following approval of the study from the relevant academic institution, an independent researcher initially approached a care organisation and, in conjunction with relevant care managers, offered service users the opportunity to take part in the study. On the scheduled day of the interview, each participant was asked if they still wanted to take part and who, if anyone they wanted present.

Seven participants were initially identified, but one of these was later withdrawn; the sample therefore consisted of six people, which is an acceptable number in qualitative research. Ogier (1998), for example, suggests that a sample size within descriptive studies should be around 5–10. All participants, by definition, lived in care settings and had done so for most of their adult lives. All displayed behaviours that had resulted in them being exposed to physical interventions. They were all able to understand the nature of the questions and give their responses to them. By definition, they were therefore quite an able group and not representative of the wider population of people with intellectual disabilities.

The participants were shown all of the methods that have been reviewed by the panel; the methods were demonstrated to the service users by the facilitator and a member of their staff. On each occasion, this took place in the service users' homes in order to make them feel as comfortable as possible. None of the five selected interventions were in use in the residential services concerned.

Once the methods had been demonstrated, the service users were asked what they thought of the interventions, using open-ended questions. Example questions included:

- What do you think of this?

- How would you feel if this was done to you?

- How would you feel if this was done to one of the people you live with?

Throughout the interviews, the researcher was careful not to lead the participants. Previous research has shown that people with intellectual disabilities are more susceptible to suggestibility and yielding to leading questions or ideas put forward by others (Sigelman et al, 1981). The researcher also had to be careful not to give an indication of what they expected or wanted to hear, as people with learning disabilities are at high risk of saying what they feel the person wants to hear (Atkinson, 1998). In addition to the structured questions, an opportunity for service users to share any additional information they wanted to disclose to the facilitators was provided. Their responses were recorded in an open-ended way and then the information analysed for trends and consensus of opinion.

All the service users questioned disliked the majority of the methods shown to them. They were unanimous in their dislike for techniques one, two, four and five. All of them made it clear that they would be unhappy at having the methods done to them or carried out on a peer. Three of them felt that technique three was acceptable, and three did not.

All service users felt that the first technique was a horrible way to be treated; two also stated it looked dangerous for both staff and service users. One person also mentioned the Health and Safety at Work Act regarding this technique! Similarly, all expressed their dislike of technique two. Several said they would report staff if they did this to them or a peer. Those that felt technique three was acceptable were putting it into context alongside prone restraint, and so were in effect saying that it was preferable to that and therefore 'ok'. Four people said that the fourth technique looked dangerous and all disliked it. Again, all disliked technique five; one person stated that it could kill someone and another stated it looked 'childish'.

An important observation from this study concerned the differences in perception about what is meant by physical interventions. Some participants stated they had never experienced any forms of physical interventions, but then went on to describe very restrictive techniques that had been carried out on them in the past. These included prone restraint, seclusion and being tied to a chair and a door handle by their belts. Those who had been exposed to more restrictive restraints/ physical interventions and seclusion in the past generally showed a more tolerant view to the techniques demonstrated. Three of the people had been restrained in prone position in the past and felt strongly about this. One person discussed having six people sitting on them, while having a broken leg, and another being dragged in prone position. Statements made while talking about prone restraint included: 'It just makes you angry and you want to fight back', 'I wish it could be banned' and 'When they let go you just feel worse – more angry'.

Discussion

The prevention and safer management of violence remains a concern for many service providers across a range of diverse settings. The significant risks to staff (both during training and workplace implementation) and service users makes the need to base training in physical interventions upon robust evidence a critical priority. The development of a tool which would facilitate a transition from a situation in which expert opinion (a concept previously noted to be questionable in this context) can be supplanted by systematically collated and robust evidence is therefore a significant first step

This chapter has described the early stages in developing and testing the utility of a risk assessment tool for physical intervention techniques.

The 39-item scale appeared to have a high degree of face validity amongst panel members and web study participants, and an acceptable level of inter-rater reliability in the panel study. The tool discriminated between the risks associated with a series of five sample physical interventions, although there was relatively limited agreement in the risk-ranking of these interventions between the panel and web-based studies. The latter is perhaps not surprising, given the differences in approach between the two studies and, most notably, the fact that the panel members were able to deliver and experience the interventions during their deliberations, whereas the web participants were not.

Much more work is clearly needed to establish the psychometric value of the tool. This will require a replication with a larger sample of procedures and a participant group of sufficient size to enable the use of factor analysis to explore the tool's structure. As already mentioned, evidence of its ability to differentiate between levels of risk in physical interventions that may initially appear topographically similar is also required. More specific work on the reliability of individual items is essential; this process will result in some of the less reliable items being dropped from the scale, thus making it easier to administer. Consideration also needs to be given to the relative weight ascribed to certain items. A positive 'trainability' score, for example, may mean little if a technique is fundamentally unsafe; similarly, a technique may be highly fragile, but at present this impacts on less than three per cent of a its score on the whole assessment tool. Pain compliance attracts slightly more attention in the scale, but is still only covered by three out of 39 items. Finally, evidence from the service user study reaffirms the importance of the scrutiny of techniques by those who are the recipients of them. This too must be captured in future versions, with a user-friendly version of a shortened tool perhaps being the most obvious way forward. Service user input could also be vital in helping construct the weightings for different scale items.

There were a number of difficulties in conducting this work, and it is important to note these. Throughout the process, panel members had to make significant assumptions about the methods they reviewed. Most notably, the amount of time devoted to teaching these methods on training courses could in most cases only be estimated. In addition, the retention of such skills will be highly context dependent. For example, a training course which teaches a technically complex method as one of several in a day needs to be reviewed slightly differently than courses which may devote an entire day to the teaching of one method only. These differences become more important given the lack of published retention and skill acquisition data for training programmes in this field (see McDonnell, this volume). Whilst training models teaching fewer procedures might be associated with better retention, trainers always have to strike a balance between the comprehensiveness of their training as a response to the range of possible situations which staff might face, and the desire to minimise the number of individual procedures taught in order to maximise opportunities for repeated practice and thus enhance retention.

In addition to the formal results, there were several clear themes that emerged from this process. The written descriptions contained in training manuals were often unhelpful and vague. A frequently encountered problem was a lack of correspondence between the text and the visual images. Several of the scenarios used to describe possible uses of the techniques also caused concern in that use of the technique appeared unwarranted from clinical perspectives, legal perspectives, or both. Other techniques reviewed were fragile in that small, potentially foreseeable adjustments in practice, either by error or wilful adaptation (by staff seeking to increase the aversiveness of the technique), would have exponentially increased the dangerousness of the procedure. Furthermore, several techniques appeared inappropriate for the organisational context and/or the clinical needs of the service user population for which they were supposedly devised.

The safe application of techniques was also felt to be heavily dependent on the competence and biomechanical understanding of the trainer. This problem is likely to be exacerbated in the context of 'off the shelf' training packages in which trainers are taught a script developed by the franchising agency, with no understanding of the underpinning biomechanical principles or safety issues involved. A number of the sample techniques were felt to be highly complex, involving multiple movements which, in team interventions, required synchronicity by several individuals. However, other, less complex techniques were also felt to be high-risk or raised concerns because of their overt use of pain compliance.

In conclusion, there are two further key recommendations about the future use of the tool that we would wish to make. The process of reviewing techniques using the tool via the panel was an important process and something that was absent from the web-based study. Once the further work on the psychometrics of the tool is complete, techniques taught by organisations seeking or already holding BILD accreditation should be assessed by panels of no less than three, and no greater than five, independent experts. This should become part of the formal accreditation procedure in order to demonstrate compliance with the Code of Practice. Second, accredited organisations should be subject to a mandatory central reporting of injuries sustained both during training and in subsequent implementation in practice of physical interventions. Over time, this exercise would do much to reduce the current risks in relation to the use of physical interventions. In addition, when techniques have been risk-assessed using the tool, such reporting will contribute significantly to the identification of its predictive validity (in that higher risk scores should be positively correlated with higher injury rates).

References

Atkinson, D (1998) Research Interviews with People with Mental Handicaps. *Mental Handicap Research*, 1, 1, 49–74.

BILD (2001) *BILD Code of Practice for the use of Physical Interventions*. Kidderminster: BILD Publications.

BILD (2006) *BILD Code of Practice for the use of Physical Interventions. A guide for trainers and commissioners of training*. Kidderminster: BILD Publications.

Bell, L and Stark, C (1998) *Measuring Competence in Physical Restraint Skills in Residential Child Care*. Edinburgh: Scottish Office Central Research Unit.

Colton, D and Covert, R W (2007) *Designing and Constructing Instruments for Social Research and Evaluation*. London: Wiley.

Department of Health and Department for Education and Skills (2002). *Guidance for Restrictive Physical Interventions. How to provide safe services for people with learning disabilities and autistic spectrum disorders*. London: Department of Health.

Deveau, R and McGill, P (2007) *As the Last Resort: Reducing the Use of Restrictive Physical Interventions*. Canterbury: Tizard Centre, University of Kent.

Harris, J, Allen, D, Cornick, M, Jefferson, A and Mills, R (1996). *Physical Interventions: A Policy Framework*. Kidderminster: BILD Publications.

Harris, J, Cornick, M, Jefferson, A and Mills, R (2008) *Physical Interventions: A Policy Framework*. Kidderminster: BILD Publications.

Hart, D and Howell, S (2004) *Report on the use of Physical Intervention across Children's Services*. London: National Children's Bureau.

Ogier, M (1998) *Reading Research*. Second Edition. London: Bailliere Tindall.

Sigelman, C K, Budd, E C, Spantel, C L and Schoenrock, C J (1981) When In Doubt, Say Yes. *Mental Retardation*, 20, 5, 339–346.

Smallridge, P and Williamson, A (2008) *Independent Review of Restraint in Juvenile Secure Settings*. London: Ministry of Justice, Department for Children, Schools and Families, Ministry of Justice.

Youth Justice Board for England and Wales (2006) *Managing Children and Young People's Behaviour in the Secure Estate: A code of practice (B250)*. London: Youth Justice Board.

Chapter 4

Physical Interventions and Family Carers

Sarah Hawkins, David Allen and Neil Kaye

> *'We've now come to terms with the fact that we have to continue to "muddle through"and not rely on outside services or agencies.* *YOU ARE ON YOUR OWN!'*
> (Family member; unpublished data: Allen et al, 2006)

Introduction

In 1997, the Mental Health Foundation highlighted the fact that services for the families of children with intellectual disabilities and severe challenging behaviour were limited in both quantity and quality, describing this group as 'the forgotten minority' (p 83).

One such area of service provision that has continued to receive little attention is the training needs of family carers in relation to reactive behaviour management. This is in stark contrast to the substantial focus over the past decade or so on training paid carers in how to safely manage the challenging behaviours of the service users that they support.

This chapter will examine family carers' experiences of managing challenging behaviour and explore the reasons why training in physical interventions is not commonly delivered to the families of children with intellectual disabilities. It will also outline why greater service attention must be given to meeting the reactive behaviour management needs of this group and highlight the ways in which training can be delivered to family carers in a manner which protects all parties.

Family carers' experiences of managing challenging behaviour

Types of challenging behaviour experienced by family carers
The prevalence of challenging behaviour has been estimated to be higher in children with intellectual disabilities than in typically developing children, with suggested differences in the type, duration, intensity and frequency of behaviours displayed (Einfield and Tongue, 1996; Saxby and Morgan, 1993).

Given that the majority of children, and a substantial proportion of adults, with intellectual disabilities and challenging behaviour continue to live at home with their families (Emerson et al, 2001; Joyce et al, 2001; Lowe et al, 2007), it is inevitable that family members will often be faced with having to manage high-risk behaviours.

A number of studies describe the types of behaviours that families may be confronted with. In her report on the experiences of 59 parents caring for 18 to 26 year olds with intellectual disabilities and challenging behaviour, Qureshi (1990) reported that 49 per cent of the young adults were said to physically attack family members, 58 per cent engaged in self-injurious behaviour, and a similar proportion displayed destructive behaviour. Likewise, 'serious or controlled' aggression was exhibited by 65 per cent of the children identified in an epidemiological study conducted by Lowe et al (2007) in South Wales, 82 per cent of whom lived within the family home.

In an exploratory study designed to better understand the behaviour management needs of the family carers of children with intellectual disabilities and challenging behaviour, Allen et al (2006) surveyed 72 parents on the database of the Challenging Behaviour Foundation (CBF), a national UK charitable organisation. The average age of the respondent's children was 13 years (range 4–38) and the majority of children (76 per cent) were resident in the family home. Seventy-five per cent of the children in the sample presented aggressive behaviours that were rated as moderately serious or severe; the corresponding figures for self-injury were 37.5 per cent and 67 per cent for destructiveness.

The impact of challenging behaviour on family carers and service users

Emotional impact

The exhibition of challenging behaviour is considered to be a major source of stress for family members (Quine, 1986; Qureshi, 1990; Shinnick and McDonnell, 2003), which in turn may impact upon the presentation of the child's behaviour (Saxby and Morgan, 1993).

The emotional impact of coping with behavioural challenges can be three-fold. Firstly, the anticipation of behaviour can lead to stress reactions in family members. Turnbull and Ruef (1996), for example, found that families often lived in the constant fear that difficult or dangerous behaviours could occur at any time, even if the behaviour in question was of low frequency. Secondly, acute emotional responses can be evident as immediate effects of the presentation of challenging behaviour, as exemplified by the following quotation from the Allen et al (2006) study: 'It's the most distressing thing possible to watch your child self-harming. As a mother, it kills you.' (p 359). Finally, stress may be a longer-term consequence of caring for a relative who displays behaviours of a challenging nature, as the result of a build up of strain. Qureshi (1990) found that almost two-thirds of the mothers in her study had been affected by behaviours in the longer-term in a mental or emotional sense.

Physical injury

By definition, challenging behaviours displayed by people with intellectual disabilities, such as physical aggression, self-injurious behaviour and environmental destructiveness, pose potential risk of injury to either the person themselves or those around them.

Qureshi (1990) reported that parents are sometimes injured as a result of the challenges posed by their children (eg 'She hit me in the ribs so hard. Oh, I was in such pain ... you've a muscle attached to your ribs and she's torn the muscle.' (p 31)) and that physical injury to the child was the second most commonly mentioned cost to the child of challenging behaviour.

Adams and Allen (2001) interviewed team members working at a specialist service for children with intellectual disabilities and challenging behaviour about the difficulties presented by 54 children (aged between 5 and 18) on their caseload. Almost a third of the group engaged in behaviours which usually resulted in quite serious consequences for either the child themselves, carers, siblings or other children (eg 'He tried to choke his sister'; 'Jumped over the banister and swung on the lampshade'; 'Bruised his mum with punches to the stomach' (p 339)).

When asked to describe the most difficult behavioural incident that they ever had to manage, 87 per cent of respondents in Allen et al (2006) reported situations that had resulted in a degree of injury to themselves or other family members. Although, in some cases, a relatively minor injury was sustained, other respondents described single or multiple incidents of physical aggression which had resulted in outcomes such as cuts, sprains, broken bones, loss of consciousness and hospital treatment (pp 358–359).

'I was attacked by my son – punched, kicked, hair pulled – then, in the same incident, pushed against a wall. Whilst I lost consciousness and was on the ground, I was repeatedly kicked.'

'I was dragged around the floor by my hair, contact with objects and prolonged and deep biting causing bleeding, bruising, infection, severe swelling and cuts needing hospital treatment.'

'Without warning, he lunged at me and bit me on the hand/arm because I held it out to protect myself. He also bit the back of my leg. I then needed hospital treatment and skin grafts.'

Accounts of injuries sustained by the children were also given and included outcomes of both physical aggression and self-injury (p 359):

'In anger, he crushed an ornament in his hand. This wasn't deliberate. He was frightened and wouldn't allow his hand to be examined or dressed.'

'My son smashed a window whilst head-banging it. A large shard of glass penetrated his shoulder and neck. He required hospital treatment (15 stitches).'

Exclusion from services/restricted opportunities

A further consequence of challenging behaviour for the family may be that a relative could be either excluded from services or have restricted opportunities to access ordinary community facilities and locations. Qureshi (1990) reported that parents in her study felt restricted in their freedom to undertake a range of social activities, largely due to concerns about behaviour occurring in public places. Green and Wray (1999) note that some individuals may be excluded from services because they are too difficult to work with, yet family carers are expected to be able to deal with the challenges presented at home.

Placement breakdown

Due to the difficulties associated with managing challenging behaviour, attempts to maintain children within the home setting can prove unsuccessful and may result in the need for individuals to move into service placements, marking the end of informal caring by families (Kiernan and Alborz, 1996; Green and Wray, 1999; Joyce et al 2001). The Mental Health Foundation (1997) reported that children with intellectual disabilities and behaviour difficulties are more likely to be placed outside their communities than children without significant behaviour problems.

Reactive behaviour management approaches used by family members

It is clear from the information presented thus far that family members caring for relatives with intellectual disabilities and challenging behaviours at home can be faced with a range of behaviours that may have far-reaching consequences. An indication of the high degree of difficulty that families experience in managing these behaviours is also documented in the literature. For example, in the Adams and Allen (2001) study, 21 per cent, 40 per cent and 17 per cent of the children respectively were considered to present family members with moderate, considerable and extreme management difficulties.

Within staffed services for adults and children with intellectual disabilities and challenging behaviour it is acknowledged that, in certain instances, physical interventions may need to be applied to protect the person and others from harm or injury. While accurate figures on the use of these strategies by formal carers are not available, there is evidence to suggest that physical interventions form a fairly frequent component of reactive behaviour management approaches with this user group (Emerson, 2002).

The true extent to which family members utilise physical interventions with their relatives (adults or children) is also largely unknown. However, there are accounts in the literature which illustrate family intervention via physical, mechanical and environmental means.

Several forms of physical and environmental restraint were described by parents interviewed by Qureshi (1990):

> *'When you're struggling with her she can use every mortal thing. Her legs are going, I mean you're trying to hold her legs, you're concentrating on the legs ...'* (p 3)

'I mean at times we've used methods with her, haven't we, that, let's put it this way you wouldn't be allowed to use inside a hospital … I used to just stick her under me arm and take her upstairs.' (p 88)

'Put her in her bedroom and put the safety chain on.' (p 88)

Adams and Allen (2001) found that physical intervention by parents was the most usual response to aggressive behaviour in 56 per cent of the children in their study. Behaviours posing moderate to serious injury risks were more likely to result in physical intervention, as were those rated as more difficult to manage.

Allen et al (2006) asked parents themselves about the extent to which they used physical interventions as a management strategy in response to challenging behaviour and what types of intervention they employed. Physical interventions had been used by 87.5 per cent of respondents, with 20.8 per cent reporting frequent use. Increasing frequency of physical intervention use was found to be positively correlated with increasing severity of injury arising from aggression for the child, but not for the family or significant others. It was also positively correlated with increasing severity of other behaviours and negatively correlated with parent age.

The qualitative data revealed that respondents used a wide range of reactive strategies. Physical removal was often detailed as a means of confining the behavioural incident to a safer area. With smaller children, this tended to involve lifting or carrying the individual: 'We had to carry him home screaming – two people, one at either end – like a log.' (p 360). In other instances, respondents reported removing the child by walking with them, usually with the assistance of another person: 'We tried to walk him, standing either side holding his hands (one each), to a quiet area.' (p 360). Personal physical restraint (ie restraint involving one person being held by others) had been used by 85.9 per cent of respondents:

'I took hold of his hand firmly so that he could not break free.' (p 359)

'He sat between my knees and I held him round the chest and held onto his arms.' (p 359)

'I managed to put my arms around her upper body and held her really tight until she calmed down (about 15 minutes).' (unpublished data)

'He became so aggressive, it took 3–4 adults to hold him down.' (p 359)

Mechanical restraint (eg via the use of ties, belts, splints etc) was used much less frequently, reported by 26 per cent of the sample (unpublished data):

'We tied her shoelaces together to prevent her from kicking out.'

'If really necessary, he has to be put in his pushchair and restrained in it with the reins on.'

'We did not know what to do so we tried wrapping him in a duvet to protect us and himself.'

Environmental restraint had been used by four per cent of respondents and included: shutting the child in a bedroom; locking doors; putting the child in a cupboard; and using a stable area as a place for containment.

Family carers' access to training in physical interventions

Paterson et al (2003) comment that where restraint is a 'foreseeable eventuality', paid care staff are increasingly being trained in systematic methods of physical intervention, with the intention of improving safety and wellbeing. In contrast, although it is clear from the evidence presented above that physical intervention use by family members could be described as a 'foreseeable eventuality', parents rarely receive training in how to apply these techniques safely and effectively (Shinnick and McDonnell, 2003). In most cases within Adams and Allen's (2001) study, the forms of restraint used had not been introduced via formal training and, despite high rates of restraint use amongst parent respondents to Allen et al's (2006) survey, only 25 per cent had actually had training in physical intervention use.

A number of key barriers to providing training for families are evident, each of which are described in turn below.

Lack of legislative drivers

Legislative requirements to provide safe working environments for paid carers (Allen, 2002) and concerns about the ethics and legality of certain approaches to physical intervention (Leadbetter, 2002; Paterson et al, 2003) have led to the development of a range of national policy and guidelines initiatives to support the need to provide training in physical interventions to staff (eg BILD, 2006; Department of Health and Department for Education and Skills (DoH and DfES), 2002; Harris et al, 2008; Welsh Assembly Government (WAG), 2005). Policy documentation also specifically supports the need for training to be provided to school teachers (eg DfES, 2007).

The legislative drivers that are at the forefront of improving training for paid carers are not in place for natural carers. Whilst it is clear that families will have to manage high-risk behaviours, this group receives very little or no attention in the above documentation. For example, governmental guidance produced by the DoH and DfES (2002) makes fairly prescriptive recommendations that: 'Staff who are expected to employ restrictive physical interventions will require additional, more specialised training' (p 29), and that 'Staff should normally only use methods of restrictive physical intervention for which they have received training ... it is not appropriate for staff to modify the techniques' (p 29), but only contains one vague reference to parents, stating that the 'information in this guidance may also be helpful to parents and those with parental responsibilities' (p 9).

This scarce acknowledgement of the need to provide similar initiatives for natural carers may well be the critical variable in understanding the current lack of training provision to the family members of those displaying challenging behaviours.

A number of the family members who responded to the survey distributed by Allen et al (2006) expressed frustration that it is deemed acceptable to train professionals and other care staff in this area, but not parents:

> 'It seems to be assumed that, as parents, we don't have the same restrictions as professionals (eg if we want to "sit" on him we can), whereas a professional requires something more "acceptable" (and probably more effective)' (pp 360–361).

Concerns about perceived conflicts with child legislation

A further barrier to the provision of training to family members links to broader debates about whether or not physical interventions should be implemented at all with children. Concerns exist about a perceived conflict with child legislation, and in particular that the application of some techniques could contravene aspects of the Children Act (DoH, 1989). Although such concerns were more than adequately dealt with by Lyon (1994) and Lyon and Pimar (2004), they remain a barrier to training access for this group

Anxieties about vicarious liability

When training is provided to statutory bodies or care provider organisations, it is on the assumption that the receiving system will cover the cost of claims from members of staff injured while undergoing training or when putting techniques into practice (Shinnick and McDonnell, 2003). A significant barrier to families accessing physical intervention training is the anxiety of training providers that they could be vicariously liable for compensating family members if they or the child subsequently became injured as a result of the application of techniques taught by its staff.

Concerns that techniques will be incorrectly applied or misused

Nunno et al (2006) state that 'All restraint positions...can be lethal, especially when misapplied or misused' (p 1341). It is believed to be more difficult to effectively control or monitor the way in which trained techniques are used in practice within the family home than in a staffed setting. It is this limitation that evokes concerns about the potential consequences of not being able to put the appropriate safeguards in place after training to prevent the incorrect application or misuse of techniques (ie abusive practices, physical injury). This, again, represents a barrier to family members accessing training.

Many of the respondents within Allen et al's (2006) study had actively pursued training to no avail. Of the 58 respondents who provided information about the difficulties that they had encountered in trying to access training, 71 per cent reported that no training was available in the geographical area within which they resided. Other barriers highlighted were: not meeting the criteria for referral; inability to afford training costs; a lack of support from local agencies;

nothing available for pre-adolescents; and organisational concerns about parental accountability.

Why must we be able to provide training in physical interventions to this group?

It goes without saying that the aim of any positive behavioural intervention within a family setting should be the introduction of strategies designed to reduce the likelihood of challenging behaviour occurring in the first place, via individualised assessment of the factors that appear to 'set up', 'set off' and 'maintain' the target behaviours. Although it is not within the remit of this chapter to research and report on the extent to which these proactive interventions are delivered to family carers, it is clear from a glance at the literature that this is an area in itself that needs to be greatly improved upon.

Behavioural approaches for changing challenging behaviours have been found to be efficacious across a range of behaviours, individuals and situations, including families (Carr et al, 1999; Lucyshyn et al, 2002). There are clear, positive examples in the literature of how family training in these broader support strategies can be provided (Bambura et al, 2004), taking into account carers' strengths and needs and being successfully incorporated into families' existing routines (Albin et al, 1996). However, there is little evidence for the widespread implementation and usage of these approaches in practice. As McGill et al (2006) note, the limited access to effective help for this population is acknowledged within professional groups. For example, the British Psychological Society's Clinical Practice Guidelines (Ball et al, 2004) state that 'the majority of people ... at home with their families are not receiving any effective psychological intervention for their challenging behaviour' (p 6).

Due to the aforementioned potential impact of supporting a relative who challenges, a clear duty of care exists to highlight the behaviour management needs of family carers and provide them with effective interventions. While the focus of behavioural approaches should be to introduce positive, proactive interventions for behaviour change, it needs to be acknowledged that elimination of challenging behaviour is unlikely and that, therefore, carers also need to be equipped with reactive skills that enable them to respond safely and efficiently to behaviours when they do occur in order to maintain the safety and wellbeing of the service user, themselves and others. In relation to the reactive component, there are a number of specific reasons why training in physical interventions should be available to this group where it is assessed as required.

Training is required to reduce risks of injury from behaviours

The fact that there is research evidence that serious or major injury to the child and others is commonly reported as usual consequences of challenging behaviour in a significant proportion of samples (eg Qureshi, 1990; Adams and Allen, 2001; Allen et al, 2006) provides firm evidence of a need for formal training in physical interventions to reduce the likelihood of such injuries occurring. There appears to be a consensus that physical interventions should be taught to paid staff when they are at risk of assault (BILD, 2006). This same principle should be applied to families.

Training is required to reduce risks that techniques will be incorrectly applied or misused

As demonstrated by the main studies conducted in this area, regardless of whether or not family members are trained, they will use physical interventions out of necessity to respond to behavioural challenges that they are faced with (eg Qureshi, 1990; Adams and Allen, 2001; Allen et al, 2006).

Without the provision of training in appropriate physical intervention skills, carers are likely to improvise their own techniques instead. Adams and Allen (2001) reported that, in most cases, the forms of restraint being used by the parents in their study had been improvised. As previously noted, in Allen et al's (2006) study, 87.5 per cent of respondents had used physical interventions, but only 25 per cent had received training. The implication of this is that a significant proportion of parents were designing their own techniques.

Of major concern is that research suggests the risk of injury to both carers and service users will increase when interventions are improvised or 'unplanned' (Spreat et al, 1986; Harris et al, 1996). Baker and Allen (2001) note that it could be hypothesised that even greater risks may be associated with strategies improvised by carers under immense emotional pressure.

The potentially lethal consequences of the use of certain forms of physical intervention have been widely highlighted in individual case reports, newspaper articles and case series reviews that have been conducted of restraint-related deaths in both the UK and USA (eg National Alliance for the Mentally Ill, 2000; Paterson et al, 2003; BBC, 2004; Nunno et al, 2006; Paterson and Bradley, this volume). A central reason for the increased risk associated with the use of 'unplanned' interventions is that carers may inadvertently use forms of physical intervention that are recognised in the literature as posing a high risk to the person being restrained, largely due to the position in which the person is held. This was certainly found to be the case in Allen et al's (2006) study, where 17 per cent of respondents reported on the use of known high-risk strategies such as basket-holds (ie a form of single-person restraint in which the service user's arms are crossed across their chest and held at the wrist by a carer standing, kneeling or sitting behind them), restraint in a prone position (ie face down), and the use of positions involving a high degree of hyperflexion of joints and/or pressure to vulnerable parts of the body:

> 'We (myself and my husband) tend to restrain him by sitting behind him on the floor and gently restrain his arms around him.' (unpublished data)

> 'Holding him pinned down on the floor with my body across his pelvis and holding down his wrists.' (p 359)

> 'Sitting on him ... restraining on the floor ... arm bent up his back ... headlock.' (p 359)

'Restrained him on the floor using arms and legs wrapped round him and rolled on the floor.' (p 359)

Additionally, without training, risks may be heightened due to the inclusion of certain procedural elements (eg the number of people involved in the techniques; the length of time that techniques are applied for; the level of observation/monitoring in place during and after techniques have been applied, etc) that are know to further heighten risk (Allen, 2008).

One of the concerns about providing training to family carers outlined earlier was that, once training had been provided, it would be difficult to ensure that techniques are used correctly and are not misused in an abusive way. In reality, due to the risks associated with the use of improvised physical interventions, it seems more likely that there is a higher probability of incorrect application and misuse of techniques occurring *without,* rather than *with,* training, and therefore, training should actually reduce risks, not generate them.

Training is required to assist families to maintain their children at home

It has already been noted that behaviour management difficulties can lead to the breakdown of family care. Joyce et al (2001) suggest that intervention and support should focus on the maintenance of family placements and the prevention of move-on to alternative accommodation occurring at crisis point, placing a heavy emphasis on the provision of advice on how to manage challenging behaviour as a key element in achieving this. Green and Wray (1999) comment that the most practical support that families require to help them to manage with their relative's behaviour at home may not actually be to reduce, modify or change behaviour, but instead simply to help to keep people 'safe'. Providing family carers with training in physical intervention skills may be an important aspect in keeping people and situations 'safe' and thus may assist in insulating against an inability to cope.

Training is required because family members say that they want it!

A final reason why family carers should be able to access training in physical interventions if they require it is because they are telling us that they need it and: 'Parents have the right to have their needs assessed, independently of the child and requests for this type of support should not go unheard.' (Green and Wray, 1999, p 37).

Although only a quarter of respondents in Allen et al's (2006) study had received formal training in physical interventions, this did not reflect actual need. Unpublished data revealed that untrained participants outlined three main reasons for requiring physical intervention training. The first of these was a desire to get techniques right to prevent injury to themselves and their child and to avoid accusations of mistreatment from others (eg 'I am desperate for training since I heard a child in America died as a result of parents using incorrect techniques when restraining their child.'; 'We feel absolutely desperate. In public, we've been afraid of being reported for not handling him properly.'). The second reason was a recognition that, although many respondents had felt confident using physical interventions with their children when they were small, they were beginning to experience management difficulties linked to the increasing size and strength of their children. This difficulty was exacerbated by parents attempting to deal with a situation on their own (eg 'He was too strong for me to hold.'; 'She is tall and I couldn't regain control on my own.'). Finally, a number of respondents whose children were in residential care/school felt that, as a consequence of not being trained, they could no longer have their children home for visits (eg 'Physical intervention is far from desirable, but without training, home visits by my son may be curtailed.').

Rather than worrying about what could go wrong if training is provided to family carers, it would be reasonable to suggest that greater emphasis is placed on concerns about the implications of not providing training to this group. In short, agencies need to be concerned about consequences of omission, not just acts of commission. Although the evidence for the effectiveness of physical intervention training is somewhat equivocal (Allen, 2001), there is evidence that training paid carers can reduce incidents (Allen et al, 1987); reduce injury rates to both staff and service users (Allen et al, 1987); reduce restraint rates (Allen and Tynan, 2000; Kaye and Allen, 2002); and improve staff confidence (Allen and Tynan, 2000). Anecdotal accounts in the literature of training that has taken place with families have highlighted some promising outcomes (eg Green and Wray, 1999; Shinnick and McDonnell, 2003). In the words of Allen et al (2006): 'Failing to train family members is hard to justify on ethical grounds, and will be hard to justify on legal grounds should serious injury or fatality arise from a failure to provide a potentially effective intervention.' (p 362).

How can we deliver training in physical interventions to family carers?

As outlined thus far, the prevailing trend at present is to concentrate on the reasons why training in physical interventions to the family carers of people with intellectual disabilities and challenging behaviour cannot be provided. The aim of this section of the chapter is to start to shift the focus to thinking about the conditions under which training can be delivered. Overcoming the highlighted barriers is the key task in hand, by developing a framework for training provision that protects all parties. The contents of *Table 1* comprise a useful checklist of considerations that, if borne in mind during planning phases, should help to support the delivery of training to this group. Naturally, any training provided should demonstrate that it complies with governmental and other published good practice guidance in the field. As these training requirements are more than adequately covered elsewhere (eg Allen, 2002; BILD, 2006; DoH and DfES, 2002; Harris et al, 1996; 2008; WAG, 2005), there is no need to restate these principles here.

A review of the existing literature identified two single-subject case reports, each of which provides an illustration of how family carer training in physical intervention skills can be delivered.

Green and Wray (1999) describe the provision of training in breakaway techniques to the family of an 11 year old boy with Prader-Willi Syndrome.

Table 1: Family training pre-considerations.

Consideration	Detail
Have all key stakeholders been involved in the decision-making process that training in physical interventions is required?	The decision to train a family in physical intervention techniques should be a multi-agency and multi-disciplinary one, with the full involvement of the family. Effective risk assessment is central to reaching the decision and should entail a balanced consideration of the risks associated with the family members being trained in and implementing physical interventions with the individual, versus the risks attached to not providing the training.
Are any contra-indicators to providing training evident?	As part of the initial multi-disciplinary risk assessment, a check should be made to see whether or not any clear contra-indicators to the family being trained are evident. A positive answer to any of the following questions would indicate a need to proceed with caution: • Is the child on the at-risk register? • Does the child have any physical health concerns that would contraindicate the use of physical intervention techniques (eg cardiac problems; severe respiratory conditions; recurrent dislocations etc)? • Does the family have a documented history of poor compliance with local services? • Are there doubts about the physical capabilities of the family members to implement intervention strategies with their relative?
Have proactive plans for promoting and working towards behaviour change been developed?	In the spirit of a true positive behavioural context to service provision, any advice targeted at the reactive management of behaviour should always be provided in conjunction with support to develop and implement positive, proactive interventions, which aim to reduce the likelihood of behaviour occurring in the first place. Training in physical interventions should never be provided in isolation.
Has the issue of vicarious liability been addressed?	Anxieties about vicarious liability need to be resolved early in the planning stages and addressed head-on in a training contract between the provider and family. Some suggestions are as follows: • The training commissioner or provider could accept liability • Training could be commissioned by more than one party, with liability shared (eg joint commissioning from health and social services) (Green and Wray, 1999) • Family members could be asked to sign a consent form for training, waiving their right to claim if injury does occur (Shinnick and McDonnell, 2003)
Has an individually tailored approach to training taken place?	The components of any physical intervention package delivered to a family should firmly map onto a thorough assessment of the actual behavioural issues that the family face in supporting their relative. Family members should only be taught the physical intervention techniques necessary to match their identified needs. Specific written guidance on when and how to use the techniques should accompany the training and be presented within a holistic support plan, containing bespoke proactive and reactive advice.

Has the 'goodness of fit' of training with the family context been considered?	It is important to strive to achieve a high degree of 'goodness of fit' between the training package, the family member, the service user and the care environment.
	A poor 'goodness of fit' will be achieved if assessment fails to go beyond the types of behaviours that the individual displays to ascertain what the expectations of family members are. Any approach to family training should take into account: overall family needs; an understanding about what help a family themselves would like; their views about how training should be provided; and who they think should be involved in the training (Engel and Powers, 1989).
Have plans for ongoing monitoring and evaluation been specified and agreed?	Shinnick and McDonnell (2003) stress that training should not be seen as one-off events. Setting-up systems for ongoing monitoring and evaluation of both behavioural incidents and the usage of techniques is an essential part of initial contract setting with families.
	The likelihood of adherence to monitoring agreements will be enhanced with the implementation of 'user-friendly' methods of recording, tailored to family need (Allen, 1999). The provision of clear instruction/training in what is required is also important.
	Monitoring outcomes should feed into a regular review of the techniques that family members require, with the aim of removing the techniques from use by the family as soon as possible.
Has a protocol for raising and addressing arising issues/concerns been specified?	In addition to the need to look carefully at completed monitoring for action implications (eg escalating patterns of use), a transparent procedure should be established for the family or involved professionals to raise any issues that emerge in relation to applying the training in practice (eg difficulty using particular techniques; new behaviours, etc).
	It is also important to be clear from the outset about the types of responses that will follow the raising of particular issues (eg refresher training; debriefing of critical incidents; requirements for training in new techniques, etc).

Proactive and early intervention strategies were in place. Risk in relation to the presenting situation was deemed to be high in that family members and the child were at significant risk of physical injury, access to the community was severely restricted and placement breakdown was a real possibility. The need for training was agreed in a multi-disciplinary team (MDT) meeting, which included the attendance of a child protection coordinator. Vicarious liability and concerns about conflicts with child legislation had to be addressed before training provision. The former was partly overcome by the joint commissioning of an external trainer by health and social services, but it is unclear how the second issue was addressed. The actual training is not described. However, it is noted that it involved theoretical and practical sessions and was based upon individual assessment of need. The authors suggest that training contributed to the child being maintained at home, the avoidance of a residential placement, and maintenance of continued safety of parent and child. The authors also comment that the parents were more able to analyse and understand their child's behaviour after the training.

Shinnick and McDonnell (2003) report on training a mother and neighbour to manage the behaviour of a 34 year old woman with a severe intellectual disability and an autistic spectrum disorder via de-escalation skills and breakaway procedures. The mother had asked for training as she had a number of health-related difficulties and was concerned that she might not be able to cope with her daughter's aggression any longer. The training consisted of: four sessions using an interactive teaching method about the use of 'low-arousal' methods with the daughter, with a significant emphasis on verbal de-escalation; and six sessions teaching three physical interventions for the target behaviours. The participants were given a copy of a videotape showing each physical intervention that they had been taught and a photograph album of the techniques with prompts. A follow-up interview and audit of the participants' physical intervention skills, conducted eight weeks after the intervention by an independent nurse indicated that both mother and neighbour demonstrated effective recall of the physical methods taught to them, the mother reported increased self-confidence in managing her daughter's behaviour and felt the relationship had improved, and there was some evidence of a reduction in behaviours in terms of two post-training measures (frequency and management difficulty).

In 2006, requests were being made for family members to be trained in a physical intervention package called Positive Behavioural Management (PBM). In light of the fact that the literature in this area consists of the above two anecdotal accounts, this was seen as an opportunity to develop our own viewpoint on the conditions under which family training can be provided, and to further the evidence-base in this area by: reviewing the effectiveness of the delivery of PBM training to family carers, using a range of outcome measures; exploring family carers' experiences of undertaking PBM training; and exploring the experiences of those directly providing the training.

A pre-training checklist was developed, which is completed at referral point by the PBM training manager, in conjunction with the multidisciplinary team of professionals involved in the service user's care. The checklist consists of eight specific criteria that have to be met before training can be provided:

- Up-to-date risk assessment confirms need for training

- Need for training has been agreed by supporting MDT

- MDT has confirmed that there are no contra-indicators to training (eg previous history of risk concerns; child on at-risk register, etc)

- MDT has confirmed that training in proactive strategies has been provided or will be provided within eight weeks of training taking place

- MDT has confirmed that family carers have the personal resources to implement PBM

- Care Manager/MDT has confirmed its external arrangements for monitoring the use of PBM within the family setting

- Care Manager has obtained confirmation that family members are fit to undertake the training

Prior to training being delivered, a contract (agreed with the NHS Trust's legal advisors) is entered into by the family, which includes issues such as liability and monitoring of techniques. All training is delivered within a positive behavioural support framework and involves the family members receiving theory and practical components, bespoke to their needs.

All families undertaking training are asked to take part in an evaluation project. The design of the evaluation is longitudinal and data at three separate time points: pre-training (no more than two weeks before); post-training immediate (immediately after training); and post-training follow-up (three to four months after training). Quantitative information is gathered via a structured questionnaire administered at the first and third time points. Separate semi-structured questionnaires are used at all three time points to gather qualitative information. The interviews are audio-taped with the carers' permission, to aid later data analysis. Five sets of family members have taken part in the evaluation to date. Initial outcome data is currently in preparation.

Conclusions

It remains ultimately desirable that we avoid any form of physical intervention. However, two points are clear. First, challenging behaviours displayed by people with intellectual disabilities within family homes may pose a major threat to the welfare of the individual themselves, family members and others. Second, risks are high from families improvising their own response strategies, in the absence of any formal training. Our attempts to reduce risk may involve the need to teach families certain physical intervention strategies.

In order to deliver training more widely to this group, the issue must be tackled head-on in legislative and policy documentation. Family training requires more mention in reviews of existing documentation but, ideally, specific policies are needed that are designed for family carers and are accessible to them. These should lay out the best practice in relation to physical interventions that has been built up and applied to paid carers being trained in and using physical interventions in practice. Policy makers should be urged to give this area more prominence by outlining the standards that services should be striving to achieve for families.

The beginnings of a framework for delivering training more widely to families is evident. It is essential that providers evaluate and report upon any training that is delivered to family carers (in terms of both process and outcome) so that we start to build up a much-needed evidence base on the effectiveness of physical intervention training with this group, to inform and shape provision in this area. Guidelines for developing evidence-based practice in the field, outlined by Allen (2001), may be of help (eg clearly specifying training content and methods; taking baselines and follow-ups of measures, etc).

More broadly, the general lack of knowledge about the needs of family members who support individuals with challenging behaviour should be addressed via future research. This will enable commissioners to develop existing and future services on the basis of accurate information about families' priorities. In particular, a true picture of the extent to which families are provided with proactive behavioural support and advice (and the usefulness of this) is essential. Whilst training in reactive behaviour management strategies is likely to assist families in coping more effectively with the challenges they face, it is the positive intervention strategies and their associated effect upon behaviour change that will have the biggest impact on insulating them in the longer-term against some of the risks associated with their support role. The early identification of children with challenging behaviour and appropriate, timely intervention, may prevent or minimise longer-term problems (Saxby and Morgan, 1993). Services need to ensure that families have access to professionals with expertise in behavioural approaches who can address the issues.

In addition, we should look in more detail at the provision of wider coping strategies for families to increase resilience to the experience of stress and burnout. Due to the proposed bi-directional relationship between parental stress and behaviours of children, failure to address this area of need may be a key precipitant of further behavioural incidents (Cottle et al, 1995; Whittington and Wykes, 1996).

References

Adams, D and Allen, D (2001) Assessing the need for reactive behaviour management strategies in children with intellectual disability and severe challenging behaviour. *Journal of Intellectual Disability Research*, 45, 4, 335–343.

Albin, R W, Lucyshyn, J M, Horner, R H and Flannery, K B (1996). Contextual fit for behavioural support plans: a model for 'goodness of fit'. In L K Koegal, R L Koegal and G Dunlap (Eds). *Positive Behavioural Support. Including People with Difficult Behaviour in the Community*, pp 81–98. Baltimore: Brookes.

Allen, D (1999) Mediator analysis: an overview of recent research on carers supporting people with intellectual disability and challenging behaviour. *Journal of Intellectual Disability Research*, 43, 4, 325–339.

Allen, D (2001) *Training Carers in Physical Interventions: Research Towards Evidence-Based Practice*. Kidderminster: BILD Publications.

Allen, D (2002) *Ethical Approaches to Physical Interventions. Responding to Challenging Behaviour in People with Intellectual Disabilities*. Kidderminster: BILD Publications.

Allen, D (2008) Risk and Prone Restraint – Reviewing the Evidence. In M Nunno, D Day and L Bullard (Eds) *Examining the safety of high-risk interventions for children and young people*. New York: Child Welfare League of America.

Allen, D, McDonald, L, Dunn, C and Doyle, A (1987) Changing care staff approaches to the prevention and management of aggressive behaviour in a residential treatment unit for persons with mental retardation and challenging behaviour. *Research in Developmental Disabilities*, 18, 2, 101–112.

Allen, D and Tynan, H (2000) Responding to aggressive behaviour: the impact of training on staff knowledge and confidence. *Mental Retardation*, 38, 2, 97–104.

Allen, D, Hawkins, S and Cooper, V (2006) Parents' use of physical interventions in the management of their children's severe challenging behaviour. *Journal of Applied Research in Intellectual Disabilities*, 19, 4, 356–363.

Baker, P and Allen, D (2001) Physical abuse and physical interventions in learning disabilities: an element of risk? *The Journal of Adult Protection*, 3, 2, 25–31.

Ball, T, Bush, A and Emerson, E (2004) *Psychological Interventions for Severely Challenging Behaviours shown by People with Learning Disabilities: Clinical Practice Guidelines*. Leicester: British Psychological Society.

Bambura, L M, Dunlap, G and Schwartz, I S (2004) *Positive Behavioural Support: Critical Articles on Improving Practice for Individuals with Severe Disabilities*. Austin, TX: Pro-Ed Inc and TASH.

BBC (2004). *Boy died after being restrained*. Available from http://news.bbc.co.uk/1/hi/england/ 3652725.stm (accessed 20 April 2009).

BILD (2006) *Code of Practice for the use of Physical Interventions: a Guide for Trainers and Commissioners of Training* (Second edition). Kidderminster: BILD Publications.

Carr, E G, Horner, R H, Turnbull, A P, Marquis, J G, McLaughlin, D M, McAtee, M L, Smith, C E, Ryan, K A, Ruef, M B and Doolabbh, A (1999). *Positive Behaviour Support for People with Developmental Disabilities: A Research Synthesis*. Washington DC: American Association on Mental Retardation.

Cottle, M, Kuipeers, L, Murphy, G and Oakes, P (1995) Expressed emotion, attributions, and coping in staff who have been victims of violent incidents. *Mental Handicap Research*, 8, 168–183.

Department of Health (1989) *The Children Act*. London: HMSO.

Department of Health and Department for Education and Skills (2002) *Guidance for Restrictive Physical Interventions. How to provide safe services for people with Learning Disabilities and Autistic Spectrum Disorder*. London: Department of Health.

Department for Education and Skills (2007) *The use of Force to Control or Restrain Pupils*. London: Department for Education and Skills.

Einfield, S L and Tongue, B J (1996) Population prevalence of psychopathology in children and adolescents with intellectual disability: II. Epidemiological findings. *Journal of Intellectual Disability Research*, 40, 99–109.

Emerson, E (2002) The prevalence of use of reactive management strategies in community-based services in the UK. In D Allen (Ed) *Ethical Approaches to Physical Interventions. Responding to Challenging Behaviour in People with Intellectual Disabilities*. Kidderminster: BILD Publications.

Emerson, E, Kiernan, C, Alborz, A, Reeves, D, Mason, H, Swarbrick, R, Mason, L and Hatton, C (2001) The prevalence of challenging behaviours: a total population study. *Research in Developmental Disabilities*, 22, 77–93.

Engel, A L and Powers, M D (1989). Behavioural parent training. A view of the past and suggestions for the future. In E Cipani (Ed) *The Treatment of Severe Behaviour Disorders. Behaviour Analysis Approaches*. Washington DC: American Association on Mental Retardation.

Green, T and Wray, J (1999) Enabling carers to access specialist training in breakaway techniques: a case study. *Journal of Learning Disabilities for Nursing, Health and Social Care*, 3, 1, 34–38.

Harris, J, Allen, D, Cornick, M, Jefferson, A and Mills, R (1996) *Physical Interventions: A Policy Framework*. Kidderminster: BILD Publications.

Harris, J, Cornick, M, Jefferson, A and Mills, R (2008) *Physical Interventions: A Policy Framework* (Second edition). Kidderminster: BILD Publications.

Joyce, T, Ditchfield, H and Harris, P (2001) Challenging behaviour in community services. *Journal of Intellectual Disability Research*, 45, 2, 130–138.

Kaye, N and Allen, D (2002). Over the top? Reducing staff training in physical interventions. *British Journal of Learning Disabilities*, 30, 129–132.

Kiernan, C and Alborz, A (1996) Persistence in challenging and problem behaviours of young adults with intellectual disability living in the family home. *Journal of Applied Research in Intellectual Disabilities*, 9, 181–193.

Leadbetter, D (2002) Good practice in physical intervention. In D Allen (Ed) *Ethical Approaches to Physical Interventions. Responding to Challenging Behaviour in People with Intellectual Disabilities*. Kidderminster: BILD Publications.

Lowe, K, Allen, D, Jones, E, Brophy, S, Moore, K, and James, W (2007) Challenging Behaviours: prevalence and topographies. *Journal of Intellectual Disability Research*, 51, 8, 625–636.

Luchshyn, J M, Dunlap, G and Albin, R W (2002) *Families and Positive Behavioural Support: Addressing Problem Behaviour in Family Contexts*. Baltimore: Brookes.

Lyon, C (1994) *Legal issues arising from the care and control of children with learning disabilities who also present with severe challenging behaviour. A Guide for Parents and Carers*. London: Mental Health Foundation.

Lyon, C and Pimar, A (2004) *Physical Interventions and the Law. Legal issues arising from the use of physical interventions in supporting children, young people and adults with learning disabilities and severe challenging behaviour*. Kidderminster: BILD Publications.

Mental Health Foundation (1997) *Don't Forget Us: Children with Learning Disabilities and Severe Challenging Behaviour*. London: Mental Health Foundation.

McGill, P, Papachristoforou, E and Cooper, V (2006) Support for family carers of children and young people with developmental disabilities and challenging behaviour. *Child: Care, Health and Development*, 32, 2, 159–165.

National Alliance for the Mentally Ill (2000) *A Summary Report of Restraints and Seclusion Abuse Received Since the October 1998 Investigation by the Hartford Courant*. Available from http://web.nami.org/update/hartford.html (accessed 20 April 2009).

Nunno, M A, Holden, M J and Tollar, A (2006) Learning from tragedy: a survey of child and adolescent restraint fatalities. *Child Abuse and Neglect*, 30, 1333–1342.

Paterson, B, Bradley, P, Stark, C, Saddler, D, Leadbetter, D and Allen, D (2003) Deaths associated with restraint use in health and social care in the UK. The results of a preliminary survey. *Journal of Psychiatric and Mental Health Nursing*, 10, 3–15.

Qureshi, H (1990) *Parents Caring for Young Adults with Mental Handicap and Problem Behaviour*. Manchester: Hester Adrian Research Centre.

Qureshi, H (1991) Challenging behaviour. *Community Living*, 5, 1, 10–11.

Quine, L (1986) Behaviour problems in severely mentally handicapped children. *Psychological Medicine*, 16, 895–907.

Saxby, H and Morgan, H (1993) Behaviour problems in children with learning disabilities: to what extent do they exist and are they a problem? *Child, Care, Health and Development*, 19, 149–157.

Shinnick, A and McDonnell, A (2003) Training family members in behaviour management methods. *Learning Disability Practice*, 6, 16–20.

Turnbull, A P and Ruef, M (1996) Family perspectives on problem behaviour. *Mental Retardation*, 34, 280–293.

Welsh Assembly Government (2005) *Framework for Restrictive Physical Intervention Policy and Practice.* Cardiff: Welsh Assembly Government.

Whittington, R and Wykes, T (1996) Aversive stimulation by staff and violence by psychiatric patients. *British Journal of Clinical Psychology*, 35, 11–20.

SECTION 2:
Controversial Topics in Behaviour Management

Chapter 5

Mechanical Restraint and Self-injury in People with Intellectual Disabilities: An Enduring Cause for Concern

Edwin Jones and David Allen

> 'In the spirit of liberty, fraternity and equality, Pinel in 1793 cast off the chains of the insane and ushered in a new humanitarian ... approach. This romanticized image ... obscures the fact that with some patients he did continue to advocate the use of restraint in the form of ... the "strait-waistcoat".'
>
> (Gordon et al, 1999, p 173)

Introduction

Mechanical restraint is by definition one of the most restrictive reactive management strategies available. In common with other forms of restrictive physical intervention, it is only recommended as a last resort, after all primary preventative, secondary preventative and alternative reactive strategies have failed (eg Commission for Social Care Inspection, 2007a; Mental Welfare Commission for Scotland, 2006; Royal College of Nursing 2008). However, in some cases mechanical restraint can become relied upon as part of routine care and appears to be the only means available to prevent severe life threatening self-injury in some situations. Whilst mechanical restraint has the potential to safeguard some people with intellectual disabilities and self-injurious behaviour (SIB), it carries the risk of severe detrimental side-effects and is surpassed only by prone restraint as a cause of death in law enforcement and care services in the USA and UK (Allen, 2008). The inappropriate use of mechanical restraint continues to feature in cases of abuse that are unfortunately, all too frequent in UK services for people with intellectual disabilities. For example, in 1995 Freda Latham, a woman with intellectual disabilities, who was being treated in an acute mental health facility in Yorkshire, died of asphyxiation after being tied to a toilet and subsequently becoming entangled in her restraints (*The Guardian*, 2005). In 2005, NHS staff in Cornwall persistently abused a blind and deaf man with intellectual disabilities by tying him to his bed or wheelchair for up to 16 hours a day in the mistaken belief that this was for his own protection (Healthcare Commission and Commission for Social Care Inspection, 2006). In

2007, a woman with intellectual disabilities in the Sutton and Merton Primary Health Care Trust was subjected to the long-term, inappropriate use of an arm splint to mechanically restrain her from placing her hand in her mouth (Healthcare Commission, 2007).

Although some form of mechanical restriction appears to be used on over ten per cent of people with intellectual disabilities who self-injure (Murphy et al, 1993; Oliver et al, 1987), most of the recent debate concerning the ethics of physical interventions has focused on the management of aggressive and destructive behaviours, thus neglecting the use of mechanical restraint and management of self-injurious behaviour (Jones et al, 2007). This policy and practice vacuum represents a major cause for concern. The present chapter therefore highlights the need for research and debate to develop good practice standards concerning the positive behavioural management of self-injury.

Prevalence of self-injurious behaviour

Murphy (1999) defined SIB as any behaviour initiated by the individual that directly results in physical harm to that individual. Amongst people with intellectual disabilities, SIB can include many different types of behaviour with numerous causes and effects (Schroeder, et al, 1980). Common characteristics of SIB include repetitive movements of various body parts that produce physical damage or potential damage if repeated frequently. Thompson and Caruso (2002) suggest that SIB occurs in two principal forms: as discrete, brief bouts lasting no longer than a few seconds; or alternatively as very protracted episodes lasting for several hours with only very brief pauses. They propose that the former tends to be environmentally determined and, whilst the latter may be initiated by environmental events, it is likely to be maintained by neurological factors.

Prevalence rates for SIB vary between 4–14 per cent of people with intellectual disabilities (Oliver et al, 1998). Self-injurious behaviour is often persistent, difficult to treat and, when untreated, has serious consequences such as major injury resulting in permanent tissue damage and secondary problems such as infection, sensory and neurological impairment and even death (Emerson, 1992). Rates of SIB are much higher amongst people with some specific syndromes or behavioural phenotypes, such as Lesch Nyhan and Cornelia de Lange, than amongst the general population of people with intellectual disabilities. These syndromes are rare; for example, Lesch-Nyhan occurs in 1 in 800,000 of the population (Harris, 1992). However, all people with Lesch-Nyhan syndrome, from the age of three years old, display severe self-injurious behaviour, usually in the form of severe biting or chewing of the lips and fingers. This has frequently necessitated extreme management strategies such as continuous mechanical restraints and even extraction of the teeth (Christie et al, 1982, cited in Hall, et al 2001; Lesch and Nyhan, 1964, cited in Oliver et al, 2001). SIB is not ubiquitous amongst people with Cornelia de Lange syndrome and rates are variable; several studies cited by Hyman et al (2002) report findings between 17 per cent and 64 per cent.

Whilst the focus of this chapter is on mechanical restraint as a specific reactive strategy to manage SIB, a brief mention of treatment approaches is relevant as the literature tends not to differentiate between treatment and management.

Treatment interventions for SIB have most typically employed either behavioural or pharmacological methods. There is little evidence that traditional psychotropic medications have any therapeutic impact in treating SIB, other than to achieve indiscriminate general sedation (Brylewski and Duggan, 2001; DeLeon et al, 2002). More recent developments have involved the use of opiate antagonists to block the effect of endogenous opiates produced by repeated SIB, thereby effectively reducing the behaviour itself (Emerson, 1992; Murphy, 1999; Oliver et al, 1987; Thompson and Caruso, 2002; Symons et al, 2004). Such medications will only be effective in cases where SIB was maintained by opiate release, however.

Interventions based on applied behaviour analysis continue to be considered the most evidence-based treatments for SIB, especially when based on detailed functional analysis (Carr et al, 1990 a, b; Emerson, 1992; Horner and Carr, 1997; Iwata et al, 1982; Kahng, et al, 2002a, b; Mace et al, 2001; Scotti et al, 1996; Schroeder, Oster-Granite and Thompson, 2002; Thompson and Caruso, 2002). Combined bio-behavioural intervention, for example, where opiate antagonists are in direct response to the results of a functional analysis of SIB, may prove to be the most effective for some types of SIB, although this remains an essentially theoretical position at the present time (DeLeon et al, 2002; Thompson et al, 1994).

While treatment is better than management, this chapter focuses on behavioural management for several reasons. Unfortunately, as is the case with most forms of challenging behaviour, available data suggests that many people with SIB in the UK are unlikely to receive effective evidence-based treatment (Emerson et al, 2000; Harris and Russell, 1989; Oliver et al, 1987; Qureshi, 1994; Robertson et al, 2005). The complete elimination of self-injury is rare, even with the most successful interventions. While from a practical standpoint, failure to 'manage' severe SIB is not an option, very little attention in terms of policy or research has been paid to the reactive management of SIB. Instead, virtually all of the ethical debate, policy development and staff training concerning reactive strategies over the last 15 years has focused on managing externally directed behaviour, most notably aggression (Allen, 2001, 2002; BILD, 2001; DoH and DES, 2002; Harris et al, 1996).

Definitions of mechanical restraint

A precise definition of mechanical restraint as used with people with intellectual disabilities and challenging behaviour is elusive. Generally mechanical restraint tends to be subsumed under the terms 'restraint' or 'physical restraint'. These all-inclusive general terms are problematic as they tend to obscure the issue of mechanical restraint and promote inconsistency in terms of whether mechanical restraint is included or excluded within such definitions (Kennedy, 2008). For example, the Department of Health guidance (DoH and DES, 2002) and the separate guidance issued by the Welsh Assembly Government (WAG) use the generic term 'Restrictive Physical Interventions'. This is defined in the Welsh guidance as:

> '... direct physical contact between persons where reasonable force is positively applied against resistance, either to restrict movement or mobility or to disengage from harmful behaviour displayed by an individual.'
>
> (WAG 2005, p 2)

SIB is briefly mentioned once in the Welsh guidance, but this contains no reference to mechanical restraint whatsoever. The DoH guidance does mention SIB and mechanical restraint briefly, but there is no detailed discussion. The Commission for Social Care Inspection, in England offers the following definition, however:

> 'the use of belts, arm cuffs, splints or helmets to limit movement to prevent self injurious behaviour (SIB) or harm to others'
>
> (CSCI 2007a, p 1)

The Mental Welfare Commission for Scotland (MWCS) guidance in Scotland contains the following definition:

> 'The commonest form of direct mechanical restraint in use is the restraining chair and/or belts for people who are mobile, or think they are mobile, but are liable to fall or otherwise injure themselves when they walk or attempt to walk. Other forms of mechanical restraint sometimes considered include limb restrictions, for those who repeatedly harm themselves, and cot sides, or secure sleeping bags for those who are restless at night.'
>
> (MWCS 2006, p 11)

A specific reference to SIB in people with intellectual disabilities is made in an exception to the general principle that under no circumstances should tying limbs or the person's body to their chair be considered, as follows:

> 'The only possible rare exception would be where the resident was specifically in danger of damaging one area of the body (eg by severe picking or scratching, or because he or she required intravenous infusion) and it was believed that a temporary use of restraint would result in a longer-term reduction in self-harming behaviour. Special nursing is always preferable to this form of physical restraint.'
>
> (MWCS 2006, p 13)

The Royal College of Nursing (RCN) distinguishes various types of restraint, including:

'Mechanical restraint involves the use of equipment. Examples include specially designed mittens in intensive care settings; everyday equipment, such as using a heavy table or belt to stop the person getting out of their chair; or using bedrails to stop an older person from getting out of bed. Controls on freedom of movement – such as keys, baffle locks and key pads – can also be a form of mechanical restraint.'

(RCN 2008, p 3)

The National Institute of Clinical Excellence (NICE) Clinical Practice Guidelines defines mechanical restraint in rather abstract terms as:

'... a method of physical restraint involving the use of authorised equipment applied in a skilled manner by designated health care professionals. Its purpose is to safely immobilise or restrict movement of part/s of the body of the individual concerned.'

(NICE 2005, pp 8–9)

This is intended to refer to the context of the short-term management of disturbed or violent behaviour in in-patient psychiatric settings. However, it is rather aspirational in tone and prompts a series of questions (What equipment is authorised? By whom? Who are designated health care professionals? etc) rather than providing answers.

Interestingly, in the early 1990s, the Council of Europe recommended that mechanical restraint should be forbidden. However, this was later retracted and replaced with the current recommendation that mechanical or other means of restraint for prolonged periods should be resorted to only in exceptional cases where there is no other means of remedying the situation. This should be interpreted in line with other Council of Europe recommendations, including the principle that people with mental disorders should have the right to individualised care in the least restrictive environment with the least restrictive treatment (Kingdon et al, 2004),

Most of the UK guidance reflects this position and refers to the principle of least restriction in some form (eg Paley, 2008; DOH and DES, 2002; MWCS, 2006). A key issue is therefore the degree of restrictiveness imposed by the specific form of mechanical appliance involved. This can range widely from the use of wrist cuffs that bring the SIB under stimulus control, but which do not restrict movement (Oliver et al, 1998), to almost complete immobilisation with the person being strapped or otherwise secured to objects such as beds (Tate, 1972) or chairs. The way in which terminology is used in the research literature, official guidance and practice can also be confusing, particularly concerning the difference between devices intended to either restrain or protect. Although the term 'mechanical restraint' implies a greater degree of restriction than the term 'protective device', they are often used interchangeably, which makes differentiating between protection and restraint problematic. For example, the Department of Health guidance (DoH and DES, 2002) briefly defines the use of a protective helmet to prevent SIB as non-restrictive, and the use of arm cuffs or splints to prevent SIB as restrictive. However, some forms of 'protective device', such as orthotic[1] helmets that cover the entire head and face, can be more restrictive than some forms of mechanical restraint, such as wrist cuffs that allow a considerable degree of movement. Such a fleeting mention in Department of Health guidance exemplifies the lack of any focused attention to the issue in UK social policy, and highlights the confusion that stems from an attempt to differentiate degrees of restrictiveness on the basis of broad intention rather than actual, specific design, function or use. This point is illustrated well in an example that contrasts good and bad practice by Harris et al, (1996; 2008) as follows:

'Good practice
The physiotherapist has recommended that Sam is placed in a standing frame for ten minutes at a time when he is undertaking a programme designed to improve his hand-eye coordination. While Sam is in the standing frame, his freedom of movement is severely restricted. The standing frame is a physical intervention to promote Sam's education and development. It is used in his best interest.

Bad Practice
When Sam is in the standing frame he is unable to move around the classroom and interfere with other pupils. Sam's teacher leaves him in the frame for longer and longer periods of time. The decision to extend the time Sam spends in the frame is based upon the teacher's concerns about classroom organisation – not what is best for Sam.'

(Harris et al, 2008, p 16)

Therefore, the term 'protective or orthotic device', although sounding more politically correct and acceptable, could sometimes serve as an euphemism to describe equipment which is used in a very restrictive manner. Furthermore, some other forms of physical restraint (for example, having your hands held at your side by a carer), although applied for short periods, could conceivably be more intrusive and restrictive than wrist cuffs that allow considerable movement but are worn continuously.

The recent BILD Principles for Practice document on the use of mechanical restraint (Paley, 2008), is one of the only documents to attempt to address the issue with a specific focus on people with intellectual disabilities and challenging behaviour. Mechanical restraint is defined as follows;

'As a last resort, the application and use of materials or therapeutic aids such as:

- *Belts*
- *Helmets*
- *Clothing*
- *Straps*

[1] A device that is applied externally to a part of the body to correct deformity, improve function or relieve symptoms of a disease by supporting or assisting the neuro-musculoskeletal system. Devices of this sort are usually made by relevant medical practitioners such as occupational therapists, etc.

- *Cuffs*
- *Splints*
- *Specialised equipment*

designed to <u>significantly</u> restrict the free movement of an individual, with the intention of preventing injury; as a result of behaviour that poses significant and proportionate risk to the individual of serious long term harm or immediate injury. The use of the device must be based on the findings of a behavioural risk assessment.'

(Paley, 2008, p 6)

Notably, the BILD definition includes the term 'therapeutic aids', an alternative term for protective devices or orthotic equipment designed by occupational therapists etc. The document contains a brief discussion of the issue of restrictiveness, and presumably this is reflected in the underlining of the word 'significantly' in the definition: this does not sufficiently operationalise the concept, but raises the question of what constitutes significant restriction in practice.

The importance of the concept of restrictiveness led Jones et al (2007) to arrange the various reactive strategies used to manage SIB along a continuum of restrictiveness. Amongst the least restrictive are reactive procedures commonly used with other forms of challenging behaviour such as distraction (Hastings, 1996), diversion to a reinforcing/compelling event and strategic capitulation (LaVigna and Willis, 2002). Verbal commands to stop or other communication, such as attempts to reassure and calm the person, including touching them (eg Hastings, 1996), can be considered as potentially more restrictive. Next come adaptations to the physical environment, such as padding furniture and fixtures or using a cushion to prevent injury (eg when hitting head against hard surfaces) (eg Spain et al, 1984, Hastings, 1996). There is then a significant leap along the continuum of restrictiveness to physical or personal restraints that involve holding the person in some way (eg Hastings, 1996; Harris, 1996). These are followed by protective devices, designed primarily to prevent or reduce injury rather than restrain individuals such as helmets (eg Dorsey et al, 1982; Duker and Seys, 1997; Murphy et al, 1993; Spain et al, 1984) The most restrictive reactive strategies are identified as various types of appliances designed to mechanically restrain individuals to prevent the occurrence of SIB such as arm splints, bed or chair ties (eg Dorsey et al, 1982; Duker and Seys, 1997; Murphy et al, 1993; Spain et al, 1984).

Whilst this continuum highlights the restrictive nature of protective devices and mechanical restraint, it does not differentiate between the varying degrees of restrictiveness of the different forms of these devices. A more objective and reliable means of measuring and describing this would therefore clearly be desirable. Duker and Seys (1997) developed the Imposed Mechanical Restraint Inventory (IMRI) to directly address some of these issues and measure restrictiveness as a dependent variable when evaluating treatment. The IMRI measures a number of dimensions in considerable detail such as: whether restraint is applied when the person is ambulant, sitting in a chair or lying in bed; the parts of the body that may be restrained; the degree of restraint applied to each body part; and a timescale to measure the duration of restraint. The IMRI is notable because it appears to be one of the only scales designed to directly address this issue. It has been found to be reliable and could be adapted to gather useful data in future research and also provides some useful concepts that could inform policy.

Prevalence of mechanical restraint

Data are sparse regarding the extent to which reactive strategies in general are used to manage SIB in practice. There are only a few epidemiological studies that report on the prevalence of mechanical restraint. For example, Oliver et al (1987) and Murphy et al (1993) report that approximately 13 per cent of people with intellectual disabilities who self-injured wore protective devices or mechanical restraints. Arm-splints were the most commonly used device, and this group of people tended to have more severe SIB and present multiple forms of challenging behaviour. They were also generally younger, and had greater sensory, cognitive and physical impairments than other people with SIB who were not subjected to mechanical restraint.

Emerson (2002) reported on a series of studies conducted over the period 1994–2000 that showed that five per cent of children with intellectual disabilities who self-injured were 'usually' or 'sometimes' managed by mechanical restraint. The equivalent figures for adults in two separate studies were seven per cent and 17 per cent . Although comparisons are difficult, taken overall, these figures suggest little change in the rate of mechanical restraint for self-injury in the UK over the last two decades. Given the lack of availability of effective therapeutic support alluded to earlier, this would perhaps be expected.

However, this lack of data should not be taken to imply that they are hardly ever used; it simply serves to highlight that currently we do not really know whether they are or not. This may be related to the general point that written management plans are only found in a minority of settings (Allen et al, 2007; Oliver et al, 1987) and, whilst organisations are required to keep an internal record of the use of all forms of physical restraint, there is no systematic requirement for organisations to report their use externally (CSCI, 2007b). Indeed, there is some evidence that staff are likely to adopt various ad hoc reactive approaches, as they, quite understandably, feel guilty if they do nothing in response to SIB (Hastings, 1996). Of course, if staff did nothing in response to severe SIB they would be in breach of their duty of care. Notably, in the study by Hastings staff reported that they were much more likely to use physical and mechanical restraint rather than the less restrictive strategies described earlier, because they reported feeling an acute need to take immediate action to prevent service users harming themselves.

The data are limited and there is a need for more, sufficient, up to date information regarding the prevalence, management and treatment of SIB in community services than is currently available. A basic research question remains regarding the current prevalence of mechanical restraint amongst people with intellectual disabilities and challenging behaviour. Additional questions concern the types of restraint used, their degree of restrictiveness, frequency of use, and possible relationships between these factors and the characteristics of the person and their environment. In common with other forms of challenging behaviour (Emerson and Hatton, 1994), it is unlikely that deinstitutionalisation and changes in the physical structure, location or value bases of services per se has resulted in a reduction in SIB or the use of restrictive mechanical devices. Further, almost half of the people identified as being subjected to mechanical restraint or using protective devices by Oliver et al (1987) and Murphy et al (1993) were living in the community. There is also some evidence that rates of SIB may by higher in 'normalised' community settings if there are many staff members involved in direct care and a high proportion are unskilled (Nottestad and Linaker, 2001).

Research using an objective measure of restrictiveness could examine whether the confusion between protective device/mechanical restraint and the euphemistic use of the former leads to an inaccurate notion of a low prevalence of mechanical restraint. Such a phenomenon could arguably be expected as similar changes in rhetoric, but not necessarily in working practice, have been identified in the historical literature on service development (Emerson and Hatton, 1994; Scull, 1993; Wolfensberger, 1975). Such 'changes in name only' result from major ideological and legislative change occurring in the absence of detailed consideration of the operational procedures required in the new service structures to achieve the desired outcomes for service users. It is not difficult to argue that recent events in the UK could give rise to such a phenomenon. Deinstitutionalisation and legislative change focusing on human rights has occurred in the context of very little research on the reactive management of SIB in community services for people with intellectual disabilities.

Future research also needs to include self-restraint. This has been estimated to be observed in between 12–50 per cent of people with intellectual disabilities and SIB (Forman et al, 2002). Self-restraint can also include the use of devices (eg a person entangling themselves in clothing, requesting or positioning themselves in mechanical restraints, holding or wearing particular items).

Main and side-effects

While mechanical restraint can be very effective in reducing self-injury and can make a major contribution to keeping people safe, it can also have a number of detrimental side-effects. A key side-effect concerns the fact that applying devices involves the provision of social attention contingent on SIB that can serve to positively reinforce (and therefore increase) rates of SIB in individuals whose behaviour is attention-driven (Hastings, 1996; Spain et al, 1984). In line with general issues concerning restrictive physical intervention, applying devices in the absence of a clear framework of guidance, training and monitoring may also risk injury to the client or staff involved (Harris, 1996). Harris also suggests that mechanical restraint may be safer than personal restraint, although other evidence would appear to question this assertion (Allen, 2008). The mechanical or protective devices themselves may assume reinforcing properties because they represent a means of escaping compulsive SIB, thus making the person dependent on wearing a device for long periods of time (Fisher, et al, 1997; Foxx and Dufrense, 1984; Spain et al, 1984). In this situation, SIB may occur at high rates in order to 'earn' access to mechanical restraint, and also when the device is removed in an attempt to secure reapplication. Mechanical restraint may also result in the development of other, alternative types of SIB that replace those controlled or eliminated through its use. Controlling one form of SIB (eg fist to head hitting) via restraint may therefore simply result in other forms (eg damaging knees by hitting objects or head butting) taking its place (Emerson, 1992; Fisher et al, 1997; Kahng et al, 2001; Lerman et al, 1994). Muscular atrophy, demineralisation of bones, shortening of tendons, arrested motor development and disuse of limbs may also occur because of long-term restriction (Emerson, 1992; Fisher et al, 1997). Mechanical restraint and protective devices can also impede or prevent a person taking advantage of opportunities to engage in a wide range of activities associated with daily living, education, leisure and reduced levels of interaction with carers (Emerson, 1992; Spain et al, 1984). There are also concerns regarding the effect of mechanical restraint on self- and public image, quality of life and the development of relationships.

Good practice guidelines

A set of good practice guidelines that could form the basis for clear standards regarding the management of SIB would be useful in improving service provision in the same way that this has helped transform the situation regarding the reactive management of aggression (Harris et al, 1996; 2008). Paley (2008) makes a valued contribution to achieving this objective, and her calls for clear organisational policy statements and more effective internal monitoring by an ethical committee are welcome. She has described a series of useful but abstract principles and produced a list of very relevant questions regarding the issue. However, more detailed practical guidance that helps to provide answers is still required.

On the basis of the available literature, a number of points emerge. As SIB is a heterogeneous class of responses that have multiple topographies which may be maintained by social, environmental and biological factors, all interventions should be based on functional analysis of SIB and follow the least restrictive alternative approach. There should be clear written behavioural management plans and treatment programmes in place, and their implementation should be regularly monitored and reviewed (Emerson, 1992; Hamad et al, 1983; Kahng et al, 2002a, b; Spain et al, 1984). Multifaceted interventions should involve both strategies for behaviour change and for situational behaviour management; where appropriate, the former should consist of combined pharmacological and behavioural intervention as described above.

The clearest and most comprehensive good practice guidance regarding the reactive management of SIB were set out by Spain et al (1984), and these continue to be relevant, especially concerning the use of protective devices. The enduring relevance of these guidelines highlights yet again the lack of focused attention given to this issue over the last two decades. Congruent with the above account, Spain et al (1984) emphasised that protective appliances may be of considerable value in the management and treatment of SIB, but that they should be used with caution and only as part of a general behavioural programme aimed to treat SIB and replace it with alternative behaviour. They recognised the need to balance the danger of a person becoming dependent on the protective device against the possible detrimental effects of the unprotected severe SIB. They suggested that the following type of key question should always be asked: Is there any alternative way of preventing damage; which would be non-reinforcing of the SIB; which would allow the person to engage in other activities; and which would be feasible in practice, given actual staffing levels? If the answer to this question is 'No', then protection may be the only alternative to prevent tissue damage, and they make a series of straightforward recommendations:

- Protection could include physical holding (depending on staffing levels), however, it may be preferable to use material restraints since physical contact may, in itself, be a powerful reinforcer in maintaining SIB. Appliances should also be easy to put on and take off, avoiding prolonged physical contact, for the same reason

- No one should be left unattended when wearing an appliance[2]

- There are no standard appliances as such; suitably skilled and experienced therapists need to adapt and make them according to individual needs

- Attempts should always be made to make the appliance look as ordinary and as pleasing as possible to promote social acceptability and positive self-image. Adapting ordinary clothing should always be considered, eg wearing a hat over a helmet

- Shorter periods of use of appliance are found to be generally more effective than longer periods (however, there are notable exceptions to this, for example people with Lesch-Nyhan syndrome)

- It may be justifiable to provide a suitable mechanical protective appliance to be used only in emergencies, mainly to allay staff anxiety

- This is because staff may be more willing to implement reinforcement based behavioural treatment programmes in the knowledge that they can use an appliance if the SIB becomes too severe

- Ideally, it should always be possible for the person wearing the appliance to engage in other activities for a large part of the day and be strongly rewarded

- Consideration should be given from the outset as to how the use of the appliance can be gradually faded over time

---

[2] This is particularly critical, as many deaths in restraint with other user groups have occurred when people have asphyxiated as a result of being entangled in their restraints.

Training staff in positive behavioural support strategies can reduce levels of personal and mechanical restraint (Sturmey, 2002). Similarly, the possible counter-therapeutic effect of restraint application acting as a social reinforcer can be reduced by ensuring that high-densities of social reinforcement are delivered non-contingently on challenging behaviour throughout the person's day (LaVigna and Willis, 2002). Where restraints are impractical (for example, the person refuses to wear a device), altering the environment to make it safer (by removing sharp corners, padding targeted areas, etc) (Harris et al, 1996; Mental Welfare Commission for Scotland, 2002) may represent a better option. Oliver et al (1998) highlight the need to base reduction strategies on functional analysis in order to avoid the inadvertent reinforcement of SIB or self-restraint. When experimental functional analysis using experimental analogue conditions may not be possible because the SIB may not vary in line with manipulations, or because free responding is too dangerous to allow, mechanical restraints should be designed so that they can be easily faded in more than one dimension (eg size, pressure, and degree of flexion).

Issues concerning consent to treatment have been appropriately highlighted by the Mental Capacity Act, and a further aspect of good practice concerns the need to use the framework set out by the act to seek informed consent wherever possible for the use of mechanical restraint, or based on clear best interest criteria in the context of a multidisciplinary approach.

Good practice must include the maintenance of accurate records concerning all instances where mechanical restraint is used, which is an existing requirement of all service providers (CSCI, 2007b)

Conclusions

Whilst many positive changes may have occurred over the last two decades in the management and treatment of challenging behaviour, the reactive management of SIB seems to have received little attention. In the mid 1980s, several authors argued that the management of SIB should be given greater attention because restraint appeared to be quite frequently used in practice and that people with SIB were at risk because treatment was either unavailable or ineffective (Griffin et al, 1986, Richmond et al, 1986; Spain et al, 1984). This position appears not to have changed significantly, and the provision of this attention is now long overdue.

The Mental Health Act Commission has repeatedly called for more debate concerning the use of mechanical restraint, mainly regarding people with mental health problems, but including people with intellectual disabilities. In 2006, for example, it argued for the extension of monitoring arrangements, which was supported by the Joint Committee on Human Rights, and reported that there had been some discussion with government concerning the introduction of a system of notifications on the use of mechanical restraint. The following statement was made:

'We are concerned as to whether non-mandatory guidance in a code of practice will be sufficient safeguard against the broad potential for abuse raised by the use of mechanical restraint ... but it may be appropriate to have this debate based upon evidence collated from the notification system'

(MHAC 2006, para 4.221)

However, it is unclear what further progress has been made concerning these issues, or whether they will be addressed by the new Care Quality Commission. The proposed regulatory powers of this Commission will extend across all health and social care provision, promising the potential for the extension called for by MHAC and improved consistent monitoring. However, if the government commitment to ensure that the abuse that occurred in Cornwall and elsewhere can never happen again is to be achieved, then renewed attention needs to be given to how a robust system of external, statutory notification of the incidence of mechanical restraint can be established.

Treatment and management are both necessary components of positive behavioural support. Unfortunately, most people with SIB in the UK appear not to receive behavioural treatment, so we need to keep them safe whilst still advocating for effective treatment. In order to do this, a clear set of guidelines and standards reflecting some of the advances made in the positive behavioural management of aggressive and destructive behaviours would be very helpful. Spain et al's (1984) account remains useful because it contains detailed descriptions and illustrations of the types of devices that are discussed, thus making it understandable, relevant and of practical use to practitioners. Any future guidelines must replicate these characteristics. Good practice guidelines, in themselves, will not solve the issues and, indeed, are likely to raise questions of service deficits in many areas, such as access to specialists who can make bespoke appliances, the general absence of behavioural inputs and the need for staff to be effectively managed as well as trained. However, debating and agreeing standards is a useful first step in improving quality. Standards are more likely to be valid if the debate engages those key stakeholders (eg researchers, service providers, staff, the various multidisciplinary professionals, relatives and people with SIB themselves) who, despite the lack of academic attention given to the issue in recent years, have been continually dealing with the reality of managing SIB in practice. With the prospect of the new quality care commission now firmly on the horizon, the next few years seem to be the ideal opportunity to have such a long-overdue debate

References

Allen, D (2008) Risk and Prone Restraint-Reviewing the Evidence In M Nunno, D Day and L Bullard *For your own Safety, Examining the safety of high-risk interventions for children and young people.* New York: Child Welfare League of America.

Allen, D (2001) *Training Carers In Physical Interventions: Research Towards Evidence-Based Practice* Kidderminster: BILD Publications.

Allen, D (2002). *Ethical Approaches to Physical interventions. Responding to Challenging Behaviour in People with Intellectual Disabilities*. Kidderminster: BILD Publications.

Allen, D, Lowe, K, Brophy, S and Moore K (2007) Predictors, costs and characteristics of out of area placements for people with intellectual disability and challenging behaviour. *Journal of Intellectual Disability Research*, 51, 6, 409–16.

British Institute of Learning Disabilities (2001) *Code Of Practice For Trainers In the Use Of Physical Interventions*. Kidderminster: BILD Publications.

Brylewski, J and Duggan, L (2001) Anti-psychotic medication for challenging behaviour in people with learning disability (Cochrane Review), In *The Cochrane Library, Issue 4, 2002*. Oxford: Update Software.

Carr, E G, Robinson, S and Palumbo, L W (1990a) The wrong issue: aversive versus nonaversive treatment. The right issue: Functional versus non functional treatment. In A C Repp and N Singh (Eds) *Current perspectives in the use of nonaversive and aversive interventions with developmentally disabled persons*. Sycamore, Illinois: Sycamore Press.

Carr, E G, Robinson, S, Taylor, J C and Carlson, J I (1990b) *Positive Approaches to the Treatment of Severe Behavior Problems in Persons with Developmental Disabilities*. Washington: The Association for Persons with Severe Handicaps.

Commission for Social Care Inspection (CSCI) (2007a) *Guidance for Inspectors: How to move towards restraint free care*. Commission for Social Care Inspection Quality Performance and Methods Directorate QPM Document Number: 301/07.

Commission for Social Care Inspection (CSCI) (2007b) *Policy and Guidance: Notification of Death, Illness and Other Event: Regulation 37* Commission for Social Care Inspection Quality Performance and Methods Directorate QPM Document Number: 025/07.

DeLeon, I G, Rodriguez-Catter, V and Cataldo M, F, (2002) Treatment: Current Standards of care and Their Research Implications. In Schroeder, S R, Oster-Granite, M K and Thompson, T *Self Injurious Behavior: Gene-brain-behavior relationships*. American Psychological Association: Washington, DC.

Department of Health and Department for Education and Skills (2002) *Guidance For Restrictive Physical Interventions Valuing People: A New Strategy For Learning Disability For The 21st Century*. London: Department of Health.

Dorsey, M F, Iwata, B A, Reid, D H and Davis, P A (1982) Protective equipment: continuous and contingent application in the treatment of self-injurious behavior. *Journal of Applied Behavior Analysis*, 15, 2, 217–230.

Duker, P and Seys, D (1997) An Inventory Method for Assessing the Degree of Restraint Imposed by Others'. *Journal of Behaviour Therapy and Experimental Psychiatry*, 28, 2, 113–121.

Emerson, E (1992) Self-injurious behaviour: an overview of recent trends in epidemiological and behavioural research' *Mental Handicap Research*, 5, 49–81.

Emerson, E (2002) The prevalence of use of reactive management strategies in community-based services in the UK. In D Allen (Ed) *Ethical Approaches to Physical interventions*. Kidderminster: BILD Publications.

Emerson, E and Hatton, C (1994) *Moving Out: Relocation from Hospital to Community*. London: HMSO.

Emerson, E, Robertson, J, Gregory, N, Hatton, C, Kessissoglou, S, Hallam, A and Hillery, J (2000) Treatment and Management of Challenging Behaviours in Residential Settings. *Journal of Applied Research in Intellectual Disabilities*, 13, 197–213.

Fisher, W W, Piazza, C C, Bowman, L G, Hanley, G P and Adelinis, J D (1997) Direct And Collateral Effects Of Restraint And Restraint Fading. *Journal of Applied Behaviour Analysis*, 30, 105–120.

Forman, D, Hall, S and Oliver, C (2002) Descriptive Analysis of Self-Injurious Behaviour and Self-restraint' *Journal of Applied Research in Intellectual Disabilities*, 15, 1–7.

Foxx, R M and Dufrense, D (1984) 'Harry': the use of physical restraint as a reinforcer, time-out from restraint, and fading restraint in treating a self –injurious man. *Analysis and Intervention in Developmental Disabilities*, 4, 1–14.

Griffin, J C, Williams, D E, Stark, M T, Altmeyer, B K and Mason, M (1986) Self-injurious behavior: a state-wide prevalence survey of the extent and circumstances. *Applied Research in Mental Retardation*, 7, 105–116.

Gordon, H, Hindley, N, Marsden, A and Shivayogi, M (1999) The use of mechanical restraint in the management of psychiatric patients: is it ever appropriate? *The Journal Of Forensic Psychiatry*, 10, 1, 173–186.

Guardian (The) (2005) *No holds barred?* Available from www.guardian.co.uk/society/2005/feb/02mentalhealth. guardiansocietysupplement (accessed 20 April 2009).

Hall, S, Oliver, C and Murphy, G (2001) Self-injurious behaviour in young children with Lesch-Nyhan syndrome. *Developmental Medicine and Child Neurology*, 43, 11, 745–749.

Hamad, C D, Isley, E and Lowry, M (1983) 'The Use Of Mechanical Restraint And Response Incompatibility To Modify Self-Injurious Behaviour: A Case Study' *Mental Retardation*, 21, 5, 213–217.

Harris, J (1996) Physical restraint procedures for managing challenging behaviours presented by mentally retarded adults and children. *Research in Developmental Disabilities*, 17, 2, 99–134.

Harris, J, Allen, D, Cornick, M, Jefferson, A and Mills, R (1996) *Physical interventions a policy framework*. Kidderminster: BILD Publications.

Harris, J, Cornick, M, Jefferson, A and Mills, R (2008) *Physical interventions a policy framework (Second Edition)*. Kidderminster: BILD Publications.

Harris, P and Russell, O (1989) The Prevalence of Aggressive Behaviour among people with learning difficulties (Mental Handicap) in a Single Health District. Bristol: Norah Fry Research Centre, University of Bristol.

Hastings, R P (1996) Staff strategies and explanations for intervening with challenging behaviours. *Journal of Intellectual Disability Research*, 40, 166–175.

Healthcare Commission and Commission for Social Care Inspection (2006) *Joint investigation into services fro people with learning disabilities at Cornwall Partnership NHS Trust*. London: Healthcare Commission.

Healthcare Commission (2007) *Investigation into the service for people with learning disabilities provided by Sutton and Merton Primary Care Trust*. London: Healthcare Commission.

Horner, R H and Carr, E G (1997) Behavioral support for students with severe disabilities: functional assessment and comprehensive intervention. *The Journal of Special Education*, 31, 88–104.

Hyman, P, Oliver, C and Hall, S (2002) Self-Injurious Behavior, Self-Restraint, and Compulsive Behaviors in Cornelia de Lange Syndrome *American Journal on Mental Retardation*, 107, 2, 146–154.

Iwata, B A, Dorsey, M F, Silfer, K J, Bauman, K E and Richman, G S (1982) Toward a functional analysis of self-injury. *Analysis and Intervention in Developmental Disabilities, 2,* 3–30.

Jones, E, Allen, D, Moore, K, Phillips, B and Lowe, K (2007) Restraint and self-injury in people with intellectual disabilities: A review. *Journal of Intellectual Disabilities*, 11, 105–118.

Lerman, D C, Iwata, B A, Smith, R G, Zarcone, J R and Vollmer, T R, (1994). Transfer of Behavioral function as a contributing factor in treatment relapse. *Journal of Applied Behavior Analysis*, 27, 357–370.

Kahng, S, Abt, K A and Wilder, D A (2001) Treatment of self-injury correlated with mechanical restraints. *Behavioural Intervention*, 16, 105–110.

Kahng, S, Iwata, B A and Lewin, A B (2002a) Behavioural Treatment of Self-Injury, 1964 to 2000. *American Journal on Mental Retardation*, 107, 3, 212–221.

Kahng, S, Iwata, B A and Lewin, A B (2002b) The impact of Functional Assessment on the treatment of Self-Injurious behaviour. In S R Schroeder, M L Oster-Granite and T Thompson (Eds) *Self Injurious Behavior. Gene-brain-behavior relationships*. Washington, DC: American Psychological Association.

Kennedy, S S (2008) Using restraint: The Legal Context of High-Risk Interventions. In M Nunno, D Day and L Bullard (Eds) *Examining the safety of high-risk interventions for children and young people*. New York: Child Welfare League of America.

Kingdon, D, Jones, R and Lonnqvist, J, (2004) Protecting the human rights of people with mental disorder: new recommendations emerging from the Council of Europe. *British Journal of Psychiatry*, 185, 277–279.

LaVigna, G W and Willis, T (2002) Counter-intuitive strategies for crisis management within anon-aversive framework. In D Allen (Ed) *Ethical Approaches to physical interventions. Responding to challenging behaviour in people with intellectual disabilities*. Kidderminster: BILD Publications.

Mace, F C, Blum, N J, Sierp, B J, Delaney, B A and Mauk, J E (2001) Differential response of Operant Self –Injury to Pharmacologic Versus Behavioral Treatment. Journal *of Developmental and Behavioural Pediatrics*, 22, 2, 85–91.

Mental Welfare Commission for Scotland (2002) *Rights, Risks and Limits to Freedom. Principles and guidance on good practice in caring for residents with dementia and related disorders and residents with learning disabilities where consideration is being given to the use of physical restraint and other limits to freedom*. Edinburgh: Mental Welfare Commission for Scotland.

Mental Welfare Commission For Scotland (2006) *Rights, Risks and Limits to Freedom. Principles and good practice guidance for practitioners considering restraint in residential care settings*. Edinburgh: Mental Welfare Commission for Scotland.

Murphy, G (1999) Self-injurious behaviour: What do we Know and Where are Going? *Tizard Learning Disability Review*, 4, 1, 5–12.

Murphy, G, Oliver, C, Corbett, J, Crayton, L, Hales, J, Head, D and Hall, S (1993) Epidemiology of self injury, characteristics of people with severe self injury and initial treatment outcome. In C Kiernan (Ed), *Research into practice? Implications of research on the challenging behaviour of people with learning disability*. Kidderminster: BILD Publications.

National Institute of Clinical Excellence (2005) *Violence: the short-term management of disturbed/violent behaviour in inpatients psychiatric settings and emergency departments*. London: RCN.

Nottestad, J and Linaker, O (2001) Self-injurious behaviour before and after deinstitutionalisation. *Journal of Intellectual Disability Research*, 45, 2, 121–129.

Oliver, C, Hall, S, Hales, J, Murphy, G and Watts, D (1998) The Treatment of Severe Self-Injurious Behavior by the Systematic Fading of Restraints: Effects on Self-Injury, Self-Restraint, Adaptive Behavior and Behavioral Correlates of Affect. *Research in Developmental Disabilities*, 19, 2, 143–165.

Oliver, C, Murphy, G H and Corbett, J A (1987) Self-injurious behaviour in people with mental handicap: a total population study. *Journal of Mental Deficiency Research*, 31, 147–162.

Paley, S (2008) *Use of mechanical devices: restrictive physical intervention, Principles for Practice* Kidderminster: BILD Publications.

Qureshi, H (1994) *Parents caring for Young Adults with Mental Handicap and Behaviour Problems*. Manchester: Hester Adrian Research Centre.

Richmond, G, Schroeder, S R and Bickel, W (1986) Tertiary prevention of attrition related to self injurious behaviours. In K D Gadow (Ed) *Advances In Learning And Behaviour Disabilities*. London: JAI Press.

Robertson, J, Emerson, E, Pinkney, L, Ceasar, E, Felce, D, Meek, A, Carr, D, Lowe, K, Knapp, M and Hallam, A (2005). Treatment and management of challenging behaviours in congregate and non-congregate community-based supported accommodation. *Journal of Intellectual Disability Research*, 49, 1, 63–72.

Royal College of Nursing (2008) *Let's talk about restraint, rights, risks and responsibility*. Royal College of Nursing: London.

Schroeder, S R, Mulick, J A and Rojahn, J (1980) The definition, taxonomy, epidemiology, and ecology of self-injurious behaviour. *Journal of Autism and Development Disorder*, 10, 417–432.

S R Schroeder, M L Oster-Granite and T Thompson (Eds) (2002) *Self-injurious Behaviour. Gene-brain-behaviour Relationships*. Washington DC: American Psychological Association.

Scotti R J, Ujcich K J, Weigle K L, Holland, C M and Kirk, K S (1996) Interventions with Challenging Behavior of Persons With developmental Disabilities: A Review of Current research Practices. *Journal Of The Association For Persons With Severe Handicaps*, 21, 3, 123–134.

Scull, A T (1993) *The Most Solitary of Afflictions: Madness and Society in Britain, 1700–1900*. New Haven: Yale University Press.

Spain, B, Hart, S A and Corbett, J (1984) 'The use of appliances in the treatment of severe self-injurious behaviour'. In G Murphy and B Wilson (Eds) *Self-Injurious Behaviour. A collection of published papers on prevalence, causes, and treatment in people who are mentally handicapped or autistic*. Kidderminster: BIMH Publications.

Sturmey, P (2002) Restraint Reduction. In D Allen (Ed) (2002) *Ethical Approaches to Physical interventions. Responding to Challenging Behaviour in People with Intellectual Disabilities*. Kidderminster: BILD Publications.

Symons, F J, Thompson, A and Rodriguez, M C (2004) Self-injurious behaviour and the efficacy of naltrexone treatment: A quantitative synthesis. *Mental Retardation and Developmental Disabilities Research Reviews*, 10, 3, 193–200.

Tate, B G (1972) Case study: control of chronic self-injurious behavior by conditioning procedures. *Behaviour Therapy*, 3, 72–83.

Thompson, T and Caruso, M (2002) Self-Injury. Knowing what we're looking for. In S R Schroeder, M L Oster-Granite and T Thompson (Eds) *Self Injurious Behavior gene-brain-behavior relationships*. Washington DC: American Psychological Association.

Thompson, T, Egli, M, Symons, F and Delaney, D (1994) Neurobehavioral Mechanisms of Drug Action on Developmental Disabilities. In T Thompson and D B Gray (Eds) *Destructive Behaviour in Developmental Disabilities. Diagnosis and Treatment*. Thousand Oaks: Sage.

Welsh Assembly Government (2005). *Framework for restrictive Physical Intervention Policy and Practice*. Cardiff: Welsh Assembly Government.

Wolfensberger, W (1975) *The Origin And Nature Of Our Institutional Models,* Syracuse, New York: Human Policy Press.

Chapter 6

Ethical use of Medication to Manage Imminent Disturbed/Violent Behaviour in Adults with Intellectual Disabilities

Shoumitro Deb

Introduction

It has been reported that 20–45 per cent of people with intellectual disability receive psychotropic medications and of these, 14–30 per cent receive those medications for the management of their challenging behaviours (Deb and Fraser, 1994; Clarke et al, 1990). Despite this high frequency of use, the evidence to support this practice currently is not well established (Deb and Unwin, 2007; Tyrer et al, 2008). There is particular concern about the adverse effects of these medications and their use outside their licensed indication (both in terms of their being used for purposes other than those originally intended and, sometimes, in dosages in excess of those ordinarily recommended). Therefore a national good practice guide has been developed recently in the UK to help the clinicians (see www.ld-medication.bham.ac.uk) in this regard. Among many things the guide recommends is the objective assessment of outcomes of medication (see Unwin and Deb, 2008, for a recent review on the outcome measures) rather than depending on only subjective view of carers and professionals.

In this chapter I will concentrate only on the use of psychotropic medication for the management of imminent violence in adults with intellectual disability and not on its routine therapeutic use. There may be separate issues relating to children with intellectual disability, but these are outside the scope of the present chapter. Its aim is to summarise existing good practice guides and review the evidence-base.

Both pharmacological and non-pharmacological strategies are used to manage imminent violence among adults with intellectual disability. In the medical literature, the use of medication in this context is known as rapid tranquillisation. However, for adults with intellectual disability, the terms 'as required' or 'pro re nata' (PRN) medication is used more frequently than 'rapid tranquillisation', particularly outside the hospital settings where most adults with intellectual disability live. Therefore in this chapter I will discuss the use of 'as required medication' first, before discussing issues relating to 'rapid tranquillisation', which may be considered as more intrusive. However, before discussing these issues, it is necessary to discuss the general issue of administration of medications, particularly in community settings.

Administration of medications

The Association for Real Change (ARC) has recently produced a guideline and training framework on the management of medication within services for people with intellectual disability. This project was funded by the Department of Health. Although this guideline is produced for use primarily in social care settings, it could be applied equally in all other settings where medication is administered to people with intellectual disability. I shall highlight the important points from that guideline here (see the full document for more information on the subject, which is available from www.arcuk.org.uk/silo/files/76.pdf). The guideline highlights the need for standardised training for people who are involved in administering medications to people who have intellectual disability. The training package is mapped against three relevant standards, namely the National Occupational Standards (NOS) NVQ, the Learning Disability Award Framework (LDAF) and the National Minimum Standards (Younger Adults) (NMS).

The emphasis on the document is on the following principles:

The right person
gets
The right medication
at
The right time
in
The right dose
using
The right method
following
The right procedure
and ensuring
The right record keeping

The right person
This should include issues relating to informed consent and capacity for consent.

The right medication
People administering the medication should have basic knowledge of the purpose of the medication, medication group, common and serious adverse effects and the action necessary to deal with them, and any contra-indication for not using the medication for the particular person.

The right time

Correct time of the day, in relation to meal times and the sequence for giving several drugs, should always be appropriate.

The right dose

The right dose of medication must always be administered. If in doubt, people should always check the instruction given by the prescriber or with other staff or the British National Formulary (BNF) (March 2008; www.bnf.org). Here communication with the prescriber is very important, particularly if any changes are made recently in the medication dosage. All who are involved in the administration of medication should be up to date with all recent changes in the dose. Recent loss or gain in weight, possible allergies and right measurement for liquid formula should always be taken into account.

The right method

People should be absolutely sure about the route of administration of medications and any changes in the instruction for that before administering the medication. People should have the right training before administering any medication (for example administration of rectal diazepam or buccal midazolam).

The right procedure

People should ensure that they have the right level of competence to undertake the administration of medication. They should always ensure that the right and safe instruments are used. The right person should be monitored after taking the medication to make sure that they do not spit out the medication or develop any adverse effects.

The right record keeping

All records should be kept in line with policy, regulations and best practice. The records should be legible and be written in an understandable way. The records should be kept confidential and up to date, and monitored regularly.

The Commission for Social Care Improvement's (CSCI) report (National Minimum Standards (www.csci.org.uk/publications/past_publications/facts_ figures/medication_report.pdf) states that improving performance on the management of medicines will require action on training, supervision, policies, the involvement of other professionals, and raising general level of awareness.

There is no specific recommendation about when to use medication in relation to a particular challenging behaviour. This has to be decided on an individual case basis after a thorough assessment and formulation, including consideration of all options for intervention and full discussion with the person with intellectual disability, their carers, and the relevant professionals involved in the care of the person.

It is good practice to always obtain and understand the drug company's patient information leaflet. It is also a good practice to obtain and read good practice guidelines produced by the local pharmacy departments. Accessible versions of information leaflets for adults with intellectual disability and their carers on commonly used psychotropic medications and accompanying audio versions could be downloaded free of charge from www.ld-medication.bham.ac.uk

As-required medications

In adults with intellectual disability, rapid tranquillisation is often used in the form of oral medication rather than injection as in intramuscular or intravenous form. As stated above, this is often described as an 'as-required' (or PRN) prescription rather than a rapid tranquillisation. If such medication is required, the following good practice standards should be observed (Deb et al, 2006).

- The prescribing of 'as-required' medications should be part of an overall 'treatment/care plan' and, when possible, should be prescribed after discussion with the service users/carers and other relevant care professionals. The service users'/carers' preferred route of administration (eg either via oral or intramuscular route) should always be considered

- The reason/indication (ie when to use) for administering 'as-required' medications must be recorded clearly in the case notes, with objectives set at the outset for measuring the outcome over a set period of time. The 'as-required' prescription must be monitored at regular intervals, the time period for which should be set at the time of prescribing

- The indication for administration of 'as-required' medications, the minimum interval between doses and the maximum dose allowed within a 24-hour period should all be clearly recorded

- The 'as-required' medications that may be administered by more than one route (eg via orally or intramuscular route) should be prescribed separately, with clear direction as to why one should be preferred

Unless there are clear clinical reasons to the contrary (which should be clearly noted), the following further guidelines should also be considered:

- Discontinuation of any 'as-required' medication that has not been used for six months or longer (exception is rescue medication for status epilepticus or prolonged seizures or prolonged cluster of seizures) should be considered

- Oral and intramuscular medications should be prescribed separately

- Oral (o)/intramuscular (i/m) abbreviations should not be used

- Two medications of the same class for the same condition (exceptions are the antiepileptic medications) should not be used

- Medications should not be mixed in the same syringe

- More than two medications should not be prescribed for any one indication

- Prescriptions must be reviewed and, where appropriate, re-written as regular prescriptions if they are needed regularly, despite the fact that they were originally prescribed as 'as-required' medications

- Medications from the same therapeutic categories that are used simultaneously as regular and 'as-required' prescription should be monitored frequently in order to avoid overdosing (if that happens, ensure that the total daily dose of the regular and the 'as-required' prescription does not exceed maximum British National Formulary (BNF, March 2008) recommended dose regularly)

Rapid tranquilisation

The recently published National Institute for Health and Clinical Excellence (NICE; www.nice.org.uk) guidelines on 'The short-term management of disturbed/violent behaviour in psychiatric in-patient settings and emergency departments' (NICE, 2005) includes guidelines for 'rapid tranquillisation'. These guidelines are equally applicable for use among adults who have intellectual disabilities. I have summarised here the main recommendations (see also the quick reference guide by Deb et al, 2006):

- The aim of rapid tranquillisation is to achieve a state of calm sufficient to minimise the risk posed to the service user or to others

- Try to predict a violent episode by using 'risk assessment', by considering appropriate 'risk factors' and looking for 'antecedents and warning signs'

- Try to avoid a violent episode by using appropriate preventative strategies such as 'de-escalation' and appropriate observation

- Rapid tranquillisation, physical intervention and seclusion are management strategies and are not regarded as primary treatment techniques

- Rapid tranquillisation should only be used once de-escalation and other strategies to control the violent episode have failed

- Clinical need, the safety of service users and others and, where possible, advance decisions should be taken into account when making decision about using rapid tranquillisation and other interventions

- The intervention selected (eg rapid tranquillisation or physical restraint or seclusion) must be a reasonable and appropriate response to the risk posed by the service user

- A crash bag should be available within three minutes in health-care settings where rapid tranquillisation might be used (this should only apply to intramuscular or intravenous administration of rapid tranquillisers)

- The crash bag should include an automatic external defibrillator, a bag valve mask, oxygen, cannulas, fluids, suction and first line resuscitation drugs

- The crash bag should be maintained and checked regularly

- At all times, a doctor should be available to quickly attend an alert by staff members when rapid tranquillisation is implemented (this should only apply to intramuscular and intravenous administration of rapid tranquillisers)

- Ensure that the service user is able to respond to communication throughout

- The prescribing and administration of rapid tranquillisation must take place within the current legal framework, particularly according to the relevant Mental Health Act or its equivalent

- Any departures from the legal guideline must be clearly recorded and justified in the service user's best interests, and reviewed as soon as possible

The guidelines also stress the importance of supporting service users appropriately throughout what is almost inevitably a traumatic process. Thus, When administering rapid tranquillisation, it is important to try to ensure that the service user does not feel humiliated (for example, respecting their need for dignity and privacy commensurate with the needs of administering the rapid tranquillisation). The reasons for using the interventions should be explained to the service user at the earliest opportunity. Finally, the service user should be supported to re-engage in their normal activities as soon as possible following the rapid tranquillisation.

Medications for rapid tranquillisation

NICE recommends the use of benzodiazepine, such as lorazepam, and antipsychotic, such as haloperidol, either via oral or intramuscular or slow intravenous route as the preferred medications for rapid tranquillisation. The medication such as oral or intramuscular chlorpromazine, intramuscular diazepam, thioridazine, intramuscular depot antipsychotics and, in particular among elderly patients with possible dementia, atypical antipsychotics such as risperidone and olanzapine should not be used for rapid tranquillisation.

Zuclopenthixol acetate (intramuscular clopixol acuphase 50–150 mgs) is not recommended for rapid tranquillisation because of long onset and duration of action. However, this could be used if the disturbed behaviour is likely to continue over a long period of time, there is a past history of good and timely response, past history showed requirement of repeated intramuscular administration, and cited in advance decisions. However, this medication should never be used on those without previous antipsychotic exposure.

Although olanzapine can be used for moderate disturbance, intramuscular lorazepam cannot be used within the one hour of administration of intramuscular olanzapine and also oral lorazepam should be used with caution.

Adverse effects of benzodiazepine and antipsychotic medication should be monitored carefully. The serious acute adverse effects of benzodiazepines include loss of consciousness, respiratory depression or arrest, cardiovascular collapse, particularly when receiving clozapine along with benzodiazepines. The serious acute adverse effects of antipsychotics include loss of consciousness, cardiovascular/respiratory complications and collapse, seizures, akathisia, dystonia, dyskinesia, neuroleptic malignant syndrome and excessive sedation. The serious acute adverse effects of antihistamines include excessive sedation, painful injection and additional antimuscarinic effects. Many acute adverse effects of benzodiazepines could be counteracted by flumazenil and of antipsychotics by anticholinergic medications such as procyclidine or benztropine.

Potential risks from using these medications involve over-sedation causing loss of consciousness or alertness, loss of airway, cardiovascular and respiratory collapse, interaction with other medications either prescribed or illicit, damage to the therapeutic relationship, and effect on the underlying coincidental physical disorders. Therefore extra care is required in the presence of congenital prolonged QTc syndrome (a cardiac dysrhythmia), medications that lengthen QTc interval directly or indirectly, hypo/hyperthermia, stress/extreme emotions, and extreme physical exertion.

Prescribers and those who administer medication should be familiar with the properties of benzodiazepines, flumazenil, antipsychotics, antimuscarinics and antihistamines; risks including cardio-respiratory effects, particularly if with high arousal, possible medication misuse, dehydration or physical illness; and the need to titrate dose to effect or adverse effect.

The risks listed above are a significant concern in themselves. However, they become potentially even more significant if rapid tranquillisation is used in combination with physical restraint (Allen, 2008) and, somewhat inevitably, physical restraint is often required to effect its administration.

Prescribers and the medication administrators should pay attention to the total dose prescribed, arrangements for review, consent, British National Formulary (BNF) requirements, physical and mental status of the person with intellectual disability.

Protocol for rapid tranquillisation (NICE, 2005)

Preferred method of administration of medication is via the oral route. If administered via the oral route, allow sufficient time for clinical response between doses. Consider lorazepam in non-psychotic conditions such as affective disorder or personality disorder, and consider lorazepam with oral antipsychotics in the presence of psychosis and mania. Consider intramuscular lorazepam in the non-psychotic context if the oral therapy has failed or has been refused or not indicated by previous clinical response or not seen as a proportionate response. Similarly, consider intramuscular lorazepam with intramuscular haloperidol in the presence of psychosis or mania if the oral medication has failed or not indicated. Only in exceptional cases intravenous administration of rapid tranquillisation is indicated.

Protocol for monitoring (NICE, 2005)

After the administration of rapid tranquillisation, monitor vital signs, record blood pressure, pulse, temperature, respiratory rate and hydration as agreed by a multidisciplinary team until the service user is active again. Pulse oximeters should be available (see Masters, 2008, for a description of their possible use also for post-restraint monitoring).

Intensive and frequent monitoring by trained staff is required if the person with intellectual disability appears overly sedated, intravenous administration is used, the dose employed exceeded BNF or SPC limit, in high risk situations, if illicit substance/alcohol is ingested, or in the presence of relevant medical such as a heart condition disorders and/or the person is taking other prescribed medication. Particular attention should be paid to respiratory effort, airway and the level of consciousness. All actions should be recorded in the care plan. If verbal response is lost, then the level of care used should be that for general anaesthesia. There should be a post-incident review within 72 hours.

Follow-up and review

The following additional good practice points have been suggested for follow up and review after rapid tranquillisation:

- All service users should be given the opportunity to discuss their experiences of rapid tranquillisation and should be provided with a clear explanation of the decision to use medication in this way. They should also be assisted in documenting an advanced directive if they desire

- Staff involved in rapid tranquillisation should be given the opportunity to discuss the incident

- Prescriptions for rapid tranquillisation should be reviewed regularly by the multi disciplinary team. If rapid tranquillisation is used on successive days, consideration should be given to increasing the regular medication

- Incidents regarding the administration of rapid tranquillisation should be reported and reviewed according to the policy of the relevant organisations that is responsible for the care of the person with intellectual disability.

Training requirements (NICE, 2005)

Training requirements for staff working within any organisation are of paramount importance, particularly when it comes to administering medication for the management of imminent violence among adults with intellectual disability. The following recommendations have been put forward to address this:

- All service providers should have a policy for training employers and staff-in-training in relation to the short-term management of disturbed/violent behaviour. This policy should specify who will receive what level of training (based on risk management), how often they will be trained, and also outline the techniques in which they need to be trained

- All key staff should receive ongoing competency training to recognise anger, potential aggression, antecedents and risk factors of disturbed/violent behaviour and to monitor their own verbal and non-verbal behaviour. Training should include methods of anticipating, de-escalating or coping with disturbed/violent behaviour

- All staff involved in administering or prescribing rapid tranquillisation, or monitoring service users to whom (im/iv) rapid tranquilliser has been administered, should receive ongoing competency training to a minimum of Immediate Life Support (ILS-Resuscitation Council, UK) (which covers airway, cardio-pulmonary resuscitation [CPR] and use of defibrillators)

The evidence base for rapid tranquillisation[1]

Most evidence on the effectiveness of rapid tranquillisation comes from studies carried out on people with psychiatric disorders but who do not have an intellectual disability. The evidence consists of mostly case studies including a small number of cohorts. There are also a small number of randomised controlled trails (RCTs). The available literature will be briefly reviewed here.

A survey of trainee doctors in psychiatry was carried out (Mannion et al, 1997) in which 55 questionnaires were returned reporting on 108 incidents of imminent aggression over the previous six months period. One medication was used on 45 (46 per cent) occasions and a combination on 53 (54 per cent) occasions. On 88 (90 per cent) occasions, intramuscular medications were used and zuclopenthixol acetate was used on a total of 45 (46 per cent) occasions. In 38 (39 per cent) incidents, the trainees used high-dose regimes.

Two studies (Battaglia et al, 1997; Bieniek et al, 1998) found that both intramuscular haloperidol (5 mgs) and intramuscular lorazepam (2 mgs) were effective individually as a rapid tranquilliser, but that the combination of these two medications faired marginally better than the individual medication. In contrast, with a group of 301 aggressive or agitated people with mental health difficulties, either intramuscular midazolam (15 mgs) or a combination of intramuscular haloperidol (5 mgs) and intramuscular promethazine (50 mgs) was used for rapid tranquillisation (TREC Collaboration Group, 2003). Both regimes were found effective, but midazolam was more rapidly sedating than the combination of haloperidol and promethazine.

Wolkowitz and Pickar (1991) analysed double blind trials on the efficacy of benzodiazepine alone (n = 14) and in combination (n = 16), and concluded that benzodiazepines are potentially most useful in the acute management of psychotic agitation if they are used in combination with neuroleptic (antipsychotic medications). However, this survey is rather dated and most studies included in the review are not of high quality.

---

[1] See Deb and Roberts, 2005 and the Royal College of Psychiatrists' Occasional Paper 41, 1998 for further details.

Chouinard et al (1993) studied people admitted to a university hospital with agitated psychotic conditions, including symptoms of mania. They were given either intramuscular clonazepam (1–2 mgs) (n = 8) or intramuscular haloperidol (5–10 mgs) (n = 8) at 0, 0.5 and one-hour intervals for up to two hours. The authors found that the scores on sub-scale for mania decreased by 50 per cent in five patients on clonazepam and six on haloperidol. On the other hand, Lenox et al (1992) found lesser adverse effects from intramuscular 4 mgs lorazepam (n = 9) than with intramuscular 10 mgs haloperidol (n = 11), both of which were used as an adjunct to lithium to control manic agitation, although there was no difference between the two medications in their efficacy.

Thomas et al (1992) compared the efficacy of intramuscular 5 mgs droperidol (n = 68) against intramuscular 5 mgs haloperidol (n = 26) among violent and agitated individuals in a hospital emergency department. Droperidol reduced combativeness index more rapidly at 10, 14 and 30 minutes after the administration. The effect size of the difference is not known. However, there was no difference between the two medications when administered via the intravenous route.

In a double-blind study Okuma et al (1989) found a neuroleptic in combination with carbamazepine (n = 82) showed more improvement in individuals with excited and aggressive state (48 per cent vs 30 per cent) when compared with a neuroleptic in combination with placebo (n = 80). In another double-blind trial on people with disruptive behaviour on a locked intensive psychiatric care unit, Salzman et al (1991) compared the efficacy of intramuscular 2 mgs lorazepam (n = 26) with intramuscular 5 mgs haloperidol (n = 21). They found no significant difference in the outcome in two groups in the Overt Aggression Scale score at two hours or at 24 hours after the administration of medications. Scores were reduced by 91 per cent in the lorazepam group and by 88 per cent in the haloperidol group after two hours of administration of these medications. However, lorazepam produced fewer adverse effects.

One study reported data on only ten secluded patients admitted to a psychiatric crisis unit (Bick and Hannah, 1986), where intramuscular 10 mgs haloperidol was administered on the first occasion for rapid tranquillisation and intramuscular 2 mgs lorazepam was used on the second occasion. The survey showed that on the first occasion, the average time to terminate seclusion was 6.8 hours, and on the second occasion it was 2.1 hours. This obviously does not mean that haloperidol is superior as a rapid tranquilliser than lorazepam.

Garza-Trevino et al (1989) showed that, in an acute psychiatric unit, 18 of 24 patients (75 per cent) who were given a combination of intramuscular 5 mgs haloperidol and 4 mgs lorazepam for psychotic agitation reached rapid tranquillisation within 30 minutes, compared with 16 of 44 patients (36 per cent) who were given these medications individually. All medications used were shown to be effective and safe.

Dorevitch et al (1999) used Overt Aggression Scale within 30 minutes of administration of intramuscular flunitrazepam (1 mg) (n = 15) or intramuscular haloperidol (5 mgs) (n = 13) in an RCT design to assess the immediate control of agitated or aggressive behaviour in acutely psychotic individuals. Both treatments exhibited acute anti-aggressive effect. Dubin (1985) randomly assigned patients with 'behavioural dyscontrol' who went through an emergency department to either oral or intramuscular thiothixene, haloperidol or thioridazine in concentrated form. The oral medication, at about twice the intramuscular equivalent dose, achieved tranquillisation in a mean of two hours, compared with 1.5 hours by injection. The authors concluded that oral administration may be suitable and welcome to some patients.

In a rare study involving people with intellectual disability, dramatic control was achieved in all three participants who received intramuscular midazolam (5–10 mgs) to control their intermittent aggression and violence (Bond et al, 1989). All three people received regularly other concurrent psychotropic medication. Buccal or nasal spray of midazolam is used to control prolonged seizures and cluster of seizures in people with epilepsy with and without intellectual disability (Marshall, 2007). Although there is no published study, anecdotal evidence suggests that buccal midazolam could be effective, easy to administer and fast acting as a rapid tranquilliser for a person with intellectual disability, which also avoids the need for either oral or intramuscular administration of medication, both of which could be difficult to administer when a person is disturbed.

Conclusions

It is sometimes necessary to use medication in order to manage imminent violence in adults with intellectual disability. If this method of management is used, it should form part of an overall care plan for the person. This care plan should have appropriate input from the person themselves, her/his carer and the other relevant professionals involved in the care of the person. Therefore, almost always, the use of medication in this context should be pre-planned and be administered against the context of preventative interventions, risk assessment, de-escalation and other strategies for managing imminent violence. Within each organisation there should be a clear policy about administration of rapid tranquillisation or as required medication, which should include a policy of analysis of events after each violent or potentially violent episode. The staff involved in the administration of medication should be appropriately trained and remain up to date with the latest evidence base.

By and large, the intramuscular route is preferred for rapid tranquillisation than the oral route because of speed of action, reliability of absorption and bypassing of liver metabolism in order to ensure that the medication is available in the person's blood (bioavailability). However, for people with intellectual disability, the oral route is often preferred and seems sufficient for rapid tranquillisation than intramuscular route. This is also in accordance with the current NICE (2005) guideline that recommends consideration of oral administration before considering intramuscular route. In some countries, particularly in Australia, the intravenous route is employed more regularly for rapid tranquillisation of people with mental health problems. This method is definitely not preferred in the UK however, and is used very rarely outside the accident and emergency departments.

Currently there is no evidence to compare directly the efficacy of pharmacological versus non-pharmacological methods of managing imminent violence. However, there is evidence to suggest that medication administered by trained and experienced staff can be used safely, rapidly and effectively to deal with violence in adults with intellectual disability when all other methods of management have failed or contraindicated and the person or others are seen to be in imminent danger. However, the contraindications for using medications should be identified and avoided. Sedative and therapeutic effects of medication can be distinguished and appropriate regimens could be prescribed, taking into account the varied causes of violence. Either an antipsychotic, such as haloperidol (5–10 mgs), or a benzodiazepine, such as lorazepam (2–4 mgs), are given independently or in combination either orally or via an intramuscular route or, in rare cases, slowly via an intravenous route. This practice seems safe if used by trained staff and is monitored carefully for adverse effects. At present, the evidence is controversial as to whether these medications are more efficacious on their own or when used in combination. There may be a marginal advantage in combining these two categories of medication.

The exact mechanism by which antipsychotics work as rapid tranquillisers is not known. It is apparent that they do not always work by sedating people. For example, clozapine has shown to have reduced aggression in people with schizophrenia without always causing sedation. On the other hand, a direct antipsychotic effect is unlikely to have been produced within such a short time scale. Antipsychotic properties take a few days, and sometimes a couple of weeks, to manifest. It is possible that antipsychotics, particularly at a low dose, may have some good effect on the underlying anxiety and arousal state, which may be associated with an aggressive incident and, therefore, indirectly influence the manifestation of aggression in a person.

Whether rapid tranquillisation should be seen as a last resort or not is a controversial issue. Like medication, physical intervention also carries risks, particularly if used by non-trained staff. Physical intervention may be contra-indicated in some people because of pre-existing medical conditions such as cardiac and respiratory impairments or physical disabilities such as abnormal chest wall or spinal curvature, etc. In fact, medication is often used in order to reduce the need for prolonged physical restraint. Furthermore, a person may see the use of physical intervention as more threatening, punitive and invasive of her/his private space than the use of medication. Medication may at least temporarily calm the person down by directly acting on her/his brain activities, whereas physical intervention tries to minimise the potential of harm to the person and others by trying to contain the situation and hoping that the nature will take its own course. The confrontational nature of physical intervention is also likely to worsen a person's aggression. As the person is likely to perceive both intramuscular injection and physical intervention as punitive and confrontational, s/he is likely to accept more easily an oral (or even buccal spray) route of administration of medication, over which s/he will have almost full control because s/he will have to agree to take the medication orally.

Given the lack of comparative data and the arguments put forward in the previous paragraph, the choice of use of physical intervention and medication to manage imminent violence will depend on individual circumstances. The service user's and the carer's choice, along with the decision taken by a multidisciplinary team, should play a major part in this decision-making. The method of management of imminent violence in an adult with intellectual disability has to be chosen within the context of an overall care plan, in which the person, their carers and the multidisciplinary team should provide full input. This should allow planned rather than non-planned interventions, with which the person and their carers are likely to comply. The method of management has to be chosen in the person's best interest and should not be used to suit the staff's or organisation's preference. The management plan has to comply with the current legal framework and has to be reviewed regularly. Regular debriefing of staff and the person following each violent incident is also recommended.

Each organisation supporting individuals likely to display such behaviours should have a policy on the management of imminent violence, including a clear policy on the use of medication for this purpose. There should be input from the multidisciplinary team and the service user and carers in drawing up this policy. The policy should comply with the current legal framework and be in line with other national and regional policies. The policy should also be reviewed and updated on a regular basis. All the staff involved in the management of violent episodes should have regular appropriate training with their competency assessed on a regular basis. The employing organisation should have the responsibility to demonstrate that the staff's practice is evidence-based and there is appropriate training to ensure that.

References

Allen, D (2008) Risk and Prone Restraint – Reviewing the Evidence. In M Nunno, D Day and L Bullard (Eds) *Examining the safety of high-risk interventions for children and young people.* New York: Child Welfare League of America.

Battaglia, J, Moss, S, Rush, J, Kang, J, Mendoza, R, Leedom, L, et al (1997) Haloperidol, lorazepam, or both for psychotic agitation? A multicenter, prospective, double blind, emergency department study. *American Journal of Emergency Medicine*, 15, 4, 335–340.

Bick, P A and Hannah, A L (1986) Intramuscular lorazepam to restrain violent patients. *Lancet*, i, 206.

Bieniek, S, Ownby, R, Penalver, A and Dominguez, R (1998) A double blind study of lorazepam versus the combination of haloperidol and lorazepam in managing agitation. *Pharmacotherapy*, 18, 1, 57–62.

Bond, W, Mandos, L and Kurtz, M (1989) Midazolam for aggressivity and violence in three mentally retarded patients. *American Journal of Psychiatry*, 146, 7, 925–926.

Chouinard, G, Annable, L, Turnier, L, Holbow, N and Szkrumelak, N (1993) Double-blind randomised clinical trial of rapid tranquilisation with IM clonazepam and IM haloperidol in agitated psychotic patients with manic symptoms. *Canadian Journal of Psychiatry*, 38, 4, 5114–5120.

Clarke, DJ, Kelley, S, Thinn, K and Corbett, J A (1990) Psychotropic drugs and mental retardation: 1. Disabilities and the prescription of drugs for behaviour and for epilepsy in three residential settings. *Journal of Mental Deficiency Research*, 28, 3, 229–233.

Deb, S and Fraser, W I (1994) The use of psychotropic medication in people with learning disability: towards rational prescribing. *Human Psychopharmacology*, 9, 259–272.

Deb, S, Clarke, D and Unwin, G (2006) Using medication to manage behaviour problems among adults with a learning disability: Quick Reference Guide (QRG). University of Birmingham, MENCAP, *The Royal College of Psychiatrists*, London, UK. Available from www.ld-medication.bham.ac.uk (accessed 20 April 2009).

Deb, S and Roberts, K (2005) *The Evidence Base for the Management of Imminent Violence in Learning Disability Settings*. Occasional Paper (OP57, March 2005). London: Royal College of Psychiatrists.

Deb, S and Unwin, G (2007) Psychotropic medication for behaviour problems in people with intellectual disability: a review of the current literature. *Current Opinion in Psychiatry*, 20, 461–466. `

Dorevitch, A, Katz, N, Zemishlany, Z, Aizenberg, D and Weizman, A (1999). Intramuscular flunitrazepam versus intramuscular haloperidol in the emergency treatment of aggressive psychotic behaviour. *American Journal of Psychiatry*, 156, 1, 142–144.

Dubin, W R (1985) Rapid tranquilization: the efficacy of oral concentrate. *Journal of Clinical Psychiatry*, 46, 11, 475–478.

Garza-Trevino, E S, Hollister, L E, Overall, J E and Alexander, W F (1989). Efficacy of combinations of intramuscular antipsychotics and sedative-hypnotics for control of psychotic agitation. *American Journal of Psychiatry*, 146, 12, 1598–1601.

Lenox, R, Newhouse, P A, Creelman, W L and Whitaker, T M (1992) Adjunctive treatment of manic agitation with lorazepam versus haloperidol: a double-blind study. *Journal of Clinical Psychiatry*, 53, 2, 47–52.

Masters, K (2008) Modernizing seclusion and restraint. In M Nunno, D Day and L Bullard (Eds) *Examining the safety of high-risk interventions for children and young people*. New York: Child Welfare League of America.

Mannion, L, Sloan, D and Connolly, L (1997) Rapid tranquillisation: are we getting it right? *Psychiatric Bulletin*, 20, 411–413.

Marshall, T (2007). A systematic review of the use of buccal midazolam in the emergency treatment of prolonged seizures in adults with learning disabilities. *British Journal of Learning Disabilities*, 35, 99–101.

Okuma, T, Yamashita, I, Takahashi, R and Itoh, H (1989) A double-blind study of adjunctive carbamazepine versus placebo on excited states of schizophrenic and schizoaffective disorders. *Acta Psychiatrica Scandinavica*, 80, 3, 250–259.

Royal College of Psychiatrists (1998) Management of imminent violence: clinical practice guidelines to support mental health services. Occasional Paper OP 41. The *Royal College of Psychiatrists*, March 1998, London.

Salzman, C, Solomon, D A, Miyawaki, E, Glassman, R, Rood, L, Flowers, E and Thayer, S (1991) Parenteral lorazepam versus parenteral haloperidol for the control of psychotic disruptive behaviour. *Journal of Clinical Psychiatry*, 52, 4, 177–180.

Thomas, H J, Schwartz, E and Petrilli, R (1992) Droperidol versus haloperidol for chemical restraint of agitated and combative patients. *Annals of Emergency Medicine*, 21, 4, 407–413.

TREC Collaborative Group (2003) Rapid tranquillisation for the agitated patients in emergency psychiatric rooms: a randomised trial of midazolam versus haloperidol plus promethazine. *British Medical Journal*, 327, 708–713.

Tyrer, P, Oliver-Africano, P C, Ahmed, Z, Bouras, N, Cooray, S, Deb, S, Murphy, D, Hare, M, Meade, M, Reece, B, Kramo, K, Bhaumik, S, Harley, D, Regan, A, Thomas, D, Rao, B, North, B, Eliahoo, J, Karatela, S, Soni, A and Crawford, M (2008) Risperidone, haloperidol, and placebo in the treatment of aggressive challenging behaviour in patients with intellectual disability: a randomised controlled trail. *Lancet*, 371, 57–63.

Unwin, G and Deb, S (2008) Psychiatric and behavioural assessment scales for adults with learning disabilities. *Advances in Mental Health in Learning Disability*, 2, 4, 37–45.

Wolkowitz, O M and Pickar, D (1991) Benzodiazepines in the treatment of schizophrenia: a review and reappraisal. *American Journal of Psychiatry*, 148, 6, 714–726.

Chapter 7

Seclusion and Time Out: Questioning and Defining Practice

Sharon Paley

Introduction

This chapter will seek to discuss and explore issues relating to the use of seclusion and time out in the field of intellectual disability. These emotive terms are often used in an unhelpful, interchangeably way both in practice and research (Powell et al, 2008). In the former context in particular, superficially more acceptable terms such as 'chill out space', 'time out room' and 'relaxation room' are used to describe spaces in which people are placed in isolation, often with no means of exiting independently. Alarmingly, these spaces are sometimes used within services that do not believe they are using seclusion. This concern was highlighted in the Eleventh Biennial Report of the Mental Health Act Commission (2005), which cited an array of euphemistic terms that were being used to justify exclusionary practices. These included:

- Therapeutic seclusion
- Open seclusion
- De-escalation rooms
- Single person ward
- Quiet room
- Calming room

The use of these variously named 'chill out' rooms and 'quiet spaces' seem to be increasing in use within services for children, young people and adults with intellectual disabilities (Paley, 2008; McDonnell, 2009), and it is possible that this movement is simply promoting seclusion by another name. If so, this poses a number of questions, including 'How informed are services and staff who work within them on the evidence for the effectiveness of such approaches?' and 'Is there any relative benefit to the person exposed to such controversial strategies?'. This chapter will explore these issues, highlight how practice is shaped and discuss how to prevent abusive practice. In doing so, the chapter will:

- Discuss seclusion, legislation, guidance and evidence base

- Discuss time out, how it is defined and used in practice

- Explore how the two terms are often used interchangeably

- Highlight the views of children, young people and adults with respect to the practice of seclusion and time out within services for people with intellectual disability

- Highlight principles for improving practice

What is seclusion?

The revised Code of Practice, Mental Health Act (1983) (Department of Health, 2008) defines seclusion as:

'... the supervised confinement of a patient in a room. Its sole aim is to contain severely disturbed behaviour which is likely to cause harm to others'

(para 15.43)

The above definition itself makes it clear that seclusion as a practice is not viewed as a proactive intervention, but as a management technique to be used only in cases of extreme risk.

However, it may be argued that the theoretical foundations of the practice are based on three possible rationales:

1. Positive therapy – the use of seclusion will to help a person to calm more quickly and enable them learn to 'manage' their own emotional states by reflecting on their behaviour and emotional expression

2. Containment – placing a person in a room alone prevents them from harming others until the time of crisis has passed

3. Punishment – seclusion is seen as an intentionally aversive intervention, the intention being to withdraw the individual from all positive experiences

Both the first and third of these options see seclusion has leading to some kind of beneficial therapeutic change in the individual, whereas the second is purely concerned with the immediate management of out-of-control behaviours. The third option blurs the use of seclusion with the use of time out, as will be seen below.

The Alliance to Prevent Restraint, Aversive Interventions and Seclusion (APRAIS) was founded in the United States in 2004 with the aim of ensuring that all children with disabilities should grow up free from the use of aversive interventions, restraints and seclusion. APRAIS describes aversive procedures as having some or all of the following characteristics:

- Produce obvious signs of physical pain

- Potential or actual physical side-effects such as tissue damage, physical illness, physical or emotional stress

- Dehumanisation of the individual

- Significant concern on the part of family members, staff or caregivers regarding the necessity of, or their own involvement, in such extreme strategies

- Obvious repulsion, stress or concern on the part of observers who cannot reconcile such extreme procedures with acceptable standard practice

- Rebellion or objection on the part of the individual against being subjected to such procedure

- Permanent or temporary psychological or emotional harm

APRAIS has also indentified a number of aversive practices that had been used in services for people with intellectual disabilities:

- Lemon juice, vinegar, or jalapeno pepper to the mouth

- Water spray to the face

- Blindfolding or other forms of visual blocking

- Withholding of meals/denial of adequate nutrition

- Teeth brushed or face washed with caustic solutions

- Prolonged restraint or seclusion.

Further to this, APRAIS states:

> *'the practice of seclusion is unsafe, potentially traumatising, and of questionable value in an emergency. Secluding children in locked rooms is experienced as a dehumanizing form of punishment and may result in intense panic, fear and even self-injury'*

As such, seclusion may be viewed as an aversive behaviour management strategy. Behaviour management strategies are in effect emergency responses to high levels of risk which, in effect, have one primary aim – establishing rapid and safe control over high-risk behaviours (Willis and La Vigna,1999). Allen (2002) states that behaviour management strategies are not constructive or concerned with changing behaviour in the long term, and that they only provide temporary control over a behaviour.

Use of seclusion with people who have intellectual disabilities

There is relatively sparse literature that discusses the use of seclusion within people who have intellectual disability. This is despite the fact that epidemiological research suggests that rates of use for seclusion may be significant within this population. Emerson (2001; 2002), for example, suggests that two-thirds of adults and children with intellectual disability and challenging behaviour may be exposed to this procedure.

Sequeira and Halstead (2001) undertook an analysis of semi-structured interviews following critical incidents with 82 people who had developmental disabilities. They found that men were more likely to be secluded as a response to their behaviour than the women interviewed (who were more likely to experience rapid tranquillisation). Seclusion was used in 19 per cent of the incidents analysed. Mason (1996) raised the concern that the use of seclusion as a strategy for managing behaviours in people who have intellectual disability may not bring about short-term improvements in behaviour as intended. Instead, he suggested the use of seclusion in the population might cause certain behaviours to increase and concluded that the use of seclusion might result in additional behavioural difficulties being generated. Contrary to this finding, a study undertaken in a long-stay hospital for people with intellectual disabilities by Rangecroft et al (1997) suggested that there may be some benefits with the use of seclusion in this population when compared to the use of emergency medication. The study focused on precipitating factors and outcomes for those people exposed to the use of emergency medication or seclusion, and concluded that seclusion has better outcomes in comparison to the use of major tranquillisers. In a sense, seclusion emerged in this paper as the 'lesser of two evils'. Notably, Rangecroft et al did not address the ethical issues associated with either practice, nor the longer term benefits or risks of their use within the population.

Use of seclusion – what do we know?

The Healthcare Commission National Audit of Violence (2007) found that 39 per cent of nurses employed within mental health services for working-aged adults reported being involved in the seclusion of patients. In the same audit, 25 per cent of patients reported that seclusion was used 'too quickly'; this view was shared by just six per cent of nurses. It is worth noting that it is not clear whether services for people with an intellectual disability were included within the audit.

The National Audit of Learning Disability Services (2007) states, 'On the whole services have appropriate practices for physical interventions, but we have concerns about medication.' It is not clear within the document what might constitute a physical intervention and whether practices such as seclusion were identified within the audit at all. It is somewhat surprising that the audit did not break down the criteria relating to the use of physical interventions more within the reporting, particularly given the findings at Sutton and Merton in 2007 and Cornwall in 2006 that suggested services or staff have poor recognition of what physical restraint, restriction or deprivation of liberty, or seclusion actually is (see below).

'Although many staff believed they were not using restraint our observations and records demonstrated otherwise.'

Healthcare Commission (2007) (p 4)

'At the time of our visit only one person was detained at Budock Hospital. Despite this all external doors and a number of internal doors were locked.'

Healthcare Commission (2006) (p 36)

'The only doors that could be locked were controlled by staff and used to restrict movement of those living in the houses ... Staff seemed unaware that it was unlawful to detain a person against their will.'

Healthcare Commission (2006, p 44)

The Cornwall enquiry in particular identified:

- The use of locked environments preventing people leaving against their wishes

- The application of prolonged restraint, restricting liberty and movement

- Health and safety concerns relating to some people being locked in bedrooms overnight.

Although limited, this evidence supports the notion that staff working within services do not recognise illegal, unethical or poor practice or understand what might constitute seclusion. All the above investigations highlighted training as a major issue within services where staff had been abusing people who had an intellectual disability.

While seclusion clearly is used within services for people with intellectual disability, it is the case that most of the available literature on its use concerns mental health service settings.

What is 'time out'?

The term 'time out' is most often used to describe a practice in which a person is removed from a situation where they are behaving inappropriately, to a less rewarding environment. Time out has been defined technically as 'the withdrawal of the opportunity to earn positive reinforcement or the loss of access to positive reinforcement for a specified time, contingent on the occurrence of a behaviour' (Copper, Heron and Heward, 2007). Yell (1994) describes four different 'levels' of time out:

1. *Non-exclusionary time out.* The person remains in the setting but is temporarily prevented from engaging in reinforcing activities. Examples include planned ignoring, and removal of reinforcing objects or activities

2. *Exclusionary time out: contingent observation*. The person is removed from the setting to another. The person is instructed to continue to watch the activities in the setting they have left, but cannot otherwise participate in them

3. *Exclusionary time out: exclusion*. The person is removed from the setting to another. The person is prevented from watching or otherwise participating in group activities. (The person should be observed at all times during exclusion time out)

4. *Exclusionary time out: isolation/seclusion*. The person is removed from the setting to a separate time out room. (Again, the person should be observed at all times)

The joint guidance published by the Department for Health and Department for Education and Skills (2002) describes time out as 'restricting the service user's access to all positive reinforcements as part of the behavioural programme'. Thus, although time out may have a physical resemblance to seclusion in some of its forms, it differs functionally from seclusion in that it is designed to be a behaviour change strategy and has empirical support for its effectiveness on this basis (eg Fabiano et al, 2004; Mace and Heller, 1990; Marlow et al, 1997).

Use of time out

In contrast with the definition above, time out is often incorrectly used to refer to a room or space in which a child, young person or adult is placed (McDonnell, 2009; Paley et al, 2009); this is clearly *de facto* seclusion.

In the USA, there appears to be some limited evidence that with increased inclusion policies within education, the use of such rooms appears to be on the increase (Stern, 2002). It is also the case that in the USA there have been several high profile instances of time out being used inappropriately, in particular with children who are identified as having special educational needs. There has also been widespread concern about the lack of guidance and oversight of such practices. For example, Wink News, a USA television news channel, found 14 'time out' rooms within elementary schools over a four-month period in Lee County:

'Oddly enough, seclusion and restraint is more closely monitored and regulated in our state psychiatric institutions than in Kansas schools.'
Rocky Nichols, Executive Director of Kansas Advocacy and Protection Services (2004)

In response to such concerns, in 2007 the State of Minnesota added to its statutes Directive 121a.67 that covers 'Aversive and Deprivation Procedures'. The directive is aimed at school employees and sets out conditions for the use of any practice defined as an 'aversive or deprivation procedure'. However, even this guidance, which one assumes was developed to prevent abusive practice, suggests that in certain circumstances a child or young person may be prevented from leaving the room.

APRAIS have collated known instances of abusive practice between 2004 and 2007 and, of these, 11 cases have included the use of 'time out,' variously described as time out, seclusion or isolation. The notion that 'time out' refers to a specifically designed space or room appears to enable staff to justify the use of such strategies. Indeed, there is evidence of a commercial demand for such spaces or rooms, and some companies are marketing specifically designed rooms and spaces. The following three quotes are extracts from adverts for such rooms, available within the UK, which are currently available on the internet:

'A safe place for children or adults with special needs – such as those with challenging behaviour, and those who may self harm ... essentially a safe room within a room. Custom-built to suit your specific requirements, the XXXX can fill a small room or be installed as a dedicated area within a large room. It can even be used as a bedroom.'

'Designed for demanding environments such as schools with challenging behaviours, offenders' institutes and prisons, these custom-made and fully installed facilities offer a safe environment for those with challenging behaviours and aggressive tendencies.'

'XXXX are used in schools all over the country as safe areas/chill-out rooms and sensory rooms. They are particularly suited to pupils with autism who seem calmed by the tent-like environment. XXXX are also used for pupils with challenging or self-harming behaviour.'

Such adverts appear to personify the use of euphemistic language to describe exclusionary practices, whilst making claims for beneficial outcomes that are not substantiated by empirical evidence, or certainly not by any which is in the public domain. Thus, for example, it is suggested by some adverts that such rooms/environments may be calming, prevent injury, reduce risk to the person and others; more tenuously, it is suggested the rooms will increase opportunities for people to learn personal coping mechanisms.

While time out is, as stated above, an evidence-based behaviour change procedure, it is nevertheless an aversive procedure; it works by introducing a punishment contingency (removal from positive reinforcement contingent upon challenging behaviour). As with any aversive procedure, it should never be employed as a first option, and certainly not until non-aversive procedures have been shown to be ineffective. If it is used, it should be subject to close scrutiny and monitoring and governed by detailed procedural protocols. The production and promotion of the rooms described above have none of these safeguards and only serve to redefine a practice and allow unacceptable interventions to 'fly under the radar'. The marketing of such rooms reinforces the idea that 'time out' is a totally acceptable generic practice and make it appear to be an appropriate, or even preferable, response to supporting children, young people or adults who exhibit severe challenging behaviour.

Some of these rooms may arguably be of benefit if used appropriately as a space where a person may spend therapeutic time in the company of supporting staff and of peers. It is difficult, though, to contemplate how a child, young person or adult who has severe intellectual disability or autism and is extremely upset might learn to 'manage their own anger' simply by being placed in a room, of any guise or description, alone. Nevertheless, what follows is an extract from an advert placed on the internet for a purpose-built room:

> *'In some cases, by replacing external factors (such as staff imposing control), these rooms can help develop internal mechanisms for calming and fostering understanding of rights and responsibilities – not least individuals are encouraged to manage their own behaviours.'*

Aristotle and Plato may have used personal isolation as a tool for self-evaluation and contemplation, but to encourage the idea that a person with an intellectual disability or autism (a diagnosis specifically referred to in the same advert) can develop an ability to reflect on their actions and develop *'internal mechanisms for calming and fostering understanding of rights and responsibilities'* is at best misleading, highly questionable and has no basis in evidence-based practice. Enhanced self-control for people with such needs is far more likely to be achieved via the use of the type of interventions described in Chapter 11 than through the use of seclusion, particularly when the results of the study by Mason (1996) are taken into consideration.

Legal and ethical considerations

It goes without saying that people with intellectual disabilities are entitled to the same protection in law as any other individuals. As a general principle, everyone has a right to freedom of movement and choice of where and when and how they spend their time. However, one must also accept that occasionally people may exhibit behaviour that presents a high level of risk to the person themselves, and those around them. It may then be appropriate and lawful to use a restrictive physical intervention or to temporarily restrict a person's liberty – for example, in the prevention of extreme self-harm or a criminal act. This section of the chapter will explore some of the legal and ethical issues related to the use of both seclusion and time out.

Lyon and Pimor (2004) state that seclusion should only be used in extreme cases; as such, it is an emergency procedure to be implemented only when there is significant risk. It should not be used when the threat only concerns destructive behaviour towards the environment. Although Lyon and Pimor propose that for some people, for example those with autism, seclusion may be preferable, this is not discussed at length or supported by substantial evidence. Theoretically, social exclusionary practices will be highly negatively reinforcing for people who naturally have difficulties with social interaction, thus leading to increased rates of challenging behaviour. It is therefore of concern that in one study reported by Emerson (2003), a diagnosis of autism was found to be predictive of seclusion use for adults with challenging behaviour in a multiple-regression model. In keeping with the discussion above, Lyon and Pimor also suggest that a failure to understand the distinction between seclusion and time out can lead to cases of abuse, when time out is, in practice, another word for seclusion.

People working within services may not have a basic awareness of legislation or guidance, or assume that if a 'professional' says you can do something, that will in some way make poor or abusive practice legal. An example of this was a service within the community which had detailed as a de-escalation procedure the following:

> 'If X continues to be physically aggressive towards staff and other householders he is to be removed to the downstairs corridor and isolated. If he continues to try to get back in the room staff will hold the handle of the door to prevent him from re-entering until he is calm.'

The staff undertaking this believed that, as a psychologist had put this plan in place, that meant it was legal and they must follow the plan without question, even though several members of the team felt unsure or unhappy about the procedure.

Another service for several adults within a community setting operated what was termed a 'lock-down' procedure, where all external doors were locked for the 'safety' of the people living there. Each named person also had a risk assessment to prove just how vulnerable they would be if they were to leave the building. One of the risk assessments even stated that the people who lived there were at risk of others entering the building and posing a threat to them! This is an example of how a service has used the risk assessment process as a means to an end, and to justify a potentially illegal practice that it has already decided to implement. In itself, the production of a risk assessment will not legitimise a practice, nor will having a policy in place that 'says it's ok'.

Another example of 'quasi seclusion' and euphemistic practice in community settings includes the removal of internal doors from rooms in which a person is placed alone, and staff then use common household furniture such as bean bags, sofas or chairs to block the gap in the door frame and prevent the person from leaving. The belief being that if you have not closed a door shut on a person, then it is not seclusion in practice. This sort of intervention is at best highly questionable and raises significant ethical, moral and legal questions.

As we move to more individualised, community services it seems staff often have less access to appropriate training, support and awareness of good practice. It is most often the least experienced, least trained team members who are delivering care and support to people. This is potentially dangerous within services where people are particularly vulnerable to experiencing poor mental health or engaging in challenging behaviour. It is therefore important that appropriate emphasis is placed in legislation, guidance and enforcement of basic practice standards.

As described previously, the Code of Practice, Mental Health Act (1983) defines seclusion in section 15.43. It further states that:

'Alternative terminology such as therapeutic isolation, single-person wards and enforced segregation should not be used to deprive patients of the safeguards established for the use of seclusion.'

(para 15.44)

The Code is actually rather helpful in enabling practitioners to understand that seclusion of persons not detained under 'the Act' is unlawful. It suggests that prolonged or repeated use of seclusion would be an indication to consider formal detention. It also states the importance of distinguishing between seclusion and the use of time out and other behavioural and psychological therapies.

The revised Code does not elaborate further on the use of time out, however. Previously advice had been that it should:

- Never take place in a locked room

- Be a practice wholly distinguished from seclusion

- Be one part of a range of approaches

- Not take place in a seclusion room

- Be clearly defined within policy

- Enable the 'patient' to lead a less restricted life

- Be part of a treatment plan leading towards the achievement of positive goals

(para 19.9, Mental Health Act Code of Practice, 1983)

The Guidance for Restrictive Physical Interventions (Department of Health and Department for Education and Skills, 2002) states that 'restricting a person's freedom of movement' should be considered a form of physical restraint. It goes on to clarify that personal freedom, Article 5 of the Human Rights Act (1998), is protected by both criminal and civil law and that seclusion must only ever be considered in exceptional circumstances.

The Children Act 1989 is clear that strategies which restrict a child's liberty are regarded as 'serious steps'. It clarifies that such actions include locking a child in a room or the use of 'time out.' It is somewhat surprising that the most recent guidance on the Use of Force to Control or Restrain Pupils (Department for Children Families and Schools, 2007) makes no reference to time out. The document focuses entirely on the use of physical intervention, as a last resort, as an approach to managing behaviour. There is almost no reference other than in the Children Act to the use of either time out or seclusion within guidance documents aimed at services for children and young people, including educational settings.

The Mental Capacity Act Deprivation of Liberty Safeguards (Ministry of Justice, 2008) specifically apply to persons over the age of 18 who have a mental disorder and lack capacity to consent to their care or treatment. It is likely that a large number of people to whom this legislation applies will be people with intellectual disability. Section 6(4) of the Mental Capacity Act 2005 states a person is using restraint if they:

- Use force or threaten to use force to make someone do something they are resisting

- Restrict a person's freedom of movement, whether they are resisting or not.

The use of seclusion and, in some instances, time out, will restrict a person's freedom of movement. It is important that any restriction placed on an individual is proportionate to the level of risk. Section 2.12 of the Code of Practice (2008) states that if any restriction or restraint is 'ongoing', it may be that consideration should be given to the deprivation of liberty safeguards, or a change in 'provision of care' may reduce the level of restraint.

It is clear from the guidance available that in legislative terms, seclusion is not supported as a therapeutic intervention and therefore not recognised as providing any therapeutic value as a form of treatment. There is also the clear danger that seclusion, and in some instances time out, could in fact constitute a deprivation of liberty.

It is therefore apparent that there is a distinct lack of guidance and clarity within services for children and young people on the use of either seclusion or time out. Given the use of time out, chill out rooms and quiet rooms within services for children and young people, and research suggesting that up to two-thirds of children with intellectual disability may be exposed to seclusion as a management strategy, this should raise a serious degree of concern at the most senior level.

When working with adults or children, it is important to be mindful of a duty of care and obligation of accountability for our own practice, as well as to act within the principles enshrined in law. Ethically it is important to consider if the approaches implemented are supportive and helpful to the child, young person or adult in the longer term – or, conversely, might the experience itself be so traumatic that it provides no immediate or longer-term therapeutic benefits? Many people with intellectual disability suffer from isolation, lack of self-worth and exclusion from society; it is possible that the use of time out and seclusion further serve to isolate the person from their immediate environment. Indeed, the practice has been described as a form of 'social control' over people already excluded from society (Morrall and Muir-Cochrane, 2002).

Effectiveness and risk

Debate will continue as to the effectiveness of seclusion. The available literature suggests that it is largely viewed as a management strategy which has limited benefits to the individuals exposed to it. Nelstrop et al (2006) undertook a review of available literature and concluded that there was insufficient evidence to support seclusion (or restraint) being safe or effective in the short-term management of people in psychiatric settings. Other studies question the practice on the basis of inconsistent practice and application (Busch et al, 2000; Gregory et al, 2005; Mason, 1994).

Restrictive physical intervention carries increased risk; the use of seclusion or 'time out' may both increase the risk to an individual. It is possible, for example, that people exposed to such strategies are at increased risk of both physical and psychological trauma (Haimowitz et al, 2006).

Research suggests that staff and service users' experiences and views of the use of seclusion generally differ. Literature suggests that staff using seclusion, or strategies which can be described as seclusion, view it as therapeutic to some extent (Powell et al, 2008). However, service users in mental health settings viewed seclusion as a form of punishment and psychological control (Martinez et al, 1999). Meehan et al (2000) found five emergent themes when exploring the impact of seclusion:

1. Inappropriate use

2. Emotional impact

3. Experience of sensory deprivation

4. Development of personal coping strategies, for example talking to one's self

5. Poor interaction and communication with staff

It is clear from this that the use of strategies that isolate an individual can have a negative impact on the relationships they form with those who are supporting them.

Conclusions

Seclusion and time out are often implemented by staff with the 'best of intentions'. It is perhaps the case that, for a small number of people, the isolation that seclusion provides can help them to calm quicker than alternate reactive strategies. Even then, as Masters (2008) has proposed, the space used to achieve these outcomes need not be a sterile, inhospitable and frightening environment that appears designed to maximise any punitive element of the seclusion process. Instead, such spaces could be appropriately decorated and stocked with equipment likely to promote calm (such as music players).

Even with these qualifications, any exclusionary approach should be treated with caution, implemented on an individual basis and form part of a wider behavioural support plan in collaboration with the person. The overall goal of such a plan would be to enable the person to develop alternative coping strategies and to reduce the reliance on seclusion as a personal management strategy.

It has to be concluded that, as with other forms of reactive strategy, the evidence base for the use of either seclusion or time out within services for people who have an intellectual disability is poor. Much of the published literature relates to mental health settings, and there is a lack of specific policy and practice guidance at any level. Children, young people and adults who have intellectual disabilities are extremely vulnerable, as evidenced in the reports of Sutton and Merton and Cornwall. In both cases, the use of restraint and the restriction of peoples liberty were highlighted as issues. It is, therefore, paramount that practice is based on good evidence and on positive outcomes for the person exposed to behavioural interventions and management strategies.

It is also the case that practice can quickly 'morph' in services; individual behaviour plans or strategies developed appropriately and risk assessed for the use with one named individual may spread and become accepted as appropriate practice within a service as a whole. In this sense, seclusion and time out are as 'fragile' as some of the physical interventions described by Leadbetter in Chapter 12. In other words, small changes in practice can change the intended purpose of the intervention, how it is delivered and its impact on the individual. Simply rebranding unacceptable interventions in an attempt to justify their use is clearly poor practice, and the use of such euphemistic terms as 'chill out', 'quiet time' or 'personal reflection time' are potential indicators of such. Drift of this type flourishes under conditions where strong service vision and leadership, clear standards, and effective monitoring of care are absent. The fact that we keep having scandals and enquiries in which restrictive interventions feature heavily is indicative that we have some way to go in terms of ensuring that these basic organisational safeguards are in place for all children and adults with intellectual disabilities who challenge services.

References

Allen, D (2002) Behaviour Change and Behaviour Management. In D Allen (Ed) *Ethical Approaches to Physical Interventions. Responding to challenging behaviour in people with intellectual disabilities*. Kidderminster: BILD Publications.

APRAIS: What are Aversive Procedures. Available from http://aprais.tash.org/faq.htm (accessed 20 April 2009).

Busch, A B and Shore, M F (2001) Seclusion and Restraint: A Review of Recent Literature. *Harvard Review of Psychiatry*, 8, 261–269.

Cooper, J O, Heron, T E and Heward, W L (2007) *Applied Behaviour Analysis* (Second Edition). Ohio: Pearson Educational International.

Department for Children, Schools and Families (2007) *The Use of force to Control or Restrain Pupils*. London: HMSO.

Department of Health (2008) *Mental Health Act 1983. Revised Code of Practice*. London: TSO.

Department of Health and Department for Education and Skills (2002) *Guidance for Restrictive Physical Interventions*. London: HMSO.

Department of Health and Welsh Office (1999). *Mental Health Act (1983) Code of Practice*. London: The Stationery Office.

Emerson, E, Green, K, Crossley, R and Rand, R l (2001) *A survey of the needs and support received by people with learning disabilities and challenging behaviour.* Lancaster: Institute for Health Research Lancaster University.

Emerson, E (2002) The prevalence of use of reactive management strategies in community-based services in the UK. In D Allen (Ed) *Ethical Approaches to Physical Interventions. Responding to challenging behaviour in people with intellectual disabilities.* Kidderminster: BILD Publications.

Fabiano, G A, Pelham, W E, Manos, M J, Gnagy, E M, Chronis, A M, Onyango, A N, Lopez-Williams, A, Burrows-McClean, L, Coles, E K, Meichenbaum, D A, Caserta, D A and Swain, S (2004) An evaluation of three time-out procedures for children with attention-deficit/hyperactivity disorder. *Behaviour Therapy*, 35, 3, 449–469.

Gregory, M, Smith, M S, Davis, R H, Bixler, E O, Lin, H M, Altenor, A, Altenor, R J, Hardenstine, B D and Kopchick, M S (2005) Special Section on Seclusion and Restraint: Pennsylvania State Hospital System's Seclusion and Restraint Reduction Program. *Psychiatric Services*, 56, 1115–1122.

Haimowitz, S, Urff, J and Huckshorn, K (2006) *Restraint and Seclusion – A Risk Management Guide.* Available from: www.nasmhpd.org/general_files/publications/ntac_pubs/R-S%20RISK%20MGMT%2010–10–06.pdf (accessed 20 April 2009).

Healthcare Commission and Commission for Social Care Inspection (2006) *Joint Investigation into the Provision of Services for People with Learning Disabilities and Cornwall Partnership NHS Trust.* London: Commission for Healthcare Audit and Inspection.

Healthcare Commission (2007) *National Audit of Violence 2006–7. Module 1: Ward Survey.* London: Commission for Healthcare Audit and Inspection.

Healthcare Commission (2007) *A Life Like No Other.* London: Commission for Healthcare Audit and Inspection.

Healthcare Commission (2007) *Investigation into the service for people with learning disabilities provided by Sutton and Merton Primary Care Trust.* London: Commission for Healthcare Audit and Inspection.

Lyon, CM and Pimor, A (2004) *Physical Interventions and the Law; legal issues arising from the use of physical interventions in supporting children, young people and adults with learning disabilities and severe challenging behaviour.* Kidderminster. BILD Publications.

Mace, F C and Heller, M (1990) A Comparison of Exclusion Time-Out and Contingent Observation for Reducing Severe Disruptive Behaviour in a 7-Year-Old Boy. *Child and Family Behaviour Therapy*, 12, 1, 57–68.

Marlow, A G, Tingstrom, D H, Olmi, D J and Edwards, R P (1997) The Effects of Classroom-Based Time-In/Time-Out on Compliance Rates in Children with Speech/Language Disabilities. *Child and family Behaviour Therapy*, 19, 2, 1–15.

Martinez, R J, Grimm, M and Adamson, M (1999) From the other side of the door: Patient views of seclusion. *Journal of Psychosocial Nursing and Mental Health Service*, 37, 13–22.

Mason, T (1994) Seclusion: An International Comparison. *Medicine, Science, and the Law*, 34,10, 54–60.

Mason, T (1996) Seclusion and Learning Disabilities: research and deduction. *British Journal of Developmental Disabilities*, 83, 2, 149–159.

Masters, K (2008) Modernizing seclusion and restraint. In M Nunno, D Day and L Bullard (Eds) *For our own safety. Examining the Safety of High-Risk Interventions for Children and Young People.* Arlington, VA: Child Welfare League of America.

McDonnell A (2009) *Reducing Restrictive Practices. Tip of the Iceberg- Developing Person Centred Specialist Services*. South Birmingham NHS Trust, 13 February 2009.

Meehan, T, Vermeer, C and Windsor, C (2000) Patients' Perceptions of Seclusion: A Qualitative Investigation. *Journal of Advanced Nursing*, 31, 2, 370–7.

Melissa Cabral (online) 2008, *Time Out Rooms*. Wink News 18 January. Available from www.winknews.com/features/education/9055756.html (accessed 20 April 2009).

Mental Health Act Commission (2005) *In Place of Fear; Eleventh Biennial Report 2003–2005*. London: TSO.

Ministry of Justice (2008). *Mental Capacity Act 2005: Deprivation of Liberty Safeguards*. London: TSO.

Minnesota Statutes (online) 2007. *Aversive and Deprivation procedures*. Available from www.revisor.leg.state.mn.us/bin/getpub.php?type=s and num=121A.67 and year=2007 (accessed 20 April 2009).

Morrall, P and Muir-Cochrane, E (online) 2002 Naked Social Control: Seclusion and Psychiatric Nursing in Post-Liberal Society. *Australian e-Journal for the Advancement of Mental Health*, 1 (2). Available from http://auseinet.com/journal/vol1iss2/morrall.pdf (accessed 20 April 2009)

Nelstrop, L et al (online) 2006 A Systematic Review of the Safety and Effectiveness of Restraint and Seclusion as Interventions for the Short-Term Management of Violence in Adult Psychiatric Inpatient Settings and Emergency Departments. *World Views on Evidence Based Nursing*, 3 (1), 8–18. Available from www3.interscience.wiley.com/journal/118634539/abstract?CRETRY= 1&SRETRY=0 (accessed 12 May 2009).

Paley, S *Round table debate: Seclusion and Time Out*. BILD Physical interventions Conference, 8–9 May 2008.

Paley, S *Defining Restrictive Practices: Mental Capacity Act and Use of Restrictive Practices*. Kidderminster: BILD Publications.

Powell, H, Alexander, A and Karatzias, T (2008) The Use of Seclusion in Learning Disability Services. *Learning Disability Practice*, 11, 5, 12–17.

Rangecroft, M E, Tyrer, S P and Berney, T P (1997) The use of seclusion and emergency medication in a hospital for people with learning disability. *The British Journal of Psychiatry*, 170, 273–277.

Sequeira, H and Halstead, S (2001) 'Is it meant to hurt is it?' Management of violence in women with developmental disabilities. *Violence against Women*, 7, 4, 462–476.

Stern, S (2002) Time Out Rooms Under Scrutiny. *The Christian Science Monitor*; 3 December. Available from www.csmonitor.com/2002/1203/p15s01-lecl.html (accessed 20 April 2009).

The Children Act 1989 (online). Available at www.opsi.gov.uk/Acts/acts1989/Ukpga_19890041_ en_1.htm (accessed 20 April 2009).

Willis, T J and LaVigna, G W (1999) *Emergency Management and Reactive Strategies within a Non-aversive Framework. Facilitators Manual*. Los Angeles: Institute for Applied Behaviour Analysis.

Yell, M L (1994) Timeout and students with behaviour disorders: A Legal Analysis. *Education and Treatment of Children*, 17, 293–301.

Chapter 8

Restraint-related Deaths: Lessons for Policy and Practice from Tragedy?

Brodie Paterson and Patrick Bradley

Introduction

Many aspects of the care of people with intellectual disabilities are the subject of controversy. Debates continue to rage regarding competing philosophies and differing interpretations of their implications for practice. This, though, is not a new phenomenon, as any competent student of social policy and disability will attest. Many of the current controversies find echoes and even parallels in much earlier debates. Restraint, the background of this chapter, exemplifies this trend, with discussions regarding whether restraint has a role to play in services for individuals experiencing mental disorder evident in the literature of the 18th and 19th century.

We might expect that contributions in the 21st century to this debate would, however, differ qualitatively from such earlier discussions in stressing the role of evidence as the basis for practice (Sailas and Fenton, 1999). Unfortunately, the practice of physical interventions in services for people with an intellectual disability have for many years represented a dirty little secret in our bright new world of evidence-based practice, in that their use is based almost solely on the opinion of 'experts'. Experts in this context are defined not by the possession of higher order knowledge, however, but by experience and, sometimes, their 'market share' of the training industry. Hence, there has been little research of acceptable quality into many aspects of the use of physical interventions, including those scenarios in which individuals have died while being restrained. While individual deaths have prompted inquiries that represent a form of case study, such inquiries sometimes appear to have focused on one aspect of a particular death (such as alleged racism in the case of the death of David Bennet), rather then examining in depth the wider implications of such deaths for policy and practice (Paterson and Leadbetter, 2006).

This lack of research into restraint-related deaths prompted an earlier survey (Paterson et al, 2003), which has been updated for the purpose of this chapter and complemented by a revised and updated discussion that focuses on the role played by physical restraint. This updated survey omitted the stages of contacting regulatory bodies and reviewing the professional literature for case studies, as those elements had proved largely unsuccessful in the original study. Instead, it extended the newspaper database search using Lexis-Nexis Executive News covering a further seven years between March 2001 and March 2008.

Two separate searches were conducted using the following criteria:

Table 1: Search terms and results.

Search	Terms	Articles identified and reviewed
1	Restraint and death and mental health articles restricted to UK broadsheets only.	210
2	Restraint and death and mental and health and disability restricted to UK newspapers between March 2001 and May 2008.	370

The inclusion criteria for cases were that:

- the individual had to have been restrained – restraint was operationally defined 'as being held against active resistance by physical or mechanical means'

- the individual had to have been described as having lost consciousness during restraint in a health or social care setting, or whilst under the care of health service staff (ie paramedic or ambulance staff)

- the individual had to have subsequently died without recovering consciousness

Deaths reported in police custody, prisons or children's services were excluded. Once a case report was identified, further details were sought in the form of an internal inquiry or other report. From these various exercises and from cases otherwise known to the authors, including involvement as an expert witness, a total of 22 cases have been identified. The process resulted, however, in a situation in which considerable detail was available on some deaths, whilst for others the details were scant and gathered only from newspaper accounts, as an internal inquiry or coroners report was not available to the authors. *Table 2* summarises the available data.

Case analysis

There is widespread anxiety about the potential for danger in 'prone restraint', and this is reflected in emerging guidance, which advises that it should be avoided (Department of Health, 2002; Scottish Institute of Residential Childcare, 2006) or proscribed (Welsh Assembly Government, 2006). In a number of the cases identified in this updated survey, prone was however not used or it appears not causal. In two of the earliest cases in this series, Bryan Marsh and Michael Martin, there is evidence that neck holds used widely in the

(Text continues on page 131)

Table 2: Restraint related deaths in health and social care in the UK.

Name	Age	Date	Location	Diagnosis	Circumstances if known
Michael Martin		1979	Broadmoor Hospital		Although he was initially restrained by a neck hold he was ultimately held face downwards and sedated. He was then left for 50 minutes, being periodically observed, before it was noted that he had not moved during this period. This case is of particular note because the subsequent inquiry called for the special hospitals to adopt 'non-violent' restraint methods and ultimately led to the adoption of control and restraint training from the prison service (Ritchie, 1985).
Orville Blackwood	31	1991	Broadmoor Hospital	Schizophrenia	He was restrained in a prone face down position by between five and seven staff while forcibly medicated. The cause of death was not, however, given as restraint, it was given as cardiac failure associated with the administration of phenothiazine drugs (Prins, 1994).
Bryan March		1992	Broadmoor Hospital		A second post-mortem suggested that he had been restrained about the neck at the time of a heart attack that caused his death.
Shaun Martin		1994	Stratheden Hospital		Restrained while lying on a bed in what was effectively a side-lying position (see Morrison and Sadler 2001 for a very detailed description of this case).
David Falconer		1994	Edith Morgan Clinic		Died of a heart attack and traumatic asphyxia. He was reported as losing consciousness the day after he had been restrained in a face down prone position for 45 minutes with his arms and legs pinned behind his back. He failed to recover consciousness and was pronounced dead the next day.
Freda Latham		1995	Stallington Hospital	Severe learning disability	Died after being 'mechanically' restrained by being tied to a toilet seat with her 'bib'. She was initially, therefore, in a seated position but appears to have slipped off the toilet seat and was then strangled by her bib, which acted as a ligature.

Name	Age	Date	Location	Diagnosis	Circumstances if known
Zoe Fairley	21	1995	Care hostel, North Yorkshire Council	Learning disability	Restrained in a prone face-down position by first two and then four staff. The post-mortem concluded that her death was caused by asphyxia due to fixation of the chest during prone restraint.
Roger Sylvester	30		St Anne's Hospital	Schizophrenia	Roger Sylvester, a 30 year old black man died in St Anne's hospital, where he had been admitted as a place of safety after being restrained by eight police officers. The coroner later recorded a verdict of unlawful killing subsequently overturned on appeal.
Michael Craig		1997	Glasgow	Learning disability	His death was not directly attributed to restraint but he suffered a myocardial infarction while restrained in a kneeling position by two staff with his knees on the floor and his torso lying face down across a bed.
John Patterson	39	1997	Poole	Learning disability	Restrained face down on a lawn by three care staff. His wrists were held behind his back by one member of staff while another secured his left arm and a third secured his legs.
David Bennett	38	1998	Norvik Clinic in Norwich	Schizophrenia	He was restrained by at least three staff after attacking a female member of staff and his heart stopped during the restraint.
Michael Goldwater	35	2000	Runwell Hospital	Schizophrenia	Died after having a heart attack whilst being restrained face down on the floor by staff.
Billy Thurgood	42	2000	St Luke's Hospital, Prudhoe	ASD and Learning disability	Died from hyperthermia following restraint, which involved him being wrapped in a duvet and then having another duvet placed on top. Death attributed to misadventure and lack of care.
Janice Jackson	50	2000	Brookland's Hospital	Learning disability	Lost consciousness during restraint by three staff.
Kurt Holland	32	2002	Cefn Coed Swansea	Schizophrenia	Lost consciousness whilst being restrained face down.
Daniel Sutcliffe	33	2002	St Luke's Hospital Huddersfield	Schizophrenia	Lost consciousness whilst being restrained face down.
Michael Lovell	38	2003	Lozells Birmingham	Schizophrenia	Details not known.

Name	Age	Date	Location	Diagnosis	Circumstances if known
Andrew Jordan	28	2003	London	Schizophrenia	Physically restrained several times, including hyper-flexion over a sofa. Reported to have lost consciousness during transport to hospital whilst strapped face down on an ambulance trolley.
Derek Lovegrove	38	2004	Castlebeck Nottingham	Autism/ severe learning disability	Lost consciousness whilst being restrained 'face up' by two staff.
Geoffrey Hodgkins	37	2004	St James' Hospital	Schizophrenia	Lost consciousness and died after being restrained by nursing and security staff face down for some 25 minutes.
Gary John Williams	46	2006	Bro Cerwyn Medical Centre, Withybush	Schizophrenia	Details not known.
Anthony Pinder	42	2004	Craegmore Healthcare, North Lincolnshire	Learning disability	Died subsequent to a period of prone restraint lasting approximately 1 hour 40 minutes and implemented following an episode of self-injury. During the restraint episode he was sat on by staff members, one of whom weighed 22 stone. Narrative verdict: 'died after a long period of agitation and restraint'.

martial arts were applied. Pressure exerted on the carotid arteries can rapidly induce unconsciousness but carries a significant risk that death, rather than unconsciousness, will result (Reay and Eisle, 1982).

The death of Freda Latham has been categorised for the purposes of this survey as mechanical restraint. A series of deaths in the USA involving the use of mechanical restraint have been reported by Miles and Irvine (1992). In the cases described, generally involving elderly people experiencing confusion, garments specifically designed for restraint purposes are often involved, and when the patient attempts to move out of restraint they become entangled – with lethal consequences (Frank et al, 1996). Such cases may not be uncommon, with Morrison (1997) recording that in the USA from 1987–96, the manufacturers of protective restraints reported 131 deaths to the Federal Drug Administration Agency. In some cases, there were similarities with the case of Freda Latham, whereby an element of the individual's own clothing, rather than a form of specialised restraint 'vest' or other garment, effectively became a ligature as they slipped out of a bed or wheelchair. The death of Billy Thurgood, who died from hyperthermia following a restraint which involved him being wrapped in a duvet and then having another duvet placed on top, was attributed to misadventure and lack of care. Given that a device, albeit in this case a duvet, was used to restrain him, it has also been classed as a mechanical death.

Two of the situations described in the previous series represented scenarios which had not previously been reported in association with restraint-related death: these relate to the deaths of Michael Craig, while restrained in a kneeling position by two members of staff with his knees on the floor and his torso lying face down across a bed, and Shaun Martin, who died whilst being restrained while lying on his side on a bed. Such deaths remain atypical, although the recent death of Gareth Myatt (which inclusion criteria prevent from being considered as part of this series as the 15 year old died in 2004 in a secure training centre ran by the Youth Justice Board in England) is worthy of note in appearing to have some similarities to that of Michael Craig. Gareth lost consciousness whilst restrained in an authorised procedure described as a 'seated double embrace', in which a member of staff sat at either side of him on chairs. However, it appears that he was then bent forward (in an unauthorised variation of the procedure), thereby bringing his head down below his waist. Sadly, the potential for impaired respiration linked to hyper-flexion during restraint was described by Paterson and Leadbetter (1998) some years earlier, who forecast that fatalities in such positions were wholly foreseeable.

However, this updated study confirms that prone restraint remains the procedure most commonly associated with adverse outcomes, with some 11 of the 22 deaths noted in this series involving prone restraint at some point in the incident. 'Prone' is, though, not one position but rather a range of procedures whose risks may vary wildly. These multiple versions of prone actually share only one variable, which is that the individual is held against resistance face down, either by being physically held via control of the limbs (the approach most commonly used in the UK), or mechanically fixated (the procedure seemingly more common in the USA), and sometimes by a combination of both. Miller (2005), a USA expert on restraint-related fatalities, argues that it is critical for restraint safety that prone restraint, *per se*, be distinguished from 'forceful prone' restraint. In 'forceful prone', pressure is applied to the back, abdomen or hips rather than, or in addition to, the holding of the limbs. Prone restraint per se, where pressure is not placed on the back, abdomen or hips, allowing thereby residual movement of the diaphragm, appears capable of use as the end point of a hierarchy of physical interventions, with minimal risks to the majority of service users (Graham, 2005). It may however, involve undue risk for those who are obese, or where other risk factors are present, and it may, where restraint is prolonged, compound the intrinsic risks associated with restraint. Hence its use should be confined to high-risk scenarios and restricted to use only by staff trained at a minimum in accordance with the National Health Service Security Management Service Promoting Safe and Therapeutic Services guidance on managing restraint risks (Miller et al, 2007).

'Forceful prone', however, is a procedure of extremely high risk for all service users, and whose use in the context of a prolonged struggle must be understood by staff to risk lethal consequences. To assert that prone, by comparison, is therefore safe, is, though, profoundly misleading. Prone restraint is a 'fragile' procedure, in that during a contested struggle for control, frightened, angry staff, whether trained or otherwise, can find themselves unwittingly drawn into the use of 'forceful' prone, as several case examples in the UK (including the death of David Bennett) illustrate. This observation might seem to create an inarguable case for a ban on the use of prone restraint, lest in practice it mutates into something much more dangerous.

However, as Mencken (1949, p 443) observed, 'There is always an easy solution to every human problem – neat, plausible, and wrong'. Unfortunately, all of the potential alternatives to prone restraint proposed have themselves been associated with fatalities and share similar potential flaws, in that unauthorised modification is potentially likely, easily achieved and can significantly increase the risks involved. The potential dangers in seated restraint related to hyperflexion have already been discussed in relation to the death of Gareth Myatt. However, there are also potential risks associated with supine restraint, sometimes advocated as a safe alternative to prone. In supine restraint (where the service user is held face up), deaths have been reported in association with aspiration. A series of deaths in the USA led to supine restraint being banned in some Californian services (Morrison et al, 2001). The death of Derek Lovegrove, reported here, illustrates the potential for weight exerted on the abdomen on a service user in supine to contribute to the risk of fatality increasing during restraint. Kneeling positions, which can obstruct movement of the diaphragm, have been associated with at least two restraint deaths in the UK (those of Michael Craig and Andrew Robinson).

Even the 'recovery position', theoretically the best position to minimise the physiological impact of being held and the potential consequences of aspiration, has been associated with a restraint-related death in Scotland. When staff were unable to secure the individual in the recovery position in this case, they eventually resorted to lying on top of them (Morrison and Saddler, 2001). Case reports in the American literature have also linked basket holds, a procedure in which the individual is restrained by a member of staff standing or sitting behind him or her, who then crosses the service user's own arms in front of him/her and secures them at the wrist or forearm, to instances of restraint related deaths (Hartford Courant, 1999). An unauthorised variation of this procedure, in which the basket hold is continued after the service user has fallen to the floor face down, resulting in a situation where the member of staff ends up lying on top of the person being restrained, may be particularly dangerous (Nunno et al, 2006).

The suggested role played by the means of restraint in related deaths is generally by the impact of the restraint position and/or the actions of staff in placing weight or pressure on the service user, restricting respiration. There are, however, also suggestions that prone restraint may affect cardio-vascular function more directly, and that blows to the chest, such as those resulting from a forceful takedown, can have cardiac consequences (Link et al, 2003). Clearly, if any part of the upper or lower airway becomes obstructed, respiration will be impeded or prevented. If the surface of the lung is diseased or damaged as a result of injury, including the aspiration of stomach content, failure of the gaseous exchange element may occur. However, even with an unobstructed airway and perfectly healthy lungs, if a failure occurs with the mechanical component of respiration (the ventilatory pump or bellows system), effective respiration cannot be achieved. Failure of the ventilatory pump will result in alveolar hypoventilation and a reduced uptake of oxygen manifested primarily by hypercapnia (Chan et al, 1998).

The mechanical element of respiration requires:

- appropriate central nervous system control of respiratory muscle activity

- the ability of the ribcage to be expanded and relaxed by action of the intercostal muscles and the diaphragm

- the ability of the diaphragm (the largest respiratory muscle) to contract in order to displace the abdominal viscera downwards and outwards

When the respiratory muscles are appropriately activated by the central nervous system, the ribcage expands and the diaphragm descends, creating a negative intra-thoracic pressure. The pressure gradient created 'draws' atmosphere into the lungs and produces inspiration. If breathing becomes difficult (for whatever reason), the accessory muscles' and the diaphragm's role becomes more important in creating the negative intra-thoracic pressure required for inspiration. A face-down position will always prevent contraction of the diaphragm to some extent, particularly where the subject is obese and excess adipose tissue is displaced upwards into the abdominal cavity. This may prevent the creation of the negative pressure gradient required for inspiration. The subject restrained in this position may therefore be reliant on whatever restricted abdominal, chest wall and shoulder movement they are able to obtain in order to achieve respiration at a time when their oxygen requirements may be high because of their exertions (Miller, 1998). These negative effects will, however, be compounded if, in addition, pressure is applied downwards on the patients back, waist or hips by staff to ensure the subject remains face down or to hold them more securely (O'Halloran and Frank, 2000a). If, for example, the wrists are pushed behind the back against resistance, and pressure is then exerted downwards on the back from behind, this may have the effect of severely limiting respiration (see the case of John Paterson).

Common misconceptions held by staff may increase the risk of restraint-related deaths in such scenarios. In a number of USA cases, it is reported the restrained individual said, 'I can't breathe,' but the staff members involved persisted with the restraint, believing that the service user was attempting to manipulate the restraint situation (Mohr and Mohr, 2000). As Mohr and Mohr (op cit) observe, 'In many death cases, patients had actually suffered respiratory arrest, but the staff thought that they had become compliant, holding them down for a few more minutes to make certain that they were calm'.

Farnham and Kennedy (1997) observed that a number of other pre-existing medical conditions will increase risk during restraint. Obesity has already been remarked upon, but the literature suggests that a range of other physical disorders, particularly those that may impair respiratory or cardiovascular function, may increase risk. Empirical support for these assertions is provided by Stratton et al (2001), who compared a series of 18 cases of restraint-related deaths associated with hobble tying with a series of 196 cases of hobble tying in which death did not occur. Factors noted to be associated with death included associated obesity, prolonged struggle, pre-existing ill health and drug misuse, particularly cocaine (Ross, 1998). There is no evidence from this series of deaths of proximal cocaine misuse; although it is reported that Roger Sylvester had previously abused cocaine, this was not found in a post-mortem blood screen.

Given the focus of this text, it is of note that eight of the twenty-one cases described in this series involved people with a intellectual disability. The 1990s were marked by an increasing awareness that people with a intellectual disability are likely to experience more health problems than the average person in the general population (Rodgers, 1994). Further, they may have higher levels of unmet healthcare needs, experiencing unrecognised and thus untreated health problems, including hypertension (Kerr et al, 1996). Particular problems identified, which occur with increased frequency in association with intellectual disability, include obesity, which is the most commonly reported health problem (Bond et al, 1997), and heart disease (Department of Health, 1994). The increased prevalence of hearing and/or visual impairment (Vitiello and Behar, 1979) may also affect the person's ability to communicate their distress or understand and respond to requests during restraint. This could, perhaps, increase the likelihood of a prolonged struggle, with its concomitant risks.

In addition to recreational drugs, the role of prescribed medication, particularly the neuroleptics, has been discussed in relation to sudden deaths in psychiatry (Wendkos, 1970). Kumar (1997) has reviewed the potential adverse effects identified, including cardiac arrhythmia and respiratory failure, and case reports have linked neuroleptic therapy, particularly the phenothiazines, with deaths involving violent struggle (Laposata et al, 1988). Administration of neuroleptics may also increase the risk of death during restraint by impairing the client's ability to swallow or expectorate effectively, leading to an increased risk of the inhalation of vomit (Wendkos, 1970). Neuroleptics drugs are used frequently in the care of people with a intellectual disability (see Chapter 6).

It must, however, be acknowledged, as in the previous study, that a number of deaths may not have been identified, and that this review, while identifying a number of further cases, is limited in the analysis it could undertake because of the varying details available. An in-depth and multi-disciplinary review across cases is needed and might yield more information regarding the factors involved in such deaths, including the role of psychotropics.

Implications for practice and policy

It is tempting to speculate with the wisdom of hindsight that alternative interventions, such as seclusion or mechanical restraint, might have avoided some of the deaths reported. Getting a violent individual into seclusion against his/her will, however, almost invariably involve some form of physical intervention – and mechanical restraint, as observed, is clearly not without its own risks and remains highly controversial in the UK. Ensuring that such interventions are used only in the tiny proportion of situations that may warrant them has, though, posed enormous problems in practice, leading many organisations to ban their use. Where, however, intervention cannot be avoided and the level of risk is extremely high, an exploration of the use of seclusion may be appropriate. Extreme care must, however, be used in its application, lest it be used in scenarios such as those involving individuals on the autistic spectrum, who may be socially avoidant. It takes little thought to recognise the potentially reinforcing properties of seclusion in such circumstances.

It remains abundantly clear that the principal means of improving both service user and staff safety (because staff are most likely to be seriously injured when attempting to implement restraint) (Stark et al, 1994) is by actively seeking to reduce the use of restraint. Such strategies seek to avoid its use by actively promoting alternative intervention and management strategies that focus on primary and secondary prevention informed by root cause analysis and individual functional analysis (Huckshorn, 2005). These, however, are not the focus of this chapter and are covered elsewhere (see chapters 9–12).

Where restraint is unavoidable, as it may be in some cases, organisations face difficult decisions. Prone restraint is clearly contraindicated in the presence of obesity and other risk factors. It should therefore be prohibited or subject to the most stringent of controls, so that its use is proportional to a threat exhibited by a service user which cannot be managed in any other way, and carried out by staff wholly trained in the assessment and management of restraint-related risk. The need for such restrictions is reinforced by the conclusions of Nunno et al (2006), who reported that, in 26 out of 45 cases of restraint-related deaths, the behaviour presented by the child recorded as precipitating the intervention was not life-threatening. However, 'life-threatening' violence presented by a child, which could not be otherwise managed, was the only scenario in the organisations concerned where restraint was authorised. The potential for high-risk interventions to be misused with fatal consequences is thus evident. Multiple inquiry reports exemplify the potential for physical interventions to be misused when cultures of care become corrupted (Wardhaugh and Wilding, 1993). However, we must also be mindful that it has long been recognised that the permission to use physical interventions, unless managed with extraordinary care, can actually be one of the fundamental causes of such corruption (Page, 1904).

Conclusions

Caution must be applied in interpreting the results of this survey. Drawing inferences from a series of infrequent events which are then subject to idiosyncratic investigation and reporting is problematic. However, the implications for services for people with an intellectual disability are significant. People with an intellectual disability comprise around two per cent of the general population, and some 17 per cent may present with challenging behaviour. They appear, therefore, over-represented in the cases presented here, something which should be a source of concern.

While a range of range of factors will increase the risk of adverse outcomes during restraint (and the role of medication in particular requires further investigation), it is now abundantly clear that certain restraint positions can lead to heightened risk. Sufficient restriction of the bellows component of respiration, such as by pressure applied to the back of an individual in prone for a sufficient time, will rapidly kill even 'the healthiest of individuals' (O'Halloran and Frank, 2000b, p 421). Consequently, any service which endorses the use of physical interventions should be actively monitoring what happens during physical interventions and striving to reduce the use of physical interventions to the absolute minimum.

A more systematic analysis of the phenomena remains warranted, however. An aggregate root cause analysis of such incidents by an authoritative body such as the National Patient Safety Agency was proposed by one of the authors in 2004. The continuing toll of deaths reported here means it is now long overdue.

References

Allen, D (2000) *Training Carers in Physical Interventions: Towards Evidence Based Practice.* Kidderminster: BILD Publications.

Baker, P and Allen, D (2001) Physical abuse and restrictive physical interventions in learning disabilities: an element of risk? *Journal of Adult Protection*, 3, 2, 25–31.

Bond, L, Kerr, M, Dunstan, F and Thapar, A (1997) Attitudes of health care practitioners towards health care for people with intellectual disability and the factors underlying these attitudes. *Journal of Intellectual Disability Research* 41, 5, 391–400.

Boyle, P (1999) Fatal hugs *Youth Today*. Available from www.ytyt.org/infobank/document/cfm/parents/529 (accessed 20 April 2009).

British Institute of Learning Disabilities (2001) *Code of Practice For Trainers in the use of Physical Interventions*. Kidderminster: BILD Publications.

Busch, A S and Shore, M F (2000) Seclusion and restraint. A review of the recent literature. *Harvard Review of Psychiatry*, 8, 1, 261–270.

Chan, T C, Vilke, G M and Neuman, T (1998) Re-examination of custody restraint position and positional asphyxia. *American Journal of Forensic Medical Pathology*, 19, 3, 201–215.

Department of Health (1994) *You Draw a Line and Put Me on One Side of It... Why Should I Suffer?* Heywood: NHS Management Executive, Health Publications Unit.

Department of Health and Department for Education and Skills (2002) *Guidance for Restrictive Physical Interventions. How to provide safe services for people with Learning Disabilities and Autistic Spectrum Disorder.* London: DoH.

Emerson, E (2003) The prevalence of use of reactive management strategies in community-based services in the UK. In D Allen (Ed) *Ethical Approaches to Physical Intervention. Responding to Challenging Behaviour in People with Intellectual Disabilities* Kidderminster: BILD Publications.

Farnham F R and Kennedy H G (1997) Acute excited states and sudden death. *British Medical Journal*, 1, 315, 7116, 1107–1108.

Frank, C, Hodgetts, G and Puxty, J (1996) Safety and efficacy of physical restraints for the elderly – review of the evidence. *Canadian Family Physician*, 42, 2402–2409.

Graham, A (2002) The use of physical interventions in managing violence in mental health settings. *Mental Health Practice* 6, 4, 10–16.

Hartford Courant (1999) *Deadly Restraint. A Hartford Courant Investigative Report*. Available at: www.courant.ctnow. com/projects/restraint/data.stm (accessed 20 April 2009).

Huckshorn, K (2005) *Six Core strategies to reduce the use of seclusion and restraint planning tool*. Alexandria Virginia: National Technical Assistance Center.

Kerr, M, Fraser, W and Felce, D (1996) Primary health care for people with a learning disability: a Keynote review. *British Journal of Learning Disabilities*, 24, 2–8.

Kumar, A (1997) Sudden unexplained death in a psychiatric patient – a case report: the role of the phenothiazines and physical restraint. *Medicine, Science and the Law*, 37, 2, 170–175.

Laposata, E A, Hale, P Jr and Polkis, A (1988) Evaluation of sudden death in psychiatric patients with special reference to phenothiazine therapy. *Forensic Pathology, Journal of Forensic Science*, 33, 432–440.

Lancaster, G A, Whittington, R, Lane, S, Riley, D and Meehan, C (2008). Does the position of restraint of disturbed psychiatric patients have any association with staff and patient injuries? *Journal of Psychiatric and Mental Health Nursing*, 15, 306–312.

Link, M S, Maron, B J, Wang, P J, VanderBrink, B A, Zhu, W and Estes, N A (2003) Upper and lower limits of vulnerability to sudden arrhythmic death with chest-wall impact. *Journal of the American College of Cardiology*, 2003, 41, 99–104.

Luiselli, J K, Kane, A, Treml, T and Young, N (2000) Behavioral intervention to reduce physical restraint of adolescents with developmental disability. *Behavioral Interventions*, 15, 317–330.

Mencken, H L (1949) The divine afflatus. In Mencken, H L, *A Mencken chrestomathy*. New York: Knopf.

Miles, S H and Irvine, P (1992) Deaths caused by physical restraints. *The Gerontologist*, 32, 6, 762–766.

Miller, C (1998). *Deaths associated with restraint use in health and social care in the UK*. Available from www.charlydmiller.com/LIB/1998chan review.html (accessed 20 April 2009).

Mohr, W K, and Mohr, B D (2000) Mechanisms of injury and death proximal to restraint use. *Archives of Psychiatric Nursing*, 14, 6, 285–295.

Morrison, A (1997) Device errors. Incorrect restraint use: deadly protection. *Nursing*, 27, 6, 32.

Morrison, A and Sadler, D (2001) Death of a psychiatric patient during physical restraint. Excited delirium – a case report. *Medicine, Science and the Law*, 41, 1, 46–50.

Nunno, M A, Holden, M J and Tollar, A T (2006) Learning from tragedy: A survey of child and adolescent restraint facilities. *Child Abuse and Neglect*, 30, 1333–1342.

O'Halloran, R L, and Lewman, L V (1993) Restraint asphyxiation in excited delirium. *American Journal of Forensic Medical Pathology*, 14, 289–295.

O'Halloran, R L and Frank, J G (2000a) Asphyxial death during prone restraint revisited: a report. *American Journal of Forensic Medical Pathology*, 21, 4, 420–422.

O'Halloran, R L and Frank, J G (2000b) Authors' Reply to Letter Re: Asphyxial death during prone restraint revisited. *American Journal of Forensic Medical Pathology*, 21, 4, 420–422.

Page, C W (1904) Mechanical Restraint and Seclusion of Insane Persons, *Boston Medical and Surgical Journal*, 590–595.

Paterson, B and Leadbetter, D (1998) Restraint and sudden death from asphyxia. *Nursing Times*, 94, 44, 62–64.

Paterson, B, McComish, S and Bradley, P (1998) The physical management of violent behaviour. *Psychiatric Care*, 5, 6, 228–231.

Paterson, B, Turnbull, J and Aitken, I (1992) An evaluation of a training course in the short term management of aggression. *Nurse Education Today*, 12, 368–375.

Paterson, B, Bradley, P, Stark, C, Saddler, D, Leadbetter, D and Allen, D (2003) Deaths Associated with Restraint Use in Health and Social Care In the United Kingdom: The Results of A Preliminary Survey. *Journal of Psychiatric and Mental Health Nursing*, 10, 3–15.

Paterson, B and Leadbetter, D (2004) Learning the right lessons: Reflecting on the David Bennett inquiry recommendations with particular reference to violence management training. *Mental Health Practice*, 7, 7, 12–14.

Paterson, B and Miller, G (2006) *Promoting Safe and Therapeutic Services, National Health Service Security Management Service. Trainers Handbook*, London: Security Management Services.

Powell, H (2008) The use of seclusion in learning disability services. *Learning Disability Practice*, 11, 5, 12–17.

Reay, D T (1995) *Positional Asphyxia and Sudden Death*. Washington: National Law Enforcement Technology Centre.

Reay, D T and Eisle, J W (1982) Death from law enforcement neck holds. *American Journal of Forensic Medical Pathology*, 3, 253–258.

Rodgers, J (1994) Primary health care provision for people with learning difficulties. *Health and Social Care in the Community*, 2, 11–17.

Ross, D L (1998) Factors associated with excited delirium deaths in police custody. *Modern Pathology*, 11, 11, 1127–1137.

Sailas, E, and Fenton, M (1999) *Seclusion and restraint as a method of treatment for people with serious mental illnesses* (Cochrane Review). In: The Cochrane Library, Issue 3. Cochrane Library Number: CD001163. Oxford: Update Software.

Stark, C and Paterson, B (1994) Violence at Work. *British Medical Journal*, 308, 62–63.

Stratton, S J, Rogers, C and Brickett, K (2001) Factors associated with sudden death in individuals requiring restraint for excited delirium. *American Journal of Emergency Medicine*, 19, 3, 187–191.

Vitiello, B and Behar, D (1979) Mental retardation and psychiatric illness. *Hospital and Community Psychiatry*, 43, 5, 484–499.

Wardhaugh, J and Wilding, P (1993) Towards an explanation of the corruption of care. *Critical Social Care*, 37, 13, 4–31.

Wendkos, M H (1979) *Sudden Death and Psychiatric Illness*. New York: SP Medical and Scientific.

Whyman, A (1976) Phenothiazine death: an unusual case report. *Journal of Nervous and Mental Diseases*, 163, 3, 214–217.

York City Council (1997) *Report of the review following the death of Zoe Fairley*. York: City Council, Social Services Department.

SECTION 3:
The Paradigm Shift

Chapter 9

Prevention is Better than Reaction – Getting Our Priorities Right

David Allen

Introduction

It is a fallacy to believe that we will significantly impact on aggressive service user behaviour by focusing our efforts on refining our approaches to physical interventions. This in itself may be viewed as a heretical statement in a book devoted to detailed consideration of such interventions, but it is nevertheless true. In the first volume of *Ethical Approaches*, a distinction was made between strategies designed to help achieve behavioural change and strategies designed to help achieve behavioural management (Allen, 2003a). Physical interventions clearly fall into the latter category and they, along with other reactive strategies, such as distraction strategies and proxemics (the use and modification of personal space zones), have a very limited role to play in improving our approaches to seriously challenging behaviour. As previously described (Allen 2003a), while behaviour management strategies are a critical component of effective support plans for people who challenge, they have restricted objectives and, consequently, limited effects:

- Their only goal is to achieve safe, rapid and ethical control over serious risk behaviours

- They only provide temporary control over difficult behaviour

- They are not constructive as they are not concerned with helping services and users change challenging behaviour in the longer term

The last of these limitations is the most serious. It has been previously suggested that physical interventions can be likened to fire fighting (Allen, 2003a); they are strategies that need to be brought into play once a 'fire' has broken out. They offer little in the sense of 'fire' prevention, and they do not indicate what needs to be done to avoid having a fire in the first instance.

The focus on physical interventions in the UK over the last 15 years has been both necessary and invaluable, in that it has allowed a previously taboo subject to be examined in (sometimes literally) forensic detail, with significant improvements in how we approach the difficult but necessary topic of physical responses to out-of-control behaviour occurring as a result. However, an unfortunate side-effect of this focus is that it has reinforced a prevailing dynamic that exists in many care services for people with intellectual disability, where the normal modus operandi is to react to problems when they occur and to do little to think about how problems could be prevented from occurring in the first instance. This is a nonsensical and ultimately self-defeating strategy. Returning to the fire analogy, we do not deal with the risk of fire simply by fighting fires whenever they erupt; if we did, the number of fires, injuries and deaths experienced would increase dramatically. In the main, we try to deal with the risk by education, by ensuring that we do not stock our homes and offices with highly combustible material or dangerous electrical hardware, by not leaving naked flames unattended, by not allowing children to play with matches, and so on. In other words, we adopt a preventative approach. In human services, the reverse is frequently true. We often provide environments and systems of care that are likely to precipitate challenging behaviour; we rarely train staff in key preventative skills; and once a challenging incident has occurred, we typically breathe a collective sigh of relief while we wait for the next one to come along.

This naturally occurring service dynamic is reinforced further by an increasingly litigious culture's overemphasis on risk management and by health and safety legislation which has been the primary driver for the development of the physical intervention industry in the UK (Allen, 2003b). Paradoxically, whereas this heavily funded and frequently championed industry is built upon a scandalously thin evidence base (Allen, 2001; McDonnell, this volume; Richter, Needham and Kunz, 2006), preventative approaches, which do have a relatively strong research foundation, have no accompanying legislative drivers to support their implementation, are poorly resourced and, consequently, are all too infrequently applied.

In short, we frequently practise approaches for which we have no evidence, and rarely practise those for which we do. People with intellectual disabilities and challenging behaviour have a history of being excluded and, in an age in which evidence-based practice is meant to be the norm for all, they are effectively being excluded again.

Systemic approaches to prevention

This chapter will explore how organisations supporting people who challenge can adopt a preventative ethos. An important first principle is to recognise that the prevention of seriously challenging behaviours cannot be achieved by improving what goes on directly at the staff member/service user interface, because what happens at this interface is in itself influenced by a wide variety of variables. These may be divided into three broad types:

- Socio-cultural
- Macro-organisational
- Micro-organisational

At the socio-cultural level, how society views a particular issue will have a great bearing on how that issue is dealt with at an operational level. In today's society, expressions like 'zero tolerance' have become a familiar mantra in relation to the management of aggression. Such expressions have emerged primarily from debates on violence management in settings such as casualty units within general hospitals, and where the behaviour of aggressive individuals is traditionally viewed as being attributable to internal, controllable causes[1] that the person displaying the behaviour can do something about if they so wish (eg aggression resulting from binge drinking). It is less clear how useful the application of 'buzz' expressions of this nature is in services such as those for persons with learning disabilities, where aggression may more accurately attributed to external, uncontrollable causes (eg aggression resulting from service user's frustration with receiving insufficient staff help to complete a difficult task).

The relationship between organisational and wider societal views is, of course, bi-directional, and how a service supports its users will in turn impact on how society views the individuals concerned. Thus, while high-profile investigations and accompanying media reports into homicides conducted by people with mental health difficulties may help create or reinforce an association between mental ill-health and violence, supporting users with mental health difficulties appropriately in community settings can help promote a positive image and illustrate how the majority do not present such high-risk behaviours.

At the macro-service level, how an organisation sets out its strategic vision, direction and intent will play a clear role in determining how violence and aggression will be addressed. If the organisation chooses to sweep these issues under the carpet, so too will its employees, with the risk of both user and staff abuse being heightened as a result. If the organisation invests heavily in reactive approaches to aggression, then reactive responses to aggression will be reinforced as the predominant approach. A more healthy organisation might be one that is defined by its taking a preventative approach to aggression. This would include it signing up to an overarching therapeutic model and ensuring that all its staff were trained in this approach, developing clear policies that reflected the chosen model and adopting quality assurance systems that ensured that these approaches were implemented in practice.

At the micro-service level, the task of management is to ensure the delivery of this over-arching service vision for individual service users. This will involve ensuring that:

- the service is user (rather than staff) led

- effective supervision systems based on direct observation of staff performance in the work place are developed

- delivery of constructive feedback on performance is routinely given

- the provision of opportunities to further refine skills are readily available

[1] See Wiener, 1985, for an explanation of attribution theory.

- the collation and utilisation of performance management data is given high priority
- there is effective micro-planning of service delivery (eg who is supporting which user to engage in which activity throughout the day)

The glue that binds a healthy organisation together is the clear vision of what the service needs to deliver therapeutically to ensure the highest quality of life for its users and the optimum level of practice by its staff. The danger of any systemic analysis is that it is typically strong on describing over-arching principles and structures, but it is somewhat weaker in articulating the specifics of actual practice. By means of illustration, while it would be hard to find a service for people with intellectual disabilities within the UK that did not claim to have some version of social role valorisation theory as its guiding philosophy, there would be a far smaller number who could describe and demonstrate in practice what they needed to do in supporting their users on a day-to-day basis to achieve community presence and participation, make meaningful choices and develop competence and respect.

Positive behavioural support

The therapeutic approach to challenging behaviour that has the strongest supporting evidence base at the present time is applied behaviour analysis. Just as many reactive approaches for responding to aggressive behaviour rejected the use of aversive pain-compliance procedures in the 1990s, many supporters of behavioural intervention rejected the use of punishment-based behaviour change strategies from the mid-1980s onwards. Although these were initially entirely independent evolutionary streams, they were entirely complementary and eventually coalesced into an approach that has become known as positive behavioural support (PBS). One of the key reasons for this coming together is that PBS includes both proactive strategies for changing behaviour and reactive strategies for managing behaviour when it occurs. It was therefore vital to have congruity across both elements, as there would be little point in having intervention packages containing non-aversive behaviour change strategies that were ethically sound and behaviour managements strategies that were not.

The essential characteristics of PBS are that it:

- is values led (in that the goal of behavioural strategies is to achieve enhanced community presence, choice, personal competence, respect and community participation, rather than simply behavioural change in isolation)
- is based on an understanding of why, when and how behaviours happen and what purposes they serve (via the use of functional analysis)
- focuses on altering triggers for behaviour (in order to reduce the likelihood of the behaviour occurring)
- uses skill teaching as a central intervention (as a lack of critical skills is often a key contributing factor in the development of behavioural challenges)

- uses changes in quality of life as both an intervention and outcome measure

- achieves reductions in behaviour as a side-effect of the above

- has a long-term focus (in that challenging behaviours are often of a long-term nature and successful interventions therefore need to be maintained over prolonged periods)

- has a multi-component focus (reflecting that the fact that challenging behaviours are often multiply determined and also that users typically display multiple forms)

- eliminates the use of punishment approaches

- contains both proactive strategies for changing behaviour and reactive elements for managing behaviour when it occurs (in recognition of the fact that even the most effective change strategies may not completely eliminate risk behaviours from behavioural repertoires)
  (LaVigna et al, 1989; Horner et al, 1990; Carr et al, 1990)

Although PBS has applied behaviour analysis as its central therapeutic stem, it is an inclusive approach. Thus, Bambara et al (2004) described PBS as being:

'... characterised by educational, proactive, and respectful interventions that involve teaching alternative skills to problem behaviours and changing problematic environments. It blends best practices in behavioural technology, educational methods, and ecological systems change with person-centred values in order to achieve outcomes that are meaningful to the individual and to his or her family.'

Although the origins of PBS are clearly within the field of intellectual disabilities, its utility is potentially much wider. In the USA, for example, its use has already extended into schools for non-disabled children (Crone and Horner, 2003; Horner et al, 2004). The central PBS intervention toolkit includes:

- Altering known conditions that increase the probability of challenging behaviour occurring (eg environmental factors such as space, light; social factors, such as the number of people in a setting; programmatic factors such as activity levels and intra-personal factors such as mental health needs, drug regimes etc)

- Changing specific triggers for behaviour (eg modifying instructional methods, interpersonal style, reducing demands, increasing choice)

- Teaching new competencies (eg general skills teaching, coping skills)

- The use of differential and non-contingent reinforcement

- Specifying changes in carer behaviour and in systems of service delivery

- Reactive strategies (eg distraction, evasion, minimal restraint etc)

The first three of these are described in detail within the chapters that follow by Baker and by Nethell and Smith; Donnellan et al (1988) cover them also, but provide particularly excellent accounts of the fourth topic, while Allen (1999) provides a review of some of the issues involved in working with carers and service systems in delivering behavioural interventions in practice.

As Emerson (2001) has observed, it is necessary for all practitioners to demonstrate that any intervention that they undertake has social validity. Interventions can be said to be socially valid when they address a socially significant problem, have clear evidence for their effectiveness in terms of achieving socially significant changes, and are undertaken using the least intrusive means acceptable to the main stakeholders involved.

How, then, does PBS fare in terms of social validity? It is well established that challenging behaviour can lead to the person concerned being excluded, neglected, abused and exposed to inappropriate interventions. Interventions for challenging behaviour are therefore clearly targeting socially significant problems. It also seems intuitively correct that most people would regard PBS methods as being less intrusive and more socially acceptable than interventions that employ aversive behavioural techniques (such as the application of physical pain or electric shock). There is also some experimental evidence in support of this proposition. Kazdin (1980), for example, showed that undergraduate students rated interventions using differential reinforcement as more acceptable than time out, drug therapy, and electric shock.[2]

Given the above, it could be concluded that PBS interventions are socially valid if it can also be demonstrated that they lead to socially significant changes for the persons concerned. The behavioural literature has traditionally been rather limited in considering this aspect of social validity. Several excellent, thorough meta-analyses of behavioural outcome research exist (Guess et al, 1987; Scotti et al, 1996; Didden et al, 1997), but these have tended to focus on a limited range of outcome measures, and mostly on changes in challenging behaviours themselves. Carr et al's (1999) meta-analysis on PBS outcomes studied a much broader range of outcomes, however. These included: changes in positive as well as challenging behaviour; stimulus transfer both across people and behaviours; the maintenance of gains over time; impact on lifestyle change; and stakeholder views on the social acceptability and effectiveness of the intervention.

The authors concluded that PBS interventions:

- were increasingly addressing severe challenging behaviours (earlier criticisms were that PBS interventions tended to focus on behaviours of lesser concern)

- produced small to significant changes in adaptive, positive behaviours

- produced 90 per cent or more reductions in challenging behaviours from baseline levels in 52 per cent of interventions and 80 per cent or more in 68 per cent of interventions

[2] See Foster and Mash (1999) for an excellent broader discussion on the social validity of treatment outcomes.

- showed successful maintenance over periods from between 1–24 months in about two-thirds of interventions (although the database here is small and inversely correlated with length of follow-up)

- could result in effective lifestyle change and positive evaluations of social validity (but once again, these outcomes were still only reported in a minority of interventions)

- were less effective for combinations of behaviours, as opposed to single behaviours

- were twice as likely to be successful if intervention was based on functional analysis

- were also likely to be more effective if interventions included changes in the structure and quality of service systems supporting the individual with behavioural challenges

- were likely to be more effective if implemented by a person's normal carers (instead of external specialists)

- could produce positive consumer ratings in terms of the acceptability and practicality, impact on levels of challenging behaviour, and impact on lifestyle change (but, once again, a very small number of studies reported such outcomes)

Although more research is required, it would therefore seem that PBS is able to meet all three social validity criteria and that, by including specific reference to reactive strategies, it has a goodness of fit with and bridge to the field of physical intervention. Critically, the adoption of a PBS model provides the potential means via which services can switch from a reactive to a proactive ethos.

From reaction to prevention: an organisational case study

The first volume of *Ethical Approaches* described how a systemic training model in reactive behaviour management was developed, delivered and evaluated within services for people with intellectual disability and challenging behaviour in South Wales (Allen, Doyle and Kaye, 2003). The training was one of the first to become BILD accredited, and has subsequently come to be used in many other parts of the UK. The outcome data from applying the programme were encouraging, and further independent evaluation (Parry and Potter, 2006) appeared to confirm a number of earlier findings. However, despite being delivered within the framework of a PBS approach, the service in question fell into the classic trap of over-emphasising the reactive element to the detriment of the proactive. This was evidenced by the fact that, while primary and secondary prevention were covered in the theory days, they were not supported by more in-depth training and not refreshed (unlike the physical intervention components of the training, which were repeated for all staff on a six-monthly or annual basis, depending on job role). This meant that there was a significant gap between what the service preached and what it actually practised.

A major change in service provision in the lead-up to the closure of the last hospital in the area, and the accompanying need to re-train a large group of staff to work within a PBS framework in new models of community provision, provided an opportunity to redress this imbalance. The community services involved included specialist behavioural teams, acute admission services and long-stay domestic scale accommodation for people with very complex behavioural and/or mental health issues. To match the fact that all service staff were required to undertake mandatory training in reactive strategies, the decision was made that training in PBS would also become mandatory, a fact that was captured in revised job descriptions for all staff working in the services concerned. A whole-organisation PBS training model adopted was selected in preference to a more traditional cascade model, because of the known limitations of the latter in achieving widespread organisational change. All service staff were therefore trained in the same concepts and practices. While staff at different levels of the organisation would undertake different levels of training, this training would vary in terms of the depth of the learning and the depth of assessment of knowledge, rather than in core content.

To fit the needs of the organisation, three levels of training were devised. In order to motivate staff to complete the courses and to demonstrate their value to the organisation, all three levels (Advanced Certificate, Advanced Diploma, and Advanced Professional Diploma in PBS) were accredited via the British Training and Education Council (BTEC). A vocational rather than university accreditation was preferred because the comparative costs of the latter were significantly greater; the vocational route therefore made the goal of a fully trained workforce much more attainable and affordable. The BTEC qualification also fitted in well with the emphasis on NVQ in the care sector, with content of the courses providing the specific underpinning knowledge required to work effectively with the service user group. The Advanced Certificate was designed for support workers (eg support workers and assistants in social care, non-registered health care support workers in NHS residential units, assistant behaviour specialists in specialist support teams etc), the Advanced Diploma for staff in middle management positions (eg unit managers), and the Advanced Professional Diploma for those staff with more senior roles in the organisation (eg behaviour specialists). To match the different job requirements, the objectives of the training varied at each level: the aim of the Certificate level was to equip staff to work within and contribute to a PBS framework; the Advanced Diploma was aimed at developing competencies in those charged with managing the implementation in practice; while the Advanced Professional Diploma was targeted at staff who would be responsible for implementing and leading the whole PBS process (from functional analysis, to plan development, staff training and outcome monitoring).

The Advanced Certificate and Advanced Professional Diploma levels of the course were originally delivered using traditional training formats. The certificate level course began with a two-week taught induction session consisting of classroom instruction utilising video-based and other group exercises, complemented by a course work book. There was also some in-vivo training on positive interaction. This was followed by a self-instructional period (which involved staff studying source material, completing a written assessment portfolio and undertaking work-based activities that were conducted under the observation and supervision of their managers) over a further 12-month period. One hundred and twenty seven health care support workers staff subsequently obtained the BTEC Advanced Certificate through this route, and the course resulted in significant changes evident in staff knowledge and confidence and positive participant evaluations (Lowe et al, 2007). Two cohorts also successfully completed the Advanced Professional Diploma in this initial phase.

While these PBS training initiatives were successful on a variety of different levels, they were also problematic for a number of reasons. The traditional format was not sufficiently engaging to promote the widespread practice changes that were sought (Perry et al, in press) and they consumed large amounts of tutor time (eg the initial two weeks' classroom element of the Certificate comprised 80 hours and was repeated 13 times in order to cover the whole staff group) from what was a fairly small tutor resource in the first instance. More crucially, they consumed even larger amounts of tutor time in terms of marking assessments at both levels. In addition, they were hard to deliver within a very dispersed service model; achieving the release of staff time from the workplace to attend training sessions was difficult and costly; ensuring that the whole workforce was trained in a service characterised by frequent staff turnover was difficult using this model; and staff had very different abilities and therefore learned at very different rates.

In response to these concerns, it was decided to deliver the training via a web-based based e-learning programme. This afforded the benefits of access to training being continuous and not dependent on course start dates or tutor availability, etc. Also, the training could be delivered in high volumes and not limited by geographical constraints, it could progress at rates suited to individual learners, required minimal release from the workplace and the whole course or specific topic refresher training could easily be achieved. Additional benefits of an e-learning approach included the availability of a variety of rich learning formats in which the content could be made interesting, interactive and attractive by using graphics, animations audio and video clips, etc. This included the use of interactive scenarios in which learners are introduced to virtual situations of working with service users who challenge.

The first students have now successfully completed the e-learning versions of the courses, and the feedback from them has been overwhelmingly positive. The implementation of the training has been supported by a number of organisational initiatives. For example, all service documentation (assessment reports, care plans, etc) were reformatted to fully reflect the content of the training, so that material learned in theory was reinforced in practice. Each user of the service has a functional analysis and PBS plan. Positive Monitoring of PBS plans (Porterfield, 1987) and the Periodic Service Review (LaVigna et al, 1994) were also introduced in every single element of the service in order to facilitate a consistent approach to quality assurance. The latter has proved to be a highly motivating and reliable tool for ensuring that the service delivers in practice what it teaches in theory (Jones et al, 2008).

Conclusions

This chapter has sought to re-establish the primacy of preventative strategies in working with people who display serious behavioural challenges, and has proposed positive behavioural support as a robust model for achieving effective intervention. It has also sought to illustrate how organisations that have established coherent approaches to reactive behavioural management can develop these approaches into a comprehensive PBS model.

The organisation at the centre of the case study has maintained its robust approach to physical intervention training, but has now properly located and contextualised this training within a broader strategic training approach to supporting people who challenge. This account can be likened to a situation that not infrequently presents at an individual clinical level. Principle 12 from the 'yellow book' on policy frameworks (Harris et al, 2008) clearly states that 'Restrictive physical intervention should only be used in conjunction with other strategies designed to help service users learn alternative non-challenging behaviours'. This is an irrefutable general principle. However, at a point where a service user is first referred for specialist intervention, but is perhaps at a point of crisis (for example, where they risk exclusion from the service and staff are being injured), implementing effective behaviour management strategies may be the first priority. Once these strategies are in place, and immediate risks managed, time and space is created that allows for proactive, preventative strategies to be developed and implemented. In such a scenario, making reactive interventions an initial priority is justified on the proviso that preventative interventions are developed subsequently. This situation is no different at an organisational level. A service is justified in prioritising physical management training to make its users and staff safe on the proviso that it then subsequently develops its strategy for prevention. Failing to do so is as ethically unacceptable as simply recommending reactive strategies in isolation at the individual user level.

As Carr et al (1994) observe, reactive behaviour management strategies 'provide a window of opportunity... for the more serious and beneficial long-term task of educating the individual in such a way as to undermine the necessity for engaging in problem behaviour in the future'. Our strategic focus on such strategies in recent years has merely helped create this window. It is now time for us to get our priorities right, to step through the window, and start implementing the strategies that will help eliminate the need for reactive interventions in the first place.

References

Allen, D (1999) Mediator Analysis: an overview of recent research on carers supporting people with intellectual disability and challenging behaviour. *Journal of Intellectual Disability Research*, 43, 4, 325–340.

Allen, D (2001) *Training Carers in Physical Interventions: Research Towards Evidence-Based Practice*. Kidderminster: BILD Publications.

Allen, D (2003a) Behaviour Change and Behaviour Management. In D Allen (Ed) *Ethical Approaches to Physical Interventions. Responding to Challenging Behaviour in Persons with Intellectual Disabilities*. Kidderminster: BILD Publications.

Allen, D (2003b). Devising individualised risk management plans. In D Allen (Ed) *Ethical Approaches to Physical Intervention. Responding to Challenging Behaviour in Persons with Intellectual Disabilities*. Kidderminster: BILD Publications.

Allen, D, Doyle, T and Kaye, N (2003) Plenty of gain, but no pain: a system-wide initiative. In D Allen (Ed) *Ethical Approaches to Physical Interventions. Responding to Challenging Behaviour in Persons with Intellectual Disabilities*. Kidderminster: BILD Publications.

Bambara, L M, Dunlap, G and Schwartz, I S (Eds) (2004) *Positive Behavioural Support: Critical Articles on Improving Practice for Individuals with Severe Disabilities*. Austin, TX: Pro Ed.

Carr, E G, Horner, R H, Turnbull, A P, Marquis, J G, McLaughlin, D M, McAtee, M L, Smith, C E, Ryan, K A, Ruef, M B and Doolabbh, A (1999) *Positive Behaviour Support for People with Developmental Disabilities: A Research Synthesis*. Washington: AAMR.

Carr, E G , Leven, L, McConnachie, G, Carlson, J I, Kemp, D C and Smith, C E (2004) *Communication-Based Intervention for Problem Behaviour. A User's Guide for Producing Positive Change*. Baltimore: Paul H Brooks.

Carr, E G, Robinson, S and Bailey, J S (1990) The Wrong Issue: Aversive vs Nonaversive Treatment. The Right Issue: Functional vs Nonfunctional Treatment. In A C Repp and N N Singh (Eds) *Perspectives on the use of Nonaversive and Aversive Interventions for Persons with Developmental Disabilities*. Illinois: Sycamore Publishing Co.

Crone, D A and Horner, R H (2003) *Building Positive Behavioural Support Systems in Schools. Functional Behavioural Assessment*. New York: Guilford Press.

Didden, R, Duker, P C and Korzilius, H (1997) Meta-analytic study on treatment effectiveness for problem behaviours in individuals who have mental retardation. *American Journal on Mental Deficiency*, 101, 387–399.

Donellan, A M, LaVigna, G W, Negri-Shoultz, N and Fassbender, L L (1988) *Progress without Punishment. Effective Approaches for Learners with Problem Behaviours*. New York: Teachers College Press.

Emerson, E (2001) *Challenging Behaviour. Analysis and Intervention in People with Learning Disabilities*. Cambridge: Cambridge University Press.

Foster, S L and Mash, E J (1999) Assessing Social validity in Clinical Treatment Research. Issues and Procedures. *Journal of Consulting and Clinical Psychology*, 67, 3, 308–319.

Guess, D, Helmstetter, E, Turnbull, H R and Knowlton, S (1987) *Use of Aversive Procedures with Persons who are Disabled: An Historical Review and Critical Analysis*. Seattle: Association for Persons with Severe Handicaps.

Harris, J, Cornick, M, Jefferson, A and Mills, R (2008) *Physical Interventions. A Policy Framework* (Second Edition). Kidderminster: BILD Publications.

Horner, R H, Dunlap, G, Koegel, R L, Carr, E G, Sailor, W, Anderson, J, Albin, R W and O'Neill, R E (1990) Toward a Technology of 'Nonaversive' Behavioural Support. *Journal of the Association for Persons with Severe Handicaps*, 15, 3, 125–132.

Horner, R H, Todd, A E W, Lewis-Palmer, T, Irvin, L K, Sugai, G and Bolond, J B (2004) The School-Wide Evaluation Tool (SET): A Research Instrument for Assessing School-Wide Positive Behavioural Support. *Journal of Positive Behavior Interventions*, 6, 1, 3–12.

Jones, E, Lowe, K, Allen, D, Andrew, J, Horwood, S, James, W and Grey, D (2008) Evaluation of Periodic Service Review (PSR) as a practice leadership tool in challenging behaviour services. *Journal of Intellectual Disability Research*, 52, 8–9, 756.

Kazdin, A E (1980) Acceptability of alternative treatments for deviant child behaviour. *Journal of Applied Behaviour Analysis*, 13, 2, 259–273.

LaVigna, G W, Willis, T J and Donnellan, A M (1989) The Role of Positive Programming in Behavioural Treatment. In E Cippani (Ed) *The Treatment of Severe Behaviour Disorders. Behaviour Analysis Approaches*. Washington: AAMR.

LaVigna, G W, Willis, T J, Shaull, J F, Abedi, M and Sweitzer, M (1994) *The Periodic Service Review. A Total Quality Assurance System for Human Services and Education*. Baltimore: Paul H Brookes.

Lowe, K, Jones, E, Allen, D, Davies, D, James, W, Doyle, T, Andrew, J, Kaye, N, Jones, S, Brophy, S and Moore, K (2007) Staff training in positive behaviour support: Impact on attitudes and knowledge. *Journal of Applied Research in Intellectual Disabilities*, 20, 1, 30–40

Parry, R and Potter, R (2006) *Positive Behaviour Management Training: An Evaluation of Staff Impressions of the Training Process and Content*. Bridgend: Bro Morgannwg NHS Trust.

Perry, J, Felce, D, Allen, D and Meek, A (In press). Resettlement Outcomes for People with Severe Challenging Behaviour Moving from Institutional to Community Living. *Journal of Applied Research in Intellectual Disabilities*.

Porterfield, J (1987). *Positive Monitoring. A Method of Supporting Staff and Improving Services for People with Learning Disabilities*. Kidderminster: BILD Publications.

Richter, D, Needham, I, and Kunz, S (2006) The effects of aggression management training for mental health care and disability staff: A Systematic Reviews. In D Richter and R Whittington (Eds) *Violence in Health Settings. Causes, Consequences, Management*. New York: Springer.

Scotti, J R, Kimberley, J, Ujcich, K L, Weigle, C M, Holland, C M and Kirk, K S (1996) Interventions with Challenging Behavior of Persons with Developmental Disabilities: A Review of Current Research Practices. *Journal of the Association for Persons with Severe Handicaps*, 21, 3, 123–134.

Wiener, B (1985) An attributional theory of achievement, motivation and emotion. *Psychological Review*, 548–573.

Chapter 10

Antecedent Interventions for People with Intellectual Disabilities who Present Challenging Behaviour

Peter Baker

Behaviour management is not behaviour change

The separation of the roles ascribed to reactive and proactive strategies in relation to aggressive behaviour presented by people with intellectual disabilities is an idea that has been around for some time. LaVigna, Willis and Donnellan (1989) described their multi-element model and argued for the explicit inclusion of reactive strategies. They clearly differentiated the functions and advised that reactive strategies should be used only to ensure the immediate safety of all those involved in the incident and, furthermore should have no responsibility to bring about longer term behaviour change. They saw this sole focus on situational management as an opportunity for the use of more creative alternatives to traditional crisis management, so much so that they labelled these alternatives as 'Counter-Intuitive Strategies' (LaVigna and Willis, 2002). However, the major focus in their multi-element model was on strategies for long-term and enduring behaviour change. These included a range of proactive strategies, focusing on creating more supportive environments and teaching the individual skills in relation to coping with everyday life. The implications here are quite profound since, if challenging behaviour is minimised through the judicious of proactive strategies, we can afford to choose from a much wider range of reactive strategies, even ones that we once would have feared using as they might reinforce the individual's behaviour. The limitations that have traditionally been put on the type of reactive strategies that we might employ have all too often created a sense of desperation, which has led to the adoption of punitive and potentially dangerous approaches (see Paterson and Bradley, this volume). The clear distinctions in the roles given to reactive and proactive strategies are enshrined in, and are fundamental elements of, positive behavioural support (PBS). This approach, described in more detail in the previous chapter by Allen, underpins the recent clinical and service guidance issued by the British Psychological Society, the Royal College of Psychiatry and the Royal College of Speech and Language Therapists (RC Psych Report CR144 2007).

The recent focus over the past ten years on practice in relation to physical management of aggression and people with intellectual disabilities was much needed, and has brought about welcome changes. In particular, Baker and Allen (2001) argued that this scrutiny of practice highlighted the extent to which individuals with intellectual disability who present aggressive behaviours can be put at risk of abuse by either no training or care planning, or by inappropriate and/or ill-informed care practices. However, this focus on physical responses has come at a cost. Balance has been lacking and, while it might seem obvious that the bulk of the energy of those responsible for the care of people with intellectual disabilities should be focused on prevention rather than reaction, this is clearly not the case currently. Possible reasons for this lack of balance are explored by Allen earlier, along with suggested organisational changes that would be required to address this. The remainder of this chapter will also attempt the task of addressing this balance by focusing on antecedent interventions. Clearly, if we are going to stop ethically dubious and potentially dangerous responses to the challenging behaviour presented by people with intellectual disabilities, then we need to be better at prevention in order for the potential of PBS to be realised.

Behaviours occur for a reason

This chapter will describe interventions designed to prevent challenging behaviour from occurring by the manipulation of the settings considered to be related to the occurrence of the behaviours. These settings will be both internal and external to the individual. This approach is reliant on having an understanding of the individual, in particular the relationship between the behaviour and the events that precede and follow it, along with the individual and environmental factors that might set the occasion for that pattern to be reproduced. Such an understanding can be arrived at through a functional assessment, a specific applied behavioural analytical procedure involving structured observations of the occurrence of the behaviour, either directly or via information gained from people in frequent contact with the individual. This understanding would generate a hypothesis regarding why the individual engages in the behaviour by identifying what the reinforcing consequences for the behaviour might be.

Durrand (1986) suggested a useful classification of possible reinforcing consequences:

- Social attention – whereby the individual will behave in ways that have previously resulted in them receiving attention

- Demand avoidance – when the behaviour is presented either to remove demands or to ensure they are presented less frequently

- Tangible reinforcement – whereby the individual's behaviour results in the acquisition of preferred objects or activities

- Sensory stimulation – where the behaviour is produced in order to receive sensory feedback

Functional assessment would also yield information regarding antecedent conditions related to the behaviour. In applied behavioural analysis, there are two broad types of antecedents: discriminative stimuli (SDs), which are environmental events that would indicate to the individual that the reinforcer was available; and motivating operations (MOs) – internal or environmental factors that would alter the motivation and therefore the likelihood of the person engaging in the behaviour. The presence or absence of either would affect the probability of the behaviour reoccurring. An example of an SD might be the arrival of a person in the environment, indicating to the individual that behaviour previously associated with attention would now be more likely to be reinforced; this association has built up from previous learning, whereby the individual's behaviour has been reinforced in the presence (ie attention has been given) and obviously not reinforced in the absence of the SD (ie when nobody is around, the behaviour has not been reinforced). An MO in this case might be a prolonged period of being alone. This condition would make attention more motivating, and the presence of the SD (the arrival of the person) in this circumstance increases the probability that the behaviour will reoccur. For the purposes of clarity within this chapter, the umbrella term of antecedent conditions will be used to refer to both SDs and MOs. For a more detailed discussion of MOs and SDs, readers are advised to read Langthorne, McGill and O'Reilly (2007).

Meta-analytical studies have indicated that the presence of a functional assessment is a key variable in determining successful outcomes in relation to intervention for people with intellectual disabilities who present challenging behaviour. While it is appreciated that currently access to sophisticated functional assessments might not be generally available to all, the need for some sort of informed understanding along the lines suggested above is nonetheless essential. O'Neil et al (1997) and Iwata and Dozier (2008) are useful resources for more detailed descriptions of functional assessment and analysis.

Consequence-based interventions

Traditionally, behavioural interventions have focused on manipulation of the relationship between the behaviour and its consequences. Such an approach would be typified by the differential reinforcement of the non-occurrence of the behaviour or the occurrence at lower rates, extinction (whereby the reinforcer for the behaviour is no longer available), or punishment-based procedures (whereby either aversive consequences follow the behaviour (type 1 punishment) or a stimulus (presumably preferred) is removed (type 2 punishment)). While the efficacy of such approaches would appear to be beyond question, various concerns remain about some specific applications of consequence-based procedures. Differential reinforcement strategies are relatively conceptually complex interventions that require high levels of supervision of the individual. They also involve identification of a deliverable reinforcer that the individual does not ordinarily have access to, and a degree of organisation that would enable these reinforcers to be delivered at precise times. It is this author's experience that services in the UK rarely have this degree of organisation and, if a differential reinforcement schedule is to be used, a substantial investment is required in terms of training and ongoing support. Furthermore, identification of reinforcers presents a considerable challenge, given the criteria that they should be both sufficiently powerful and not ordinarily available. When such a reinforcer can be found, a further ethical dilemma becomes apparent; a highly preferred object or activity has been found for the person which, in order to be maximally effective in bringing about behaviour change, is then, albeit temporarily, rationed.

The use of punishment as a consequence has attracted strong criticism and, although it has widespread use within wider society, it is out of place in current services that espouse human rights and person-centred approaches. The use of extinction has been demonstrated to be effective; however, the reduction in behaviour is sometimes preceded by an extinction burst (a temporary increase in severity and/or frequency of the behaviour). In the case of dangerous behaviours, this may be ill-advised, with serious safety implications. In addition, responses that occur after an episode of aggressive behaviour may also be seen as occurring far too late in the behavioural chain, especially for the victim of that aggression. Perhaps more fundamental is the supposition that the use of consequence-based approaches is limited in that they often do not address the conditions that set the occasion for the behaviour. These conditions are often related to the adequacy of the environment in which the individual exists and receives care. These concerns have influenced the increasing emphasis on antecedent-based intervention for people with intellectual disabilities who present challenging behaviour, changing the focus to addressing the range of environmental and personal setting events that are responsible for such behaviours.

Removing and/or altering antecedent conditions

In the case of antecedent interventions, the general principles are that antecedent conditions for the behaviour are removed or altered in some way in order to weaken their effect on the behaviour. Removal is conceptually straightforward and would involve identification of the antecedent conditions that set the occasion for the behaviour and, where possible, removing them. This is essentially one of the principles that underpin the advice in the low arousal approaches described by McDonnell et al in the first volume of *Ethical Approaches* (ie the reduction of points of conflict around an individual by decreasing staff demands and requests). This is based on the assumption that such demands and requests from staff constitute antecedent events that are functionally related to the challenging behaviour (ie that the individual seeks to avoid these demands through the use of the challenging behaviour). Alteration, rather than removal, of the antecedent conditions is a strategy that may well need to be employed in situations where it is not possible to remove the antecedent. This is a less intuitive approach, and one that perhaps requires a bit more detailed discussion. Horner at al (1997) used the term 'neutralising routines' to describe this type of alteration of antecedent conditions. They demonstrated that, for some of the participants in their study, being told that a planned activity was cancelled or delayed, and then being requested to comply in tasks together, was an antecedent condition for distressed and problematic behaviour. Similarly, for another participant, getting less than five hours sleep has a similar effect on their behaviour when combined with a request to comply. The first participants were given the opportunity to engage in a preferred activity and to formally reschedule the cancelled activity prior to the requests for compliance. The last individual was given a one-hour nap prior to the request. Both procedures effectively reduced the problem behaviours. In such a situation, we can assume that events such as cancellation of activity and not getting enough sleep were absolutely unavoidable. When these events occurred, they affected the individual's motivation to engage in the presented tasks to such an extent that they exhibited difficult and problematic behaviour. If the option of not presenting the demand was available, this would have been an example of removal of an aspect of the antecedent condition. However, in this study this was not possible – hence the need for alteration of a further aspect of the antecedent condition and the use of effective neutralising routines to minimise the problematic behaviours

Non-contingent reinforcement

Where the reinforcer for the behaviour is known, presenting the reinforcer independently of the behaviour, thus reducing the frequency of that behaviour, can alter the link between them. This will usually be achieved by delivering large amounts of the reinforcer at times determined by the clock rather than the behaviour. This procedure is commonly referred to as non-contingent reinforcement. For example, if the identified reinforcer for the behaviour is attention, attention will be provided to the individual on a fixed time basis, for example every ten minutes. If there are concerns about the attention being delivered and accidentally being paired with the behaviour, then a brief delay of delivery can be employed in such circumstances. Non-contingent reinforcement effectively weakens the relationship between the behaviour and the attention, with a resulting decrease in the behaviour. This may be considered analogous to a situation whereby an employee goes to work in order to earn money. This employee wins a large sum on the Lottery, with the resulting effect of him no longer going to work. The relative value of his wages have been reduced by the amount of money he has now, so this affects his motivation to work for what has now effectively become loose change.

Positive behavioural support also uses skills teaching as a key intervention. This is dealt with in detail in the following chapter by Nethell and Smith. However, a brief mention may be warranted, as there may well be some overlap in situations where skills teaching may be used to alter motivation to engage in the challenging behaviour by the elimination of an MO. For example, with an individual with mobility problems, where the MO for attention-motivated challenging behaviour was deprivation of attention, the intervention involved teaching the individual to use an independent mobility aid. With independent mobility, they could seek out attention when needed, thus eliminating attention deprivation and hence the need for challenging behaviour. Similarly, when augmented communication systems (such as the use of picture cards) are used to teach an individual a response to gain access to a reinforcer that was previously associated with challenging behaviour, this acts directly on the motivation by reducing deprivation in relation to the desired object or activity. This effect may well be twofold, in as much as the individual has generally greater access of the reinforcer and, as the communication is easier to comprehend by those who can deliver the reinforcer, the likely of delivery also increases.

The reinforcers most commonly implicated in the motivation for aggression in people with intellectual disabilities would be deprivation of attention, deprivation in relation to objects or activities, inadequate levels of stimulation and demands. Thus, effective intervention may seek to involve such things as the provision of higher levels of attention, increased access to object/activities, adjustment to prevailing stimulation and specific changes in the way in which demands are presented, in order to reduce aversiveness.

Antecedent interventions associated with demand-related behaviours

Whilst the provision of higher levels of attention, increased access to objects/activities and adjusting prevailing stimulation are conceptually straightforward, antecedent interventions concerned with demand are arguably more complex. Variables influencing demand-related behaviour might include the frequency, difficulty, predictability, timing, length and choice of the task. In addition, there is some evidence that suggests that demand is the common identified reinforcer for challenging behaviour, representing 35 per cent of cases of self-injury (Iwata, Pace, Dorsey et al, 1994) and 48 per cent of cases of self-injury and aggression (Derby et al, 1992). As such, this perhaps warrants some more detailed discussion.

Miltenberger (2006) suggested a number of procedures aimed at reducing challenging behaviours associated with escape from demand:

- *Fading demands.* This includes decreasing either the frequency or difficulty of the tasks and then gradually increasing to a level necessary for optimal learning. This is assumed to be effective, as it will initially diminish the aversiveness of the task and, with a gradual increase in frequency or difficulty, result in the likelihood of the behaviour not re-emerging

- *Altering the pace of demands.* In contrast to the strategy above, for some individuals, presenting the demands more frequently can have the effect of reducing related challenging behaviour. When this is effective, it is assumed that increasing the frequency of the demands results in more opportunities for success, and therefore a larger amount of reinforcement

- *Interspersal of easy tasks.* Combining tasks that are associated with a higher chance of correct responses (easy) with those that have a lower chance (hard) may well have an effect of reducing the aversiveness of the hard tasks and, consequently, the associated challenging behaviours

- *High-probability sequence.* This requires preceding the request that is related to the challenging behaviour with requests that not only are unlikely to trigger the behaviour, but also are likely to be met with by compliance. For example, ask the person to shake your hand, show you what they are wearing, or drink some tea before the more difficult request to vacuum the lounge. Thus the individual 'gets on a roll of compliance'. This procedure is also known as Behavioural Momentum or pre-task requesting

- *Modify task features.* Some specific aspects of the task that the individual finds aversive can be altered to make it more acceptable to the individual – for example, the task length, fine motor versus gross motor tasks, morning versus afternoon, individual versus group, tape versus book, etc. Thus the task remains essentially the same, but a slight aspect is altered

- *Alter the timing.* Deliver requests when the individual is not engaged in a preferred activity. If the individual is engaged in a highly reinforcing activity, a request to perform a task is likely to result in challenging behaviour if the behaviour increases the chances of the demand being removed and the preferred activity continuing. Waiting until the person has finished watching their TV programme before asking them to complete the washing-up may well be wise advice

- *Provide assistance.* The simple expedient of the provision of help to complete the task may well decrease the difficulty and the aversiveness of the task. This could be combined with a Functional Communication Training approach, whereby the individual is taught to request this assistance (see chapter by Nethell and Smith)

- *Provide non-contingent attention.* The provision of attention unrelated to the challenging behaviour may well serve to decrease the aversiveness of the task. The important aspect here is not that the attention is continuous throughout the task, but rather that it is not paired with the challenging behaviour. This would serve to weaken the link between the behaviour and escape from demand.

- *Embedding tasks.* This involves placing the demand in a context not associated with the occurrence of the challenging behaviour, presumably an enjoyable activity for the person. For example, if the disliked task is getting dressed in the morning, this could perhaps be made more acceptable by embedding it within the activity of listening to music on the radio. This is more likely to be effective if compliance with the demand does not interfere with the reinforcing properties of the context. For example, this would not work if you tried to embed vacuuming in the activity of listening to music, as obviously the noise from vacuuming would interfere with the enjoyment of the music

- *Increase predictability.* Being able to predict upcoming demands may well result in them becoming less aversive. This could well be achieved by the use of accessible timetables, for example using photographic sequences. The issue of predictability for the person may well be not only what they are being asked to do, but also for how long or how much. In this case, careful preparation of the environment so that the task is unambiguous in all its aspects would be important. For example, when trying to encourage the person to wash up their dishes, compliance is more likely if the kitchen is clear of all other dirty implements and has just the plates, cutlery, etc that belong to the individual, thus giving a clear signal about the extent of the task

Miltenberger (2006) also argued that the provision of choice of tasks has been shown to decrease the likelihood of associated challenging behaviour. This could be choice between tasks, or a choice regarding some aspect of the task, such as time or location. Also, the use of non-contingent access to escape from the task could potentially weaken the link between reinforcer (escape) and the challenging behaviour. This procedure would involve removal of the task based on time and not the individual's behaviour. This could perhaps be achieved by the scheduling of regular and frequent breaks. The individual would learn that escape from the task would be forthcoming, irrespective of what they did, thus weakening motivation to engage in the behaviour (see previous discussion in this chapter).

Environmental enrichment

The procedures described above require specific understanding of the features of the demand that appear to be functionally related to the challenging behaviour, in order for there to be confidence that manipulation of that specific feature will reliably alter the probability of the reoccurrence of the behaviour. Thus again, the importance of conducting a thorough functional assessment is emphasised.

In general, when the reinforcers are not known or poorly understood, arbitrary non-contingent reinforcement may be used. This is simply providing a high density of preferred objects/activities according to a time schedule and not as a result (thus non-contingently) of the behaviour. This tactic is also known as environmental enrichment (Horner et al, 1990). Most studies that have used this procedure have followed the precedent of Vollmer et al (1993), utilising high-density of reinforcement, that is a large amount of reinforcement delivered frequently. This can be difficult to sustain and often, when the behaviours have reduced to acceptable levels of intensity, the schedule is thinned – that is, the amount and timing of delivery of reinforcement is gradually reduced to sustainable levels.

McGill (1999) noted that the implications for the consideration of antecedent factors in analysis and intervention in challenging behaviour have extended the influence and remit of applied behaviour analysis. Intervention in relation to these factors is not about the manipulation of contingencies, but rather on the provision of a better quality of life for the recipient of the intervention. People with intellectual disabilities frequently find themselves in environments that provide a poor fit for their basic needs and, as such, can be conceptualised as challenging environments. For example, environments that are austere and barren, with low levels of social interaction, where preferred objects and activities are either absent or are under the control of or rationed by staff, are environments that would provide the motivation for challenging behaviour. Thus environmental enrichment can be conceptualised as an antecedent-based intervention. Of note is that not all of these strategies necessarily require a sophisticated functional assessment before they are implemented, and they could well be put in place via a robust person-centred planning regime.

Health – environment interactions

This chapter thus far has concentrated on the influence of external environmental variables on challenging behaviour. Up until recently, the role of health conditions in the causation of challenging behaviour had seen little attention both as an explanatory variable and as a potential for intervention. For the purposes of this discussion, health conditions are conceptualised as including both chronic and acute conditions that negatively affect the person's well-being. The lack of attention to these variables may be particularly remiss, given the evidence of a greater prevalence of health care needs amongst people with intellectual disabilities. Where the individual's well-being is adversely affected by a health problem, this may well exacerbate some aspect of the relationship between the environment and the behaviour. For example, a person who suffers from epilepsy may well experience subjective discomfort prior to a seizure. This discomfort may make them more sensitive to environmental events that ordinarily would be tolerated. In this state, a request to comply with a task might be more likely to be met with aggression, as the pre-seizure state will have affected motivation, having increased the relative aversiveness of the task and thus making its removal more reinforcing. This would be especially likely to be the case in people with intellectual disabilities who have problems in regard to expressive language, where they would experience difficulty in communicating that they were in pain, with the resulting difficulties in obtaining help

The rationale for their inclusion in this chapter is that the medical conditions or their associated symptoms may well be amenable to medical intervention; this in itself would be an antecedent intervention. When the condition has fluctuating influence over behaviour, this might necessitate making specific environmental changes around the time where painful symptoms are in evidence.

Sleep

Studies suggest a relatively high prevalence of sleep disorders in people with intellectual disabilities (Brylewski and Wiggs, 1999). The negative effects of sleep deprivation include reduced attention, impaired memory and altered immune system functioning, in addition to the effects on subjective well-being. These variables are likely to impact on behaviour, and intervention strategies may well focus on sleep hygiene strategies, provision of additional opportunities during the day to catch up on sleep or the use of medication. O'Reilly (1995) examined the relationship between sleep deprivation and environmental conditions in a young man with an intellectual disability and aggression. Aggression occurred in demand conditions when the young man had less than five hours' sleep Durand (1998) provides a comprehensive description of interventions for sleep problems.

Gastrointestinal disorders

The two most common gastrointestinal disorders in people with intellectual disabilities are gastroesophageal reflux disease (GERD) and constipation. GERD is a painful condition where there is a dysfunction of the sphincter at the top of the stomach, whereby stomach contents are allowed to wash back into the oesophagus; this results in heartburn and regurgitation. Less obvious and rarer symptoms may include asthma, chronic coughing, chronic laryngitis, sore throat and non-cardiac chest pain. The incidence in people with intellectual disabilities may be as high as 48 per cent (Bohmer et al, 1999). Kennedy and Becker (2006) demonstrated how a relationship between these symptoms and self-injurious behaviour can exist, and how the symptoms can be relieved by medication, surgery or dietary adjustments, with a subsequent decrease in self-injurious behaviour.

Constipation involves decrease in frequency of, or incomplete, defecation, and may result in abdominal pain or discomfort. Most cases are due to decreased fibre and fluid intake, but may also be a side-effect of certain psychotropic medications. The prevalence in people with intellectual disabilities is significant, with Bohmer et al (2001) reporting rates as high as 69 per cent . The pain associated with GERD and constipation may well constitute antecedent conditions for challenging behaviour, either by acting as direct triggers or interacting with the environment by altering the individual's sensitivity and tolerance of environmental triggers.

Allergies

Allergic reactions are atypical physiological responses (usually inflammation), whereby the individual has either inhaled, ingested or simply come into contact with a foreign body. The foreign bodies that trigger allergic reactions are specific to the individual and may include pollen, animal hair, dust mites, cosmetics, insect stings, etc. The areas most affected are the respiratory tract and skin. The most common condition is allergic rhinitis, where the membrane of the nose becomes inflamed results in nasal discharge and sneezing. This may also be associated with irritation to the eyes, asthma, and inflammation in the sinuses and ears, with accompanying pain and discomfort. The effect of such symptoms on challenging behaviour was demonstrated by Kennedy and Meyer (1996), where the presence of self-injury in a boy with autism was related to demands, with this relationship exacerbated by the presence of allergy symptoms. Alleviation of symptoms is possible through the use of medication and avoidance of allergens.

Dysmenorrhoea and Premenstrual Syndrome (PMS)

Dysmenorrhoea and PMS are conditions occurring in women in relation to their menstrual cycle. Dysmenorrhoea is abdominal and/or pelvic pain occurring around the time of menstruation, while PMS is a recurrent cyclic condition associated with mood disturbance, including irritability, depression, crying and mood swings, along with sleep disturbances and changes in appetite and libido. Carr et al (2003) demonstrated a relationship between demand situations and menses in four women with intellectual disabilities. As with allergy related conditions, alleviation of symptoms is possible through the use of medication.

Otitis Media

Otitis Media involves the infection of the inner and middle ear. Prevalence in people with intellectual disabilities is estimated as 25 per cent , with a particular association with cleft palate and Down Syndrome (Mitchell et al, 2003). The symptoms are reported to be painful, with some evidence that they can be relieved by head–hitting, and indeed there is a reported association with head-hitting and acute otitis media in typically developing children (Bramble, 1995). A number of studies have demonstrated a relationship between the condition and self-injurious behaviour in people with intellectual disabilities. In particular, O'Reilly (1997) demonstrated the relationship in a child with intellectual disabilities between otitis media, noise and demand. As with conditions mentioned above, alleviation of the condition can be achieved through the use of analgesia and antibiotics.

Epilepsy

Epilepsy is a seizure disorder, involving loss of consciousness and motor (muscular) control. The frequency of epilepsy occurring in people with intellectual disability is fifteen to thirty times higher than in the general population and increases in proportion with the severity of their disability (van Schrojenstein Lantman-de Valk, 2005). Several studies have suggested an association between epilepsy and challenging behaviour in people with intellectual disabilities, with effective medical control of epilepsy being associated with improvements in behaviour (Scheepers et al, 2004). There is a lack of knowledge regarding the causal mechanisms that underlie this relationship However, it is plausible, and in keeping with the evidence concerning other health conditions, that the neurological status (either permanent or fluctuating) could well interact with the environment, affecting tolerances and sensitivities and resulting in challenging behaviour.

Mental illness

Studies of the prevalence of psychiatric disorder among people with intellectual disabilities are beset by methodological difficulties, including sampling, reliability of diagnosis and definitional problems. There is evidence that the overall rate of psychiatric disorder is higher in people with severe intellectual disability than with people with mild intellectual disability or those without intellectual disability. There is, as yet, no evidence that the overall rate of psychiatric disorders for adults with mild intellectual disabilities (IQ 50–70) is any higher than that for the population as a whole (Whitaker and Read, 2006). A number of studies have suggested links between mental illness and challenging behaviour in people with intellectual disabilities. For example Reiss and Rojahn (1993) found that individuals who displayed aggressive behaviour were four times as likely to suffer from depression than those who were not aggressive. Emerson at al (1999) suggested the possibility of an interactive effect between environment and some psychiatric conditions. For example, depression is associated with a number of physical, cognitive and emotional symptoms, including fatigue, loss of energy, insomnia and hypersomnia (American Psychiatric Association, *Diagnostic and Statistical Manual* (4th ed), 1994). The presence of such symptoms may well affect the person's responses to environmental antecedent conditions, resulting in challenging behaviour.

Interventions for psychiatric conditions might include shorter-term modification of the environment and expedient use of as-required medication when symptoms are present and, in the longer term, psychotherapy and/or medication.

Psychotropic drugs and behavioural toxicity

The use of medication for people with intellectual disabilities who present challenging behaviour is widespread, with estimates between 50–60 per cent (Kiernan et al, 1995; Fleming et al, 1996). Langthorne et al (2007) argued that the direct and side-effects of such medication could well constitute antecedent conditions for the presentation of challenging behaviour. For example, Dicesare et al (2005) reported the effects of the drug methylphenidate on the behaviour of a young man diagnosed with Attention Deficit Hyperactivity Disorder. His challenging behaviour occurred exclusively in relation to attention and was less frequent when taking the medication. Behavioural toxicity refers to the indirect and unintended side-effects of drugs. There is an acknowledged paucity in the knowledge regarding psychotropic behavioural toxicity in people with intellectual disability (Advocat et al, 2000) and this, set against the acknowledged rates of polypharmacy in the population (Robertson et al, 2000), is likely to increase the risk. This highlights the importance of good prescribing practice in relation to this population (see RC Psych Report CR144 2007 and Deb, this volume).

Summary and conclusion

PBS has attempted to bring together a set of person centre values and an applied behavioural technology to assist in the process of bringing about better lives for people with intellectual disabilities who have been presenting challenging behaviour. The principles that underpin antecedent interventions are key to PBS, in that they attempt to address and make better the fit between the person and their environment. Looking for solutions using this paradigm takes us away from less helpful approaches where the person is forced to fit in, irrespective of their particular needs, and confronted (often physically) and punished if they do not. This is based on the premise that the person will eventually be forced into submission and will change their behaviour. For many people who continue to present severe and enduring challenging behaviour, this has obviously not worked. Using antecedent interventions and the other elements of PBS will involve a paradigm shift for many who work in this area. As a culture we have been taught that the way to manage the behaviour of others is through reaction: we punish bad behaviour and reward (although, as is often the case, ignore) good behaviour. Once a good understanding of the person is achieved, the ideas contained here in many cases are simple. The real challenge is implementation – investment in training, supervision and supportive infrastructures is essential.

References

Advokat, C D, Mayville, E A and Matson, J L (2000) Side effect profiles of atypical antipsychotics, typical antipsychotics, or no psychotropic medications in persons with mental retardation. *Research in Developmental Disabilities*, 21, 75–84.

American Psychiatric Association (1994) *Diagnostic and statistical manual of mental disorders* (Fourth Edition). Washington, DC: APA.

Baker, P A and Allen, D (2001) Physical abuse and physical Interventions: An element of risk for people with learning disabilities? *Journal of Adult Protection*, 3, 2, 25–32.

Bohmer, C J, Niezen-de Boer, M C, Klinkenberg-Knol, E C, Deville, W L, Nadorp, J H and Meuwissen, S G (1999) The prevalence of gastro-esophageal reflux disease in institutionalized intellectually disabled individuals. *American Journal of Gastroenterology*, 94, 804–810.

Bohmer, C J, Taminiau, J A, Klinkenberg-Knol, E C and Meuwissen, S G (2001) The prevalence of constipation in institutionalized people with intellectual disabilities. *Journal of Intellectual Disabilities Research*, 45, 212–218.

Bramble, D (1995) Two cases of severe head-banging parasomnias in prepubertal males resulting in otitis media in toddlerhood. *Child: Care, Health, and Development*, 21, 247–253.

Brylewski, J and Wiggs, L (1999) Sleep problems and daytime challenging behaviour in a community-based sample of adults with intellectual disability. *Journal of Intellectual Disability Research*, 43, 504–512.

Carr, E G, Smith, C E, Giacin, T A, Whelan, B M and Pancari, J (2003) Menstrual discomfort as a biological setting event for severe problem behavior: Assessment and intervention. *American Journal on Mental Retardation*, 108, 117–133.

Derby, K M, Wacker, D P, Sasso, G, Steege, M, Northup, J, Cigrand, K and Asmus, J (1992) Brief functional assessment techniques to evaluate aberrant behavior in an outpatient setting: A summary of 79 cases. *Journal of Applied Behavior Analysis*, 25, 713–721.

Dicesare, A, McAdam, D B, Toner, A and Varrell, J (2005) The effects of methylphenidate on a functional analysis of disruptive behavior: A replication and extension. *Journal of Applied Behavior Analysis*, 38, 125–128.

Durand, M V (1986) Self-injurious behavior as intentional communication. *Advances in Learning and Behavioral Disabilities*, 5, 141–155.

Durand, M V (1998) *Sleep Better. A Guide to Improving Sleep for Children with Special Needs*. Baltimore: Paul H Brookes.

Emerson, E, Moss, S and Kiernan, C (1999) The relationship between challenging behavior and psychiatric disorders. In N Bouras (Ed) *Psychiatric and behavioral disorders in developmental disabilities and mental retardation*. Cambridge: Cambridge University Press.

Fleming, I, Caine, A, Ahmed, S and Smith, S (1996) Aspects of the use of psychoactive medication among people with intellectual disabilities who have been resettled from long-stay hospitals into dispersed housing. *Journal of Applied Research in Intellectual Disabilities*, 9, 3, 94–205.

Horner, R H, Day, M H and Day, J R (1997) Using neutralizing routines to reduce problem behaviors. *Journal of Applied Behavior Analysis*, 30, 601–614.

Horner, R H, Sprague, J R, O'Brien, M and Heathfield, T H (1990) The role of response efficiency in the reduction of problem behaviors through functional equivalence training: A case study. *Journal of the Association for Persons with Severe Handicaps*, 15, 91–97.

Iwata, B A, Pace, G M, Dorsey, M F, Zarcone, J R, Vollmer, T R, Smith, R G, Rodgers, T A, Lerman, D C, Shore, B A, Mazaleski, J L, Goh, H L, Cowdery, G E, Kalsher, M J, McCosh, K C and Willis, K D (1994) The functions of self-injurious behavior: An experimental-epidemiological analysis. *Journal of Applied Behavior Analysis*, 27, 215–240.

Iwata, B A and Dozier, C L (2008) Clinical application of functional analysis methodology. *Behavior Analysis in Practice*, 1, 3–9

Kiernan, C, Reeves, D and Alborz, A (1995) The use of anti psychotic drugs with adults with learning disabilities and challenging behaviour. *Journal of Intellectual Disability Research*, 39, 4, 263–274.

Kennedy, C H and Meyer, K A (1996) Sleep deprivation, allergy symptoms, and negatively reinforced problem behavior. *Journal of Applied Behavior Analysis, 29*, 133–135.

Kennedy, C H and Becker, A (2006) Health conditions in antecedent assessment and intervention of problem behavior. In J K Luiselli (Ed) *Antecedent Assessment and Intervention: Supporting Children and Adults with Development Disabilities in Community Settings*. Baltimore: Paul H Brookes.

Langthorne, P, McGill, P and O'Reilly, M (2007) Incorporating motivation into the functional analysis of challenging behaviour: On the interactive and integrative potential of the motivating operation. *Behavior Modification, 31*, 466–487.

LaVigna, G W, Willis, T and Donnellan, A (1989) The role of positive programming in behavioral treatment. In E Cipani (Ed) *The Treatment of Severe Behavior Disorders. Behavior Analysis Approaches*. Washington: American Association on Mental Deficiency.

LaVigna, G W and Willis, T (2002) Counter-intuitive strategies for crisis management within a non-aversive framework. In D Allen (Ed) *Ethical approaches to physical interventions. Responding to challenging behaviour in people with intellectual disabilities*. Kidderminster: BILD Publications.

McDonnell, A, Waters, T and Jones, D (2002) Low arousal approaches in the management of challenging behaviour. In D Allen (Ed) *Ethical approaches to physical interventions: Responding to challenging behaviour in people with intellectual disabilities*. Kidderminster: BILD Publications.

McGill, P (1999) Establishing operations: Implications for the assessment, treatment, and prevention of problem behaviour. *Journal of Applied Behavioral Analysis*, 23, 3, 393–418.

Miltenberger, R G (2006) Antecedent interventions for challenging behaviors maintained by escape from instructional activities. In J K Luiselli (Ed) *Antecedent Assessment and Intervention: Supporting Children and Adults with Development Disabilities in Community Settings*, Baltimore: Paul H Brookes.

Mitchell, R B, Call, E and Kelly, J (2003) Ear, nose and throat disorders in children with Down Syndrome. *Laryngoscope,* 113, 259–263.

O'Neill, R, Horner, R, Albin, R, Sprague, J, Storey, K and Newton, J (1997) *Functional Assessment and Program Development for Problem Behavior: A practical handbook* (Second Edition). Pacific Grove, CA: Brooks/Cole.

O'Reilly, M F (1995) Functional-analysis and treatment of escape-maintained aggression correlated with sleep–deprivation. *Journal of Applied Behavior Analysis,* 28, 225–226.

O'Reilly, M F (1997) Functional analysis of episodic self-injury correlated with recurrent otitis media. *Journal of Applied Behavior Analysis,* 30, 165–167.

Reiss, S and Rojahn, J (1993) Joint occurrence of depression and aggression in children and adults with mental-retardation. *Journal of Intellectual Disability Research*, 37, 287–294.

Robertson, J, Emerson, E, Gregory, N, Hatton, C, Kessissoglou, S and Hallam, A (2000) Receipt of psychotropic medication by people with intellectual disability in residential settings. *Journal of Intellectual Disability Research*, 44, 666–676.

Royal College of Psychiatrists, British Psychological Society and Royal College of Speech and Language Therapists (2007) *Challenging Behaviour: A Unified Approach*. London: Royal College of Psychiatrists.

Scheepers, B, Salahudeen, S and Morelli, J (2004) Two-year outcome audit in an adult learning disability population with refractory epilepsy. *Seizure,* 13, 529–533.

van Schrojenstein Lantman-de Valk, H, (2005) Health in people with intellectual disabilities: Current knowledge and gaps in knowledge. *Journal of Applied Research in Intellectual Disabilities*, 18, 4, 325–333.

Vollmer, T R, Iwata, B A, Zarcone, J R, Smith, R G and Mazaleski, J L (1993) The role of attention in the treatment of self-injurious behavior: Noncontingent reinforcement and differential reinforcement of other behavior. *Journal of Applied Behavior Analysis,* 26, 9–21.

Whittaker, S and Read, S (2006) The prevalence of psychiatric disorders among people with intellectual disabilities: An analysis of the literature. *Journal of Applied Research in Intellectual Disabilities*, 19, 330–345.

Chapter 11

Teaching New Skills to People with Learning Disabilities who Engage in Aggressive Behaviour

Gillian Nethell and Mark Smith

Introduction

Within the framework of positive behavioural support (PBS), it is recognised that primary prevention (or 'proactive') strategies are a key component of a comprehensive intervention package (Horner et al, 1990). Primary prevention focuses on helping the person behave in non-challenging ways and is therefore concerned with behaviour *change*. In the absence of primary prevention, it is unlikely that an intervention package will lead to significant long-term change in an individual's behaviour, as secondary and reactive strategies, albeit important, are concerned with behaviour *management*.

It is in the context of primary prevention that we present ideas for teaching new skills to people with intellectual disabilities who engage in aggressive behaviour. While primary prevention involves a number of other important strategies (eg broad-based ecological strategies, setting event intervention, antecedent intervention and reinforcement-based interventions), these share the common characteristic of requiring a degree of external control, usually in the form of implementation via paid carers or staff, for their effectiveness. This is a potential limitation to these strategies, as the need for such external controls is often ongoing and can result in service users having to remain in services that can provide this level of support, which can seriously limit independence (Whitaker, 2001). In theory, skills teaching does not have this limitation. Once the person has gained the skills that enable them to cope better with provoking situations, they should be able to draw upon the skill without the need for ongoing external controls (Whitaker, 2001; La Vigna, Willis and Donnellan, 1989).

Skills teaching approaches

A useful starting point for considering skills teaching approaches is a framework put forward by La Vigna and colleagues (La Vigna, Willis and Donnellan, 1989). They use the collective term *positive programming* for skill teaching, and define this as follows:

'... a longitudinal, instructional programme designed to give the learner greater skills and competencies for the purpose of controlling or eliminating problem behaviour in order to facilitate and enhance social integration ...'

(La Vigna, Willis and Donnellan, 1989, p 59)

Within positive programming, La Vigna and colleagues suggest four variations:

General skill development

This involves increasing the person's *general* competence as a preventative strategy. It is based on the principle that eliminating challenging behaviour can create a 'behavioural vacuum' – that is, in the absence of socially acceptable alternative behaviours, there is always a risk that the behaviour of concern will re-emerge, or that another problematic behaviour will develop. As La Vigna et al (1989, p 64) state:

'a positive programme, with instructional objectives that are functional and that give the person ample opportunity to learn and engage in a wide variety of relevant and/or interesting activities, would remove the conditions that are discriminative for many problem behaviours.'

Functionally equivalent skills

This involves teaching specific skills that serve the same function as the problem behaviour, and therefore reduces the need to engage in the behaviour. The teaching of communication skills (eg speech, manual signs/gestures or graphic symbols) has been prominent in this area and this is frequently referred to in the literature as functional communication skills teaching. An example of this would be teaching a person who engages in aggressive behaviour to obtain a drink by pointing to a symbol for 'drink' which results in a staff member providing a drink.

Functionally related skills

Functionally related skills teaching involves teaching skills that produce a similar, but not exactly the same, outcome as the challenging behaviour. To follow the above example, this could involve teaching the same person to make a drink for themselves rather than teaching them to request a drink.

Coping skills

This involves teaching the individual skills that can enhance their ability to cope with situations that provoke challenging behaviour. This variation recognises that there are often unavoidable stressors and naturally occurring aversive events in one's life, and that teaching new coping skills can reduce the individual's need to engage in challenging behaviour in these situations. Within this variation of positive programming, there has been a considerable focus on applying cognitive-behavioural interventions with people with intellectual disabilities, especially interventions to address underlying issues of anger and its relationship with aggressive behaviour ('anger management').

Essentially, all the above variations involve working *directly* with the individual to develop skills that either reduce or eliminate the need to engage in challenging behaviours. Although this framework can apply to a range of other behaviours (eg self-injury, stereotypy, sexually inappropriate behaviour), we will consider its applicability to aggressive behaviour in this chapter. As general skills development is a very broad topic, we will focus on the three areas of functionally equivalent skills, functionally related skills and coping skills in this chapter.

Theoretical basis of positive programming approaches

The wide range of interventions under the umbrella term of 'positive programming' have evolved from a number of theoretical perspectives. For example, functionally equivalent skills training can be seen to emerge from theories that emphasised skills deficits as explanations for aggressive behaviour in people with intellectual disability. There is some research evidence to support this theory. For example, Duncan et al (1999) found that individuals who displayed aggressive behaviour (and also self-injurious behaviour, or a combination of both) differed significantly on a measure of social skills when compared to a matched control group There is also considerable evidence to suggest a link between communication difficulties and challenging behaviour, which sets a context to communication-based interventions. Desrochers et al (1997) found that only 32 per cent of service users referred to challenging behaviour services were able to communicate most or all wants and desires, and earlier research has also shown that challenging behaviours typically increase in frequency, intensity or duration when communication difficulties increase (eg Talkington et al, 1971).

Another set of theories that have shaped positive programming interventions, concern the relationship between aggressive behaviour and anger. There is clearly a close link between anger and aggression, particularly under conditions of high arousal intensity, which can serve to override inhibitory controls (Novaco, 1994). Indeed, anger has shown to be predictive of aggression in both psychiatric and forensic populations (Novaco, 1994). There is also evidence of a relationship between anger and aggression in relation to people with intellectual disabilities. For example, Lindsay and Laws (1999) reported that more than 60 per cent of individuals referred to a community-based service for challenging or offending behaviours had clinically significant anger problems.

Novaco's (1994) model is one of the most widely cited in the literature on anger and aggression. This presents aggressive behaviour as a product of the reciprocal connection between (1) the cognitive processing of environmental circumstances, (2) conjoined physiological arousal, and (3) behavioural reactions. It is this framework that has underpinned many of the anger management approaches described in this chapter.

While there is evidence of a relationship between anger and aggression, it is also important to recognise that anger as an emotional state is not necessarily required for aggression to occur (Konecni, 1975; Novaco, 1979; Zillmann, 1979). In fact, Novaco (1986) has argued that a simple way of classifying aggression is by thinking of it as occurring with or without anger. This is an important distinction, as not all of the approaches reviewed in this chapter take anger as their starting point, and it would therefore be misguided to assume that 'anger management' will be an appropriate positive programming approach in all cases of aggressive behaviour.

Assessment and functional analysis

As with any other intervention strategy, positive programming should be based on a full functional analysis of the individual's behaviour (La Vigna, Willis and Donnellan, 1989). It is only when the *function* of a behaviour is understood that the appropriate approach can be taken to change the behaviour, and this applies equally to positive programming approaches.

We will not present a full discussion on functional analysis in this chapter, as there are several excellent texts on this topic (eg O'Neil et al, 1990; Sigafoos et al, 2003; Cooper et al, 1987). However, for the purposes of this chapter it is perhaps helpful to reiterate the key aims of functional analysis, which are to:

- accurately describe the behaviours of concern

- identify general and more immediate factors that predict the occurrence (and non-occurrence) of the behaviour

- identify potential functions of the behaviour in relation to the consequences that are maintaining it

- develop summary statements describing relationships amongst these variables

(O'Neill et al, 1997)

To achieve this, a detailed assessment is required, based on multiple sources of information (interviews, direct observation, questionnaire measures, analogue conditions) and following a process of hypothesis development, testing and refinement (Royal College of Psychiatry, British Psychological Society/College of Speech and Language Therapists, 2007).

In relation to positive programming, it is imperative that the assessment provides a detailed understanding of the person's current repertoire of skills, as the ultimate goal of positive programming will be to build upon and enhance what the person is currently able to do. In this context, there are certain areas within the assessment that are particularly salient to consider:

Communication skills
- What expressive and receptive communication skills does the person have in his/her current repertoire?

- How does the person communicate his/her basic needs, likes/dislikes, preferences etc?

Intellectual skills
- What is the person's level of intellectual disability?

- Is the person able to show any insight into his/her difficulties?

- Is the person able to articulate his/her thoughts/feelings?

Coping skills

- Does the person always respond with aggressive behaviours or does s/he already have some other skills in his/her repertoire? If so, what variables predict whether the person uses these skills versus engaging in aggressive behaviour?

- Does the person's environment enable him/her to use these skills effectively (eg if the person can express basic needs through Makaton, are any of his/her carers trained in Makaton)?

- Have any positive programming interventions been tried before? Were they successful? If not, what were the reasons for lack of success?

The key question that needs to be asked in determining whether an intervention plan needs to include positive programming is, 'Could any of the variables identified in the functional analysis potentially be reduced or eliminated if the individual was taught new skills?' This question should be answered in relation to all of the variables that are identified in the summary statements for a given behaviour.

If the answer to the above question is 'yes', then a related question is whether positive programming is the most effective or appropriate way to achieve this; it is important to note that this may not always be the case. For example, if crowded shops are the main setting event for a person's aggression, they could be taught relaxation skills to cope in this environment. However, an antecedent intervention that involves choosing quiet times of day to go to the shops may be a more effective and efficient intervention in this instance.

To illustrate the importance of a detailed assessment, we will present two case examples. Both individuals engaged in aggressive behaviour which were similar in terms of their functions, but the context of their behaviour varied greatly.

'Josephine'

Josephine presented with aggressive behaviour (verbally abusing staff, throwing objects, and punching). Her functional analysis identified that the key antecedent for this was prompts from staff to undertake personal care tasks, and that the behaviour resulted in staff withdrawing, suggesting the aggression was maintained by demand avoidance. In addition, through asking the questions relating to her communication skills noted above, the following facts were established:

- Josephine had a severe intellectual disability and limited ability to articulate her thoughts and feelings

- Josephine experienced extreme sensitivity to touch and found this very difficult to cope with

- Josephine was extremely competent in the use of Makaton, but none of the carers in the current setting had ever received any training in its use

- Josephine had limited expressive communication skills but reasonable receptive communication skills

'Loui'

Loui presented topographically similar aggressive behaviour, and the functional analysis identified very similar functions to Josephine's behaviour – his aggressive behaviour was triggered when staff prompted him to undertake personal care tasks and this led to staff withdrawing, which maintained the behaviour through demand avoidance. However, the questions listed above led to a very different formulation:

- Loui had a mild intellectual disability (Full Scale IQ of 68) and very good expressive communication skills

- Loui was able to identify that he becomes angry when staff prompt him with personal care tasks, and stated that this was because 'they treat me like a child'

- Loui was also able to say that he became 'wound up' on waking in the morning, before staff tried to support him with his personal care. In the past, staff had given Loui the chance to carry out personal care without support, but he found this too difficult and his standard of personal hygiene deteriorated

In view of this contextual information, positive programming approaches were implemented for both Josephine and Loui, but the choice of approach varied considerably. We will return to these case examples later in the chapter.

Assessing internal processes

As positive programming involves teaching skills to enhance the individual's *internal* control over his/her behaviour, it is also important to attend to internal processes in an assessment. This is particularly relevant for cognitive behavioural approaches, where the person's thoughts (cognitions) and emotions are the focus of intervention.

It is accepted within the functional analytic approach that cognitions are a legitimate focus of analysis. Jones et al (1997) present case examples of how an understanding of cognitive processes can enrich the assessment and add to the potential intervention options. One case involved a 20 year old woman with mild intellectual disabilities who presented aggressive behaviour. Through the process of functional analysis, it was identified that the behaviour was maintained by staff attention. However, further discussion with the woman identified a number of relevant thought processes – she believed she was personally responsible for the resignation of a favourite staff member, and she was jealous of an older sister who had recently been married. From this wider perspective, the options for intervention become broader and add context (and meaning) to the relationship initially identified between aggressive behaviour and staff attention.

Writing on from a cognitive behavioural therapy (CBT) perspective, Black et al (1997) suggest that key issues to address in an assessment of an individual are (1) the nature of the anger problem; (2) motivation for treatment; and (3) ability to engage in treatment. We will briefly discuss each of these in turn.

Nature of the anger problem

Attention should be paid to the service user's own narrative around their anger, and the thoughts and beliefs that underpin this narrative. The physiological arousal which the person experiences should also be identified, as should a description of the person's behaviour when experiencing anger. This is particularly important as there may be a mismatch between objective data and what the person him/herself reports about his/her behaviour.

Motivation for treatment

Cognitive behaviour therapy requires active involvement from the service user, so therefore acceptance that there is a 'problem', and motivation to address the 'problem', is an important consideration. Willner (2005) points out that motivational interviewing techniques (Millner and Rollnick, 1991) have shown to be effective in increasing motivation in non-intellectually disabled clinical populations, and suggests that consideration should be given to using some of these techniques to support individuals with intellectual disability to develop motivation to take action.

Ability to engage in treatment

It is recognised in the literature on CBT that a number of skills and abilities are prerequisite for successful engagement in CBT. Willner (2005) summarises these as (1) an ability to distinguish between antecedent events and associated cognitions and emotions; (2) an ability to recognise that cognitions mediate the effect or events on emotions; and (3) an ability to engage in the process of questioning the accuracy of cognitions.

There are now a number of assessment formats for assessing an individual's ability to understand the basic concepts required to engage in CBT. For example, Dagnan and Chadwick (1997) put forward an assessment framework for exploring the key concepts required to engage in this approach, and there is growing evidence that some people with intellectual disabilities do possess the necessary prerequisite skills.

Standardised measures of anger and aggression

If it is established through functional analysis that there is an underlying anger regulation problem involved in the person's aggressive behaviour, a number of standardised measures have been developed that can add value to the behavioural assessment. Some of these are adaptations of well-established tools used in the adult mental health/forensic field, while others have been developed specifically for use with people with intellectual disability. Taylor and Novaco (2005) provide a detailed review of these tools, including information on their psychometric properties.

The most well known are probably the State Trait Anger Inventory (STAXI) by Spielberg (1996), the Novaco Anger Scales (NAS) by Novaco (1994; 2003) and the Provocation Inventory (PI) by Novaco (1975, 1988). These are service user-rated measures and, as such, the wording has been adapted for people with intellectual disability from their original use in the mental health field.

In addition to these measures, there are several staff-rated measures that can be used. These include the Ward Anger Ratings Scale (Novaco, 1994) and the Profile of Anger Coping Skills (PACS) (Willner et al, 2005). The PACS was developed in response to a lack of available instruments for assessing either the coping skills an individual has at their disposal or the extent to which those skills are actually used in the person's day to day life. A key carer is first asked to identify three situations in which the service user often displays anger. They are then asked to rate the extent to which the service user is able to use each of eight coping strategies in that specific situation (these eight strategies are then taught during the group intervention).

It is important to note that a potential limitation to all these measures is that they are informant-based. While this is an essential aspect of any assessment, it is important that this is supplemented with objective measures of the frequency, intensity and duration of *actual incidents* of aggression. Some aggressive behaviour can be high intensity but low frequency (which can make the task of accurately recalling specific details difficult when done retrospectively). Aggressive behaviour can also create strong emotional responses from carers, and this can potentially influence the perception, and subsequent reporting, of incidents.

Positive programming approaches

Functionally equivalent skills

As noted earlier, functionally equivalent skills involves teaching specific skills that serve the same function as the problem behaviour and thereby reduce the need to engage in the behaviour. One of the most widely reported variations of this approach is functional communication training (FCT) (Carr and Durand, 1985). Functional communication training is based on the notion that challenging behaviours have communicative functions. The approach consists of teaching an individual to 'mand' (make a verbalisation, gesture, sign, etc) and then reinforcing the individual for this. This reinforcement then increases the manding behaviour. At the same time, whenever the person displays the challenging behaviour (instead of manding), the problem behaviour is not reinforced, ie the problem behaviour is extinguished. For example, if the results of a functional analysis suggest that the individual's behaviour is maintained by negative reinforcement (escape from demands), FCT could consist of providing brief breaks contingent on the person using a mand (eg holding up a 'break' card, or saying 'break, please'), while not providing breaks when the challenging behaviour occurs. So, the individual learns that manding provides breaks from tasks.

The literature on FCT points to two considerations that are key to success. First, the new replacement behaviour must be truly equivalent to the challenging behaviour (ie serves exactly the same function). Second, the replacement behaviour must be a more 'efficient' response than the person's challenging behaviour. If these conditions are not met, there is a risk that the replacement behaviour will not sufficiently 'compete' with the behaviour of concern and will fail to bring about change.

The FCT approach

The key procedure in an FCT approach is to successfully teach the communication skill to the individual using prompts and reinforcement. Taking an example of an individual being taught to mand for breaks from task demands, a task would be presented, then about every 15–30 seconds the individual would be prompted to mand for a break (eg make a gesture, sign, point, ask, etc). Prompts are then faded as soon as an individual begins to demonstrate occasional independent mands. When the individual mands, they are provided with a break, usually between 30 seconds and one minute. During this break, the person does preferred things. At the end of the break, the individual is prompted on task again. If the individual mands again, another break is provided, and so on. If the individual does not mand, the task continues. If the individual engages in problem behaviour during the task, they are requested to carry on with one more task before being able to request a break. The sessions usually last about 15 minutes at a time and can occur once a day.

Effectiveness

Functional communication training as an approach to teaching functionally equivalent skills has been successfully implemented across many different types of behaviours and has a good evidence base (eg Peterson et al, 2005; Bailey et al 2002; Braithwaite and Richdale, 2000; Hanley et al, 2001; Richman et al 2001; Durand, 1999; Hagopian et al, 2001; Peck et al, 1996). In a recent study, Peterson et al (2005) reported on two case studies, where the individuals were taught to mand for breaks instead of engaging in disruptive and aggressive behaviour. The training resulted in both individuals manding independently 100 per cent of the time and in challenging behaviour lessening or being eradicated altogether (as compared to baseline).

Bailey et al (2002) taught a young man to ask for social interaction from staff instead of engaging in aggressive behaviour to achieve this. Two FCT conditions were used: condition one required pointing to a picture of two people interaction (point condition), while condition two required spelling the word 'talk' on a laminated paper replica of a computer keyboard. The results were that aggressive behaviour occurred less in the point condition than in the spell condition. Also, independent requests occurred exclusively in the point condition. Follow-up data indicate maintenance of treatment for two years, and the daily use of several additional picture requests.

Braithwaite and Richdale (2000) evaluated functional communication training for the reduction of multiply controlled, self-injurious and aggressive behaviour. Treatment consisted of teaching an alternate request, while challenging behaviours were concurrently placed on extinction. Acquisition of the alternate requests was associated with a decrease to zero levels of self-injury and aggression across the two behavioural outcomes, which was maintained when a five-second delay was implemented.

Mirenda's (1997) review, which included the above studies on FCT, concluded that FCT ranged from 'fairly effective' to 'highly effective'. An advantage to FCT is that it typically results in very rapid and durable reductions in challenging behaviour.

However, a potential limitation is that individuals can sometimes request continuous reinforcement once they have been taught to mand. Using the example described above, individuals who are taught to mand to receive breaks may request breaks whenever a demand is delivered, so that they are continuously 'on a break'. Thus, although problem behaviour may be dramatically decreased, so has time spent engaged in tasks. However, introducing varying dimensions of reinforcement for engaging in a task can resolve this issue. For example, you could alter the 'quality' of the break when the individual mands for this. So, when the person mands for a break without having engaged in any of the task, they receive a very short break and no preferred activities during that break. However, if they have engaged in the task for a short while and then mand for a break, they receive a longer, better quality break with preferred activities in that break. This encourages only manding for a break after completing the task or part of the task. Of course, if they engage in the challenging behaviour in order to receive a break, then the presentation of the task continues until the person mands for a break. This may give rise to a temporary 'extinction burst' of behaviour where the person may escalate their behaviour in order to achieve a break. Extinction bursts, however, are usually short-lived and eventually dissipate. However, the fact that the person is being taught another skill (manding) to achieve their needs acts to combat the occurrence of an extinction burst and eventually reduces/eradicates their reliance on challenging behaviour to get their needs met.

Also, when using FCT with escape-maintained problem behaviours (as in the example here), the literature suggests the importance of including positive reinforcement contingencies with the FCT (DeLeon et al, 2001; Golonka et al, 2000; Harding et al, 1999; Lalli et al, 1999; Piazza et al, 1997). An example could be the provision of reinforcement other than the natural reinforcement that would be gained from manding, such as staff praise, activity rewards, token systems, etc.

Case example of FCT

Earlier in the chapter we presented Josephine – a lady with severe intellectual disability and limited communication skills but good use of Makaton (despite the fact that staff currently supporting her had no training in this). Her behaviour was triggered by prompts from staff to undertake personal care tasks which resulted in staff withdrawing, the function therefore being demand avoidance. Based on the functional analysis, FCT was implemented as part of a wider intervention package.

Josephine was taught to use Makaton signs to indicate when she was feeling pain. The staff were taught to recognise the Makaton signs and respond consistently to this. This involved staff stopping the personal care task for five minutes, then using Makaton to ask Josephine if it was ok to try again. Josephine could already indicate 'yes' and 'no' through Makaton, and staff were trained to recognise these signs. If Josephine indicated 'no', staff would give her a further five minutes before trying again.

Alternative/functionally related skills

The defining feature of functionally related skills is that they produce a similar, but not exactly, the same outcome as the challenging behaviour. As noted earlier, this could involve teaching a person to make a drink for themselves rather than teaching them to request a drink (the latter being a functionally equivalent skill). The outcome of this is the same (the person gets a drink), but the process is different (the person is not asking someone else to do it). However, both achieve the goal of reducing the need to engage in challenging behaviour to achieve the desired outcome (a drink).

There are several examples of functionally related behaviours in published case studies (eg McClean et al, 2005; Eccles and Pitchford, 1997). For example, an individual responded to teasing from others with screaming and aggression. The individual was taught the skill of making assertive statements designed to stop teasing. The individual was taught to say, 'Please don't say that, I don't like it.' Other examples could include teaching someone to make themselves a sandwich when hungry, to leave a noisy environment when they need to, or to ask for some help when they need it. Individuals may engage in a range of difficult behaviours because they don't have the skills themselves to do anything different, and also because environments are often set up where the individual has no control.

Another strategy for teaching functionally related behaviours is teaching rule-governed behaviours. Here, individuals who enjoy rules and work well within a rule-based environment can be taught to follow the rules as an alternative to engaging in challenging behaviour. For example, a young man found it difficult not to hit out at his younger sister in the car. A number of other types of interventions had failed. As the young man always liked having rules in his life, a new rule became that he must not hit his sister in the car, as this was very dangerous. This eradicated the behaviour immediately (see LaVigna, Willis and Donnellan, 1989).

The teaching of social skills could be placed under the heading of functionally related skills. Social skills problems are pervasive among individuals with intellectual disabilities (Siperstein, 1992). As challenging behaviours, such as aggression, can greatly effect the development and display of appropriate social skills (Duncan, et al, 1999), social skills deficits in people with intellectual disabilities are an important concern for clinicians. When developing interventions, clinicians need to pay attention to social skills deficits as they are essential for successful social interactions and relationships, which are necessary for healthy emotional functioning and psychological adjustment (Guralnick, 1986) and also for general day-to-day functioning.

Cognitive behavioural approaches to anger and aggression

Cognitive behavioural approaches have increasingly been applied to people with intellectual disabilities, and the literature on the effectiveness of this approach has greatly increased over the last decade. It is helpful to view the literature on cognitive behavioural approaches as being underpinned by two approaches – a cognitive *deficits* approach and a cognitive *distortions* approach (Kendall, 1985). The former relates to deficits in the processes by which information is acquired and proceeded, the latter relates to distortions in the content of thoughts, assumptions and beliefs.

Cognitive behavioural approaches – addressing cognitive deficits

A very prominent technique here is self-management. This is a cognitive behavioural technique that is often used with people with intellectual disabilities for problem behaviours. Self-management (Smith, 1990) has been defined as 'obtaining the skills involved to change one's own behaviour, and providing intervention for oneself'. Self-management includes a range of techniques: *self-monitoring, self-instruction, self-evaluation, self-reinforcement, relaxation and social problem-solving*.

Self-instructional training (SIT)

This is a useful self-management technique and came out of the work of Vygotsky (1962), in which language exerts control over behaviour. With SIT, the clinician first models the statements to be used, then the individual is encouraged to make overt self-statements, and finally the individual is encouraged gradually to make the statements covert. The self-statements could include self-monitoring, self-evaluation and self-reinforcement statements.

Relaxation

This is another self-management technique and can be a useful way for individuals to learn to cope with their 'symptoms'. There is a range of relaxation techniques that are widely used, but the main relaxation training that tends to be adapted comes from Ost (1987). Whichever technique is chosen, it is important that relaxation should be presented as a skill to be learned through repeated practice, with the aim being not to just relax in the chair at home, but also to be able to use relaxation during everyday activities and when needed.

Social problem-solving

This is another self-management technique, where individuals learn to discover an effective course of action to deal with everyday problems by generating and evaluating potential solutions (D'Zurilla and Goldfried, 1971). In people with intellectual disabilities, this technique has been used primarily in the treatment of anger and challenging behaviour (Willner, 2005). It is often one part of a cognitive behavioural intervention package.

Evidence base

Whitaker's (2001) review showed that self-monitoring alone brought about large decreases in the frequency of inappropriate behaviours, which were maintained at six-month follow-ups. Similar benefits have been described when service users were taught to reinforce themselves appropriately, either verbally or with pictures or coins (Williams and Jones, 1997).

Self-instructional training

Lancioni et al (1997, 2001) and Embregts (2000, 2002) carried out studies with people with mild to moderate intellectual disabilities. They found that the techniques required an adequate level of verbal ability, so may not work well with those less able. However, simplifying instructions (Williams and Jones, 1997) or adding picture prompts to verbal instruction (Lancioni et al, 1998) can achieve success with less able individuals.

Relaxation
A number of studies have reported that relaxation can be effective in decreasing anger and anxiety in people with mild or moderate intellectual disabilities (eg Morrison and Lindsay, 1997; To and Chan, 2000; Whitaker, 2001).

Social problem-solving
This technique has been evaluated in its use alone by Benson (1986). She compared self-instruction, problem-solving and relaxation as single interventions used alone with a package of all three, and found no differences.

Case example of cognitive behavioural self-management
Earlier in the chapter we presented Loui, a man with a mild intellectual disability (Full Scale IQ of 68) and very good expressive communication skills. Loui presented aggressive behaviour and the functional analysis identified that the behaviour was triggered when staff prompted him to undertake personal care tasks. This led to staff withdrawing, which maintained the behaviour through demand avoidance.

Due to Loui's level of intellectual ability and his communication skills, a range of self-management techniques were identified that would be appropriate to help him overcome and cope with the difficult situation. These are outlined below:

1. Problem-solving
The first part of the intervention was to sit down with Loui and discuss the best way to manage the situation. It was important that Loui was fully in control of this problem-solving and that he 'owned' the potential solutions. With staff input, Loui came up with the rest of the intervention (below).

2. Self-instructional training
Following the problem-solving above, Loui came up with a few statements that could help him manage staff prompting him around self-care. Because the problem-solving had occurred first, Loui was fully aware why staff needed to prompt him. Loui was then helped to learn and remember the self-instruction statements to help him cope with staff prompting him to around personal care. These were:

- 'staff are just trying to help me'
- 'they are helping me remember to do it'
- 'stay calm and relaxed'

3. Relaxation – for the morning time, prior to getting up
Loui also problem-solved that he would like to be able to feel more relaxed in the morning time, prior to personal care. He was therefore taught relaxation

techniques to help him cope with feeling wound up in the morning. He was taught a brief number of techniques that would only take ten minutes to complete. The self-instructional statement of 'stay calm and relaxed' was also taught within the relaxation training.

Cognitive behavioural approaches – addressing cognitive distortions

Anger treatment approaches are usually based on the model by Novaco (1975) and Black et al (1997). This model views anger as an emotion with three components – physiological, behavioural and cognitive – which are addressed in therapy by, respectively, relaxation, coping skills and cognitive restructuring. So, anger treatment models are not pure cognitive distortion models – they usually combine both self-management and cognitive distortion methods.

Behavioural methods and, to some extent, anger management methods (self-management techniques) do little to address the emotional problems of individuals with intellectual disabilities, and many studies demonstrate that emotional problems are more prevalent in this group (Prosser, 1999). So, there can be no justification for denying psychotherapy to those clients who have the necessary cognitive skills (Dagnan and Chadwick, 1997).

It is now widely accepted by clinical psychologists who work with people with intellectual disabilities that, with appropriate modification, the methods and models of therapy that are used in able populations can also be applied to people who are less intellectually able (Willner, 2006). Equally, it is recognised that not all clients with intellectual disabilities will be suitable for therapy (Willner, 2006). A decision whether or not to offer cognitive therapy should be derived from a comprehensive formulation and should not be based solely on a client's performance on cognitive tests (Willner, 2006).

Willner (2005) found that the research suggests that CBT can only be used with more able individuals where individuals need to possess the necessary cognitive skills. This has led to therapeutic disdain and 'can we overcome this difficulty of cognitive deficits and teach the necessary cognitive skills to be ready for CBT?' Most clinicians believe that the answer to this is 'yes' and that we need to use more ingenious and creative CBT methods to overcome this difficulty (eg simplifying language, using pictures, proceeding slowly, extensive rehearsal, supporting homework, providing aides memoir and using carers for assistance). Much can be done to increase accessibility without undermining the underlying principles of cognitive therapy (Stenfert-Kroese et al, 1997). Also, Dagnan and Chadwick (1997) found that a substantial proportion of individuals with mild to moderate intellectual disabilities possessed the necessary cognitive skills for CBT.

Evidence base

Lindsay (1999) reviewed cognitive therapy with people with intellectual disabilities referred for anger. The anger treatment was: cognitive reframing of anger-provoking situations; arousal reduction through relaxation; and acquisition of coping skills using simplified versions of standard procedures (from Black et al, 1997). As mentioned above, although a large part of the treatment was focused on cognitive distortion work, there were also elements of anger management approaches (eg relaxation, coping skills).

There is evidence of positive outcomes from this approach from two randomised controlled trials from Taylor et al (2002) and Willner et al (2002), where individuals who received treatment were compared to waiting list control groups. However, both studies relied on outcome data based on self-report (both clients and staff) and no behavioural data was reported on.

Generally, there is little evidence for 'pure' cognitive approaches. It is the non-cognitive methods (eg self-management techniques and behavioural methods) that have a much more robust evidence base. As mentioned above, all of the cognitive distortion work is paired with cognitive deficit work, ie cognitive work *and* self-management work. Willner (2005) reports that even though there is good evidence, including RCTs, for cognitive work from a range of studies, there is little evidence as yet for the effectiveness of cognitive therapy by itself with people with intellectual disabilities. So, it remains to be robustly shown that the cognitive components of anger treatment packages are effective.

Barriers to positive programming

As with any other component of a comprehensive intervention package, there are a number of potential barriers to the successful implementation of positive programming. Failure to identify and address these from the outset can lead to interventions being incorrectly labelled as unsuccessful.

Willner (2005) suggests a useful framework for understanding barriers to intervention and separates barriers that stem from service user variables from those that stem from external variables. Willner (2005) further classifies the 'external variables' as (a) the setting/context of delivering the intervention; (b) the therapist/person delivering the intervention; and (c) the intervention itself. Willner (2005) also suggests that it can be helpful to separate the concepts of 'motivation' (being willing to engage in the intervention) and 'ability' (having the skills to engage in the intervention), and this can apply to both the service user and the external context. Although writing from a CBT perspective, Willner's framework can be usefully applied when thinking about barriers to other positive programming interventions. Here we have listed some pertinent barriers to consider under these headings:

Service user variables:
1. The person may not recognise the aggressive behaviour as a 'problem' due to the reinforcement (either positive or negative) which the behaviour provides

2. The person may have low self esteem and a poor sense of self-control

3. History of failed relationships/difficulties engaging with professionals

4. Limitations to general cognitive abilities and specific abilities such as linking thoughts → feelings → behaviour

5. Limitations to mobility, dexterity, motor skills, etc which could impact on ability to benefit from certain approaches (eg using manual signs and gestures as a replacement for aggressive behaviour)

External variables:

1. Staff/family members not understanding the intervention or the rationale for it

2. Staff/family members not having the skills to successfully implement the intervention and not being provided with adequate training

3. Inadequate resources to fully implement the intervention (eg high use of agency staff who are not familiar with the plan, low staff-to-service user ratios)

4. Interventions that are developed in 'unnatural' settings and fail to generalise in the environment where behaviour is actually problematic.

5. Interventions being delivered without any adaptations, creating a mismatch with the individual's abilities

Overcoming barriers

As part of a comprehensive assessment, it is important to attend to barriers so that appropriate solutions can be identified. Some of these solutions will involve preliminary work with the service user, carers/family members or adaptations to the intervention itself before it is delivered. From our review of the literature, we have listed some of the adaptations made to various positive programming approaches:

1. In the literature on CBT, there are many examples of adaptations to the basic approach which include changing language to be more basic and understandable, using visual materials, providing short but frequent sessions (eg 30 minutes twice a week rather than one hour once a week), and building in extensive rehearsal into sessions (Willner, 2005). It has also been suggested (Rose et al, 2000) that anger management training should be more tailored so that it is specific to the situation/s in which the individual has problems with anger/aggression. Here, the individual would learn how to manage situations specifically rather than managing anger generally. Rose et al (2005) also found that outcome following anger management group work is improved if the individual is accompanied by a member of their care staff.

2. Recruiting carers to support the individual in sessions and/or supporting the individual to practice in between sessions.

3. Thorough training for staff/family members on the intervention, with a focus on developing an accurate understanding of the intervention (and the rationale for it), and ensuring competency that mediators achieve competency in delivering the intervention.

4. 'Pre-therapy' work with the individual to develop the skills required to successfully engage in positive programming (if the skills are not already part of the person's repertoire). Examples of this could include educative work on the link between thoughts and feelings before cognitive behavioural intervention (eg Dagnan and Chadwick, 1997), or input to enhance a person's verbal expressive skills before training in the use of vocalisations as a replacement behaviour in FCT (eg Durand and Carr, 1991).

5. Combining the positive programming intervention with other strategies to enhance the impact of the intervention. For example, if a person is taught to say 'help' when struggling with a task, as an alternative to becoming verbally aggressive, the person could be given reinforcement for correctly saying 'help' in the initial stages of the intervention (eg verbal praise, access to a desired tangible, etc).

6. Ensuring that positive programming takes place in natural settings and targets the situations that are specific issues for the individual. For example, if a person is taught to make his own drinks as a functionally related alternative to shouting at staff (who then make drinks for him), then the teaching should take place in the setting(s) where this happens (eg the day centre, the person's home).

Conclusions

In this chapter, we have reviewed different approaches to positive programming. The underpinning principle of all these approaches is that teaching new skills to people who engage in aggressive behaviour can displace the need to engage in the behaviour in the first place: the key to selecting the appropriate intervention being an accurate assessment and functional analysis of the person's behaviour. Although the application of CBT approaches have developed as a significant approach to positive programming, this is by no means the *only* approach available, and we have presented favourable reviews of other approaches in this chapter, particularly FCT.

We would conclude that consideration should *always* be given to positive programming when developing an intervention package, and that failure to do so would be difficult to justify. If individuals who engage in aggressive behaviour are not given the opportunity to develop skills that reduce the need for such behaviour, then there will be an ongoing reliance on external management of behaviour, which often has significant implications for their quality of life.

References

Ager, A and O'May, F (2001) Issues in the definition and implementation of 'best practices' for staff delivery of interventions for challenging behaviour. *Journal of Intellectual and Developmental Disability*, 26, 3, 243–256.

Bailey, J, McComas, J J, Benavides, C and Lovascz, C (2002) Functional assessment in a residential setting: identifying an effective communicative replacement response for aggressive behaviour. *Journal of Developmental and Physical Disabilities*, 14, 353–369.

Baumeister, A A, Sevin, J A and King, B H (1998) Neuroleptics. In S Reiss and M G Aman (Eds) *Psychotropic Medications and Developmental Disabilities: The International Consensus Handbook*. Columbus, OH: Ohio State University.

Black, L, Cullen, C and Novaco, R W (1997) Anger assessment for people with mild learning disabilities in secure settings. In B Stenfert Kroese, D Dagnan and K Loumidis (Eds) *Cognitive-behaviour therapy for people with learning disabilities*. London: Routledge.

Royal College of Psychiatry, British Psychological Society, Royal College of Speech and Language Therapists (2007) *Challenging Behaviour: A Unified Approach*. London: Royal College of Psychiatrists.

Braithwaite, K L and Richdale, A L (2000) Functional communication training to replace challenging behaviours across two behavioural outcomes. *Behavioural Interventions*, 15, 21–36.

Brylewski, J and Duggan, L (2000) Antipsychotic medication for challenging behaviour in people with learning disability. *Journal of Intellectual Disability Research*, 43, 360–371.

Carr, E G and Durand, V M (1985) Reducing behaviour problems through functional communication training. *Journal of Applied Behaviour Analysis*, 18, 111–126.

Cooper, J O, Heron, T E and Heward, W L (1987) *Applied Behaviour Analysis*. Upper Saddle River, NJ: Prentice-Hall.

D'Zurilla, T J and Goldfried, M R (1971) Problem-solving and behaviour modification. *Journal of Abnormal Psychology*, 78, 107–126.

Dagnan, D and Chadwick, P (1997) Cognitive-behaviour therapy for people with learning disabilities: assessment and intervention. In B Stenfert Kroese, D Dagnan and K Loumidis (Eds) *Cognitive-behaviour therapy for people with learning disabilities*. London: Routledge.

DeLeon, I G, Neidert, P, Anders, B M and Rodriguez-Catter, V (2001) Choices between positive and negative reinforcement during treatment for escape-maintained behavior. *Journal of Applied Behavior Analysis*, 34, 521–525.

Desrochers, M N, Hile, M G and Williams-Moseley, T L (1997) Survey of functional assessment procedures used with t individuals who display mental retardation and severe behavioural problems. *American Journal of Mental Retardation*, 101, 535–546.

Duncan, D, Matson, J L, Bamburg, J W, Cherry, K E and Buckley, T (1999) The relationship of self-injurious behaviour and aggression to social skills in persons with severe and profound learning disability. *Research in Developmental Disabilities*, 20, 441–448.

Durand, V M (1999) Functional communication training using assistive devices: Recruiting natural communities of reinforcement. *Journal of Applied Behavior Analysis*, 32, 247–267.

Durand, V M and Carr, E G (1991) Functional communication training to reduce challenging behaviour: maintenance and application in new settings. *Journal of Applied Behaviour Analysis*, 24, 251–264.

Embregts, P J C M (2000) Effectiveness of video feedback and self-management on inappropriate social behaviour of youth with mild mental retardation. *Research in Developmental Disabilities*, 21, 409–423.

Embregts, P J C M (2002) Effects of video feedback on social behaviour of young people with mild intellectual disability and staff responses. *International Journal of Disability, Development and Education*, 49, 105–116.

Golonka, Z, Wacker, D P, Berg, W, Derby, K M, Harding, J and Peck, S (2000) Effects of escape to alone versus escape to enriched environments on adaptive and aberrant behavior. *Journal of Applied Behavior Analysis*, 33, 243–246.

Guralnick, M J (1986) *Children's social behaviour: Development, assessment and modification.* Orlando, FL: Academic Press.

Hagopian, L P, Wilson, D M and Wilder, D A (2001) Assessment and treatment of problem behavior maintained by escape from attention and access to tangible items. *Journal of Applied Behavior Analysis*, 34, 229–232.

Hanley, G P, Iwata, B A and Thompson, R H (2001) Reinforcement schedule thinning following treatment with functional communication training. *Journal of Applied Behaviour Analysis*, 34, 17–38.

Harding, J W, Wacker, D P, Berg, W K, Cooper, L J, Asmus, J, Mlela, K and Muller, J (1999) An analysis of choice making in the assessment of young children with severe behavior problems. *Journal of Applied Behavior Analysis*, 32, 63–82.

Horner, R H, Dunlap, G, Koegel, R L, Carr, E G, Sailor, W, Anderson, J, Albin, R W and O'Neil, R E (1990) Towards a technology of 'nonaversive' behavioural support. *Journal of Association for Persons with Severe Handicap*, 15, 3, 125–132.

Jones, R S, Miller, B, Williams, H and Goldthorp, J (1997) Theoretical and practical issues in cognitive behavioural approaches for people with learning disabilities: a radical behavioural perspective. In B Stenfert Kroese, D Dagnan and K Loumidis (Eds) *Cognitive-behaviour therapy for people with learning disabilities.* London: Routledge.

Kendall, P C (1985) Toward a cognitive-behavioural model of child psychopathology and a critique of related interventions. *Journal of Abnormal Child Psychology*, 13, 357–372.

Konecni, V J (1975) The mediation of aggressive behaviour: arousal levels versus anger and cognitive labelling. *Journal of Personality and Social Psychology*, 32, 706–712.

Lakin, K C, Hill, B K, Hauber, F A, Bruininks, R H and Heal, L W (1983) New admissions to a national sample of public residential facilities. *American Journal on Mental Retardation*, 88, 13–20.

Lalli, J S, Vollmer, T R, Progar, P R, Wright, C, Borrero, J, Daniel, D, et al (1999) Competition between positive and negative reinforcement in the treatment of escape behavior. *Journal of Applied Behavior Analysis*, 32, 285–296.

Lancioni, G E, O'Reilly, M F, Oliva, D and Pellegrino, A (1997) Persons with multiple disabilities acquiring independent task performance through a self-operated verbal instruction system. *Irish Journal of Psychology*, 18, 419–429.

Lancioni, G E, O'Reilly, M F and Oliva, D (2001) Self-operated verbal instructions for people with intellectual and visual disabilities: Using instruction clusters after task acquisition. *International Journal of Disability, Development and Education*, 48, 303–312.

Lancioni, G E, Van den Hof, E, Furniss, F, Boelens, H, Rocha, N and Seedhouse, P (1998) A computer-based system providing pictorial instructions and prompts to promote task performance in persons with severe developmental disabilities. *Behavioural Interventions*, 13, 111–122.

La Vigna, G W, Willis, T J and Donnellan, A M (1989) The role of positive programming in behavioural treatment. In E Cipani (Ed) *The Treatment of Severe Behaviour Disorders: Behaviour Analysis Approaches.* Washington, DC: American Association on Mental Retardation.

Lennox, D B, Miltenberger, R G, Spengler, P and Efranian, N (1988) Decelerative treatment practices with persons who have mental retardation: a review of five years of the literature. *American Journal on Mental Retardation*, 92, 492–501.

Lindsay, W R (1999) Cognitive therapy. *Psychologist*, 12, 238–241.

Lindsay, W R and Law, J (1999) *Outcome evaluation of 161 people with learning disabilities in Tayside who have offending or challenging behaviour.* Paper presented at BABCP 27th Annual Conference, University of Bristol, Bristol, 14–17 July 1999.

Matson, J L, Bamburg, J W, Mayville, E A, Pinkston, J, Bielecki, J, Kuhn, D, et al (2000) Psychopharmacology and mental retardation: a 10 year review (1990–1999). *Research in Developmental Disabilities*, 21, 263–296.

Millner, W R and Rollnick, S (1991) *Motivational Interviewing: Preparing People to Change Addictive Behaviour.* New York: Guilford.

Mirenda, P (1997) Supporting individuals with challenging behaviour through functional communication training and AAC: Research review. *Augmentative and Alternative Communication*, 13, 207–225.

Morrison, F J and Lindsay, W R (1997) Reductions in self-assessed anxiety and concurrent improvement in cognitive performance in adults who have moderate intellectual disabilities. *Journal of Applied Research in Intellectual Disabilities*, 10, 33–40.

Novaco, R W (1975) *Anger control: The development and evaluation of an experimental treatment.* Lexington: D C Health.

Novaco, R W (1994) Anger as a risk factor for violence among the mentally disordered. In J Monahan and H J Streadman (Eds) *Violence and Disorder: Developments in Risk Assessment*, pp 21–59. Chicago: University of Chicago Press.

Novaco, R W (1988) Novaco Provocation Inventory. In M Hersen and A S Bellack (Eds) *Dictionary of Behavioural Assessment Techniques.* New York: Pergamon.

Novaco, R W (1986) Anger as a clinical and social problem. In R Blanchard, and C Blanchard (Eds) *Advances in the Study of Aggression*, Vol 2. New York: Academic Press.

Novaco, R W (1979) The cognitive regulation of anger and stress. In P C Kendall and S G Hollon (Eds) *Cognitive Behavioural Interventions.* New York: Academic Press.

O'Neil, R E, Horner, R H, Albin, R W, Storey, K and Sprague, J R (1990) *Functional Analysis of Problem Behaviour: A Practical Assessment Guide.* Pacific Grove, CA: Brooks/Cole.

Ost, L G (1987) Applied relaxation: description of a coping technique and review of controlled studies. *Behaviour Research and Therapy*, 25, 397–410.

Peck, S M, Wacker, D P, Berg, W K, Cooper, L J, Brown, K A, Richman, D, et al (1996) Choice-making treatment of young children's severe behavior problems. *Journal of Applied Behavior Analysis*, 29, 263–290.

Peterson, S M P, Caniglia, C, Royster, A J, Macfarlane, E, Plowman, K, Baird, S J and Wu, N (2005) Blending functional communication training and choice making to improve task engagement and decrease problem behaviour. *Educational Psychology*, 25, 257–274.

Prosser, H (1999) An invisible morbidity? *Psychologist*, 12, 234–237.

Piazza, C C, Fisher, W W, Hanley, G P, Remic, M L, Contrucci, S A and Aitken, T (1997) The use of positive and negative reinforcement in the treatment of escape maintained destructive behavior. *Journal of Applied Behavior Analysis*, 30, 279–298.

Richman, D M, Wacker, D P and Winborn, L (2001) Response efficiency during functional communication training: Effects of effort on response allocation. *Journal of Applied Behaviour Analysis*, 34, 73–76.

Rose, J (2002) *An investigation into factors associated with the efficacy of interventions for anger.* Paper presented at 2nd Seattle Club Conference on Research in Intellectual Disabilities, Birmingham, UK. December 2002.

Rose, J, Loftus, M, Flint, B and Carey, L (2005) Factors associated with the efficacy of a group intervention for anger in people with intellectual disabilities. *British Journal of Clinical Psychology*, 44, 305–317.

Rose, J, West, C and Clifford, D (2000) Group interventions for anger in people with intellectual disabilities. *Research in Developmental Disabilities*, 21, 171–181.

Scotti, J R, Evans, I M, Meyer, L H and Walker, P (1991) A meta-analysis of intervention research with problem behaviour: treatment validity and standards of practice. *American Journal on Mental Retardation,* 96, 233–256.

Sigafoos, J, Arthur, M and O'Reilly, M (2003) *Challenging behaviour and developmental disability.* Philadelphia: Whurr Ltd.

Smith, M D (1990) *Autism and life in the community: Successful interventions for behavioural challenges.* Baltimore, MD: Paul H Brookes.

Spielberg, C D (1996) *State-trait anger expression inventory professional manual.* Odessa, FL: Psychological Assessment Resources Inc.

Stenfert Kroese, B, Dagnan, D and Loumidis, K (1997) *Cognitive-behaviour therapy for people with learning disabilities.* London: Routledge.

Talkington, L W, Hall, S and Altman, R (1971) Communication deficits and aggression in the mentally retarded. *American Journal of Mental Deficiency*, 76, 233– 237.

Taylor, J L (2002) A review of the assessment and treatment of anger and aggression in offenders with intellectual disability. *Journal of Intellectual Disability Research*, 46, 57–73.

Taylor, J L and Novaco, R W (2005) *Anger treatment for people with developmental disabilities: A theory, evidence, and manual based approach.* London: John Wiley and Sons.

Taylor, J L, Novaco, R W, Gillmer, B T and Robertson, A (2004) Treatment of anger and aggression. In W R Lindsey, J L Taylor and P Sturmey (Eds) *Offenders with developmental disabilities* (pp 201–219). Chichester: John Wiley and Sons.

Taylor, J L, Novaco, R W, Gillmer, B and Thorne, I (2002) Cognitive-behavioural treatment of anger intensity among offenders with intellectual disabilities. *Journal of Applied Research in Intellectual Disabilities*, 15, 151–165.

To, M Y C and Chan, S (2000) Evaluating the effectiveness of progressive muscle relaxation in reducing the aggressive behaviours of mentally handicapped patients. *Archives of Psychiatric Nursing*, 14, 39–46.

Vygotsky, L S (1962) Thought and language. New York: Wiley.

Whitaker, S (2001) Anger control for people with learning disabilities: a critical review. *Behavioural and Cognitive Psychotherapy*, 29, 277–293.

Williams, H and Jones, R S P (1997) Teaching cognitive self-regulation of independence and emotional control skills. In B Stenfert Kroese, D Dagnan and K Loumidis (Eds) *Cognitive-behaviour Therapy for People with Learning Disabilities*. London: Routledge.

Willner, P (2006) Readiness for cognitive therapy in people with intellectual disabilities. *Journal of Applied Research in Intellectual Disabilities*, 19, 5–16.

Willner, P (2005) The effectiveness of psychotherapeutic interventions for people with learning disabilities: a critical review. *Journal of Intellectual Disability Research*, 49, 73–85.

Willner, P, Jones, J, Tams, R and Green, G (2002) A randomised controlled trial of the efficacy of a cognitive-behavioural anger management group for clients with learning disabilities. *Journal of Applied Research in Intellectual Disabilities*, 15, 224–235.

Wu, N (2005) Blending functional communication training and choice making to improve task engagement and decrease problem behaviour. *Educational Psychology*, 25, 257–274.

Zillmann, D (1979) *Anger and Aggression*. New York: Erlbaum Associates.

Chapter 12

Restraint Reduction

David Leadbetter

> *'Whether you think you can do it*
> *Or, whether you think you can't do it.*
> *You're probably right'*
> (Chinese proverb)

Introduction

Once upon a time, in a university far, far away, a good fairy appeared to a researcher and granted him a pot of gold. She said, 'Put down your statistical tables and copy of *The Guardian*, take this research grant, and go forth from your ivory academic tower and do something to actually make people's lives better.' The researcher pondered mightily, as only academics can ponder. He knew that restraint injury was a big problem. Eventually, the thought came to him that he might design an experiment to determine how to reduce restraint use and stop people getting hurt. So he selected two human service agencies (equally matched to ensure experimental validity, of course). In one, he spent thousands of pounds training the staff in conflict management, breakaway techniques and physical restraint (British Institute of Learning Disabilities (BILD) accredited, naturally). In the other, he simply got the Chief Executive to stand up in a staff meeting and say, 'I want fewer restraints!'

At this point I woke up, so readers will have to supply their own outcome data. Pity – there might have been a Nobel prize in it, although I suspect I might have difficulty getting the research design past an ethics committee.

Whether simply defining restraint reduction as a formal service aim would actually reduce it (Davidson et al 1984, cited in CWLA 2004), or simply drive it underground, is a complex question. However, it speaks to a basic truth. Motivation is an essential pre-requisite for restraint reduction. Hence, the first question must be 'Do the human services actually want to reduce restraint use?' and, if so, why restraint reduction merits such a low priority within national and service level agendas (Deveau and Mc Gill, 2007).

Underpinning assumptions

The current widespread use and acceptance of physical, mechanical, and chemical restraint in human services is based on an implicit, unconscious set of assumptions, as listed by Tumeinski (2007):

- All human problems, including violence or injuring oneself, are solvable

- The people we serve are dangerous to themselves and/or to others

- The benefits of restraints outweigh the costs

- The use of restraint has a negligible long-term effect on the restrained person, their relationships with others, etc

- Restraints are a valid helping form

- Control and violence are useful in stopping violence in others

- Human service restraint is the only way to control violence, aggression, etc

- My comfort (or job, security, time, etc) is more important than the devalued person

- The programme's needs and interests are more important than the devalued person

- What works for most people will not work for socially devalued people

- We (the service worker/programme) know better than the devalued person, their family, friends, etc

- The devalued person is a menace and dangerous to others

- The devalued person is a child, or child-like

- This devalued person is like every other devalued person

- The devalued person cannot do (*fill in the blank*) and never will

- The devalued person needs to be controlled rather than given mutual help, freely given help, engagement, friends, family, etc

As with Hitler's 'Final Solution', such implicit assumptions act to frame, depersonalise and dehumanise the target population. As Bauman (1990) (cited in Wardhaugh and Wilding, 1993) suggests, they become objectified specimens of a category, rather than human beings, and are thus placed beyond the bounds of moral obligation. Hence it becomes easy to justify repressive measures to control their behaviour whilst silencing normal moral considerations.

Zeitgeist and social change

Restraint misuse has become a focus of concern in both the USA and UK, and the UN Committee on the Rights of the Child has again recently condemned the UK for the overuse of restraint. There are also widespread concerns around the legality and ethics of many restraint systems, notably the pain-based methods employed by the control and restraint (C and R) model and its derivatives that are still used widely in the National Health Service in the UK. These concerns relate to the general compliance of such interventions with the Human Rights Act (1998), and specifically with the proscription of torture and inhuman methods or degrading treatment or punishment under Article 3. Presumably the Court of Appeals recent finding against the Government (Supreme Court of Judicature, Court of Appeal, 2008), in addition to previous judgements by the European Court of Human Rights (1995), is likely to have wide-ranging repercussions for the legality and continuing use of such methods. Any future appeal to the House of Lords will speak volumes about the Government's priorities. However, the actual legality of pain infliction during restraint appears to be effectively ignored by the recent independent review of restraint use in juvenile secure settings (Smallridge and Williamson, 2008), which endorsed pain compliance in extreme situations on practical and ethical grounds – a confusing contradiction which will no doubt await clarification through due legal process.

In the interim, the absence of centralised data reporting systems at national levels ensure restraint fatality, injury and trauma remains a hidden epidemic. Condemnation by the UN and the UK courts has provided the oxygen for a fire of publicity in the wake of a series of UK restraint fatalities, and most recently the death of 15 year old Gareth Myatt in secure care.

In the context of a total of 29 deaths of children in penal custody since 1990, the Youth Justice Board (YJB) (cited in *The Independent*, 2008) reported that physical restraint, including pain-based 'distraction techniques' were used on 3,036 occasions in 2005–2006 in English secure training centres, and on over 2,000 occasions across the secure estate over a three-month period in 2008. On 80 occasions, medical treatment was required following restraint. A confidential YJB report reported in *The Observer* (2007) indicated that young people '*report that they frequently experience difficulty in breathing during restraint. There have been numerous reports from trainees indicating that many had experienced difficulty in breathing and other distress during restraints*'. The single restraint death to date in this service is perhaps the tip of a very large iceberg of near misses.

We are therefore in a period of national debate, and perhaps at something of a crisis point regarding restraint use. Beyond the political rhetoric around social inclusion and the merits of the welfare state, the narrow UK focus on restraint method masks more fundamental questions about civil rights and the basic ability of services to safely support the rapidly growing population of individuals with challenging behaviour.

Restraint itself clearly generates widely conflicting views. The paucity of a valid research literature (Sailas and Fenton, 1999) has maintained an essentially subjective, 'reductionist' debate, plagued by opinion and vested interest, which underlines the crucial importance of the BILD risk assessment initiative described in Chapter 3. Reflecting the debate on the Millfield Charter, a petition to ban prone restraint in the UK (McDonnell, 2007; Leadbetter, 2007; Paterson, 2007), the principal arguments range along a continuum. At one pole, the use of restraint is viewed as a necessary aspect of control and discipline in services for the deviant and/or vulnerable; at the other, restraint is considered to be morally reprehensible, overused, never legitimate, and easily eradicated in human services where the will exists. The middle-ground perspective is that the use of restraint as a last resort response is legitimate in specific, extreme situations, to prevent a greater harm.

In 'The Structure of Scientific Revolutions', Thomas Kuhn (1962) suggested that:

'Scientific advancement is not evolutionary, but rather is a series of peaceful interludes punctuated by intellectually violent revolutions, and in those revolutions one conceptual world view is replaced by another.'

To effect a paradigm shift (ie a major change in the prevailing beliefs and attitudes), the bankruptcy of the prevailing view must therefore be demonstrated. Restraint acts as a barometer of the moral climate. It is a shifting zeitgeist, involving a dialectic process, with more powerful moral arguments gradually replacing preceding orthodoxy through discourse. It is possible to map historical attitudes to restraint and transition points at which these attitudes have changed; these phases are shown below. With the current debate on restraint use, it is conceivable that we may be at another such point.

- **Phase 1: Clinical restraint use.** *'Restraint forms the very principle on which the sound treatment of lunatics is founded.'* (Dr Samuel Hadwin of Lincoln Asylum, 1841) Physical, primarily mechanical, restraint was widespread in European mental health services, up to the 19th century. Indeed, it was seen as a fundamental aspect of treatment, important to coerce the 'insane' away from deviant, into socially compliant, behaviour.

- **Phase 2: The anti-restraint movement.** *'So negligible is the amount of mechanical restraint, or of any form of physical coercion... that we frequently omit all reference to it in our entries.'* (Mental Health Board of Control, 1927) Visionaries in both France and the UK successfully challenged this prevailing attitude, replacing it with a more humane and person-centred approach to mental illness which placed importance on actually talking to the patient.

- **Phase 3: The development of ad hoc methods:** Industrialisation and increased stress and mental illness brought in the era of mass hospitalisation, which precluded such a time-intensive approach. The hegemony of the psychiatric profession and its reliance on pharmacology also required compliant patient behaviour to ensure control and the smooth running of institutions. However, restraint remained ad hoc, placing a premium on the tradition of toughness and the frequent use of large, unqualified and mostly male staff as the agents of control.

- **Phase 4: The development of systematic training:** The Ritchie Report (1985) on the restraint-related death of a patient at Ashworth Special Hospital heralded the introduction of the control and restraint model.

Developed from techniques from the martial art of Jiu Jitsu, C and R techniques rely heavily on the infliction of pain through the hyper-extension of joints (see Leadbetter 2003). Control and restraint perhaps no longer constitutes a single model. However, its methods remain in widespread use, given the consequent expansion of C and R, and its derivatives, from the adult criminal justice system into services which now include frail elderly, intellectual disability and children's services (for discussion, see Stubbs et al, 2008; 2009). Concerns continue regarding its toxic impact, methods, legality and the security-based confrontational attitudes promoted, which arguably frame patients primarily as dangerous (eg Deveau and McGill, op cit; Carlile, 2006; BILD, 2006; RCP, 2005). This is a legacy reflected by the high injury rates incurred operationally – 19 per cent (SNMC, 1999) and in training – 29 per cent (Lee et al, 2001) (see also Hart, 2008). Logic might suggest that, given the obligation imposed by the UK Health and Safety at Work legalisation to reduce risk to the 'lowest practicable level', such data might suggest it may be safer not to train in C and R, rather than to train.

- **Phase 5: The market economy.** The 1980s saw the introduction of a wide range of restraint methodologies, many imported from the USA. There are thought to be as many as 700 training provider organisations in the UK. The marketing methods employed by sections of the 'Fear industry' (Mc Donnell, 2007) and *'the defensive cult mentality and restrictive role played by guru trainers from the USA'* (Allan, 1999) to suppress debate and valid criticism continue to attract concern.

- **Stage 6: Transition.** The uncritical acceptance of restraint is currently under attack and a fierce debate ensues. At its heart lies the key dilemma: the balance of rights between staff and service users. As a major Scottish child care report suggested, 'It may be a moment when the boundaries of Equal Opportunity can recede a little in favour of the rights of children.' (HMSO, 1997)

It is clear that in specific services, a small minority of service user behaviour does constitute a real and significant danger. In others, restraint is routine and has become 'normalised', leading to overuse and the uncritical acceptance of inherently dangerous and 'fragile'[1] methods (Leadbetter et al, 2005; Paterson and Duxbury, 2007; Paterson et al, 2008).

Discriminating between those individuals and services where restraint is necessary from those where risk behaviour can be prevented, avoided and/or managed by alternative means is, therefore, crucial. Alternative approaches also require motivated, knowledgeable and reflective practitioners and managers (Royal College of Psychiatrists, British Psychological Society and Royal College of Speech and Language Therapists, 2008). High restraint use may therefore reflect basic structural inadequacies at both a service and national level.

---

[1] 'A technique is deemed fragile if small adjustments (movement or pressure) to the procedure (either intentionally or unintentionally) are likely to result in intentional, or unintentional injury or severe pain to an individual.' (Leadbetter et al, 2005)

Framing

Irvine Goffman (1974) suggested we employ specific cognitive schemas, or 'frames' to make sense of reality. To date, the dominant 'master frame' (Paterson et al, 2008) applied to challenging behaviour has been the neo-conservative (or security) perspective which advocates that restraint is necessary for safety. This is based on an internal attributional stance (see Crighton, 1997; 1999) which locates the causation of problem behaviour within the pathology of the challenging person. As Fisher (2003) suggests, *'Restraint rationales focus on consumer pathology divorced from the context of interpersonal relating'*. The task, then, is to control the behaviour through coercive responses which effectively punish the person for the behaviour.

Competing, more liberal frames tend to recognise that a significant proportion of challenging behaviour is functional, often taught to the person by a process of differential and intermittent reinforcement in which staff/carer responses to specific behaviours are experienced as rewarding, thus leading to their repetition and strengthening over time (eg Hastings and Remington, 1994).

Whatever its nature, the underlying frame will also correlate significantly with the quality of organisational practice and culture, staff morale and team dynamics (see Cambridge, 2002; Bloom, 2006). The prediction of challenging behaviour within human services is more accurately achieved by assessment of specific organisational indicators, rather than the pathology of service users (Forquer et al, 1996), a fact that is obscured where the security paradigm predominates.

An over emphasis on internal factors is almost routine in explanations of behavioural causation within many services. Such a 'universal attribution error' (Heider, 1958) also provides the basis for the development of blame cultures, in which staff incompetence forms the primary explanation for critical incidents. As an alternative, the core aim of any organisational restraint reduction strategy should be the promotion of a co-creationist (Paterson and Miller, 2006) or public health model (Paterson et al, 2008) approach that moves explanatory causal and remedial beliefs along the attribution continuum, from internal (ie personality, pathology etc) towards external explanations (ie behaviour is influenced by contextual factors). In advocating such an approach, based on positive behavioural support, the recent exemplary joint report (2008) by the Royal College of Psychiatry, the British Psychological Society and the Royal College of Speech and Language Therapy concluded:

> *'Staff teams should not be looking for quick fix solutions to what may be lifelong patterns of behaviour. They need to be trained, supported and managed in such a way that they can promote positive interactions that may bring about increased participation, independence, choice, and inclusion within local communities. Limitations in "placement competence" appear to reflect a lack of training, or relevance of training, and "practice leadership" and different perceptions by front line staff about priorities in their work. The rhetoric of "treatment" in which*

challenging behaviour is seen as entirely located within the individual and amenable to medical or psychological treatment, actually helps perpetuate unsophisticated support for individuals presenting challenging behaviour in residential or in their family homes. The requirement for staff to work in skilled, well organised ways is diminished by the belief that the problem lies in the person and that they can be cured, usually somewhere else.' (p 44)

The report states that the dominance of the internal attributional perspective has promoted poor practice, resulting in a focus on crisis management, to the exclusion of longer-term therapeutic work. When problems arise, the priority becomes finding alternative placements, invariably out of area, which increases costs exponentially. Such exclusionary responses also serve to label and stereotype the service user, confirming their challenging reputation and preventing community integration. Ultimately, these dynamics reward weak management and poor training and perpetuates 'passing the buck' as a service response.

Common myths and confounding factors

According to Gournay (2000), the evidence that training reduces both violent incidents and associated injuries is 'reasonably sound'. This is, however, a contentious conclusion as the impact of training is subject to competing claims, and 'training' in this field encompasses a very broad church of approaches. If, as successive reports suggest, conflict management and restraint training represents the principal agency response to challenging behaviour, a systematic evaluation of its impact is required in order to be able to distinguish evidenced-based claims from simple marketing rhetoric. At present, common claims about training include the following.

Training can improve safety

Despite counter-arguments from training providers based on single studies (eg Nunno, Holden and Leidy, 2003), successive literature reviews offer limited support for this premise (Allen, 2001; Royal College of Psychiatrists, 1998, 2005; McDonnell et al, 2005; Zarola and Leather, 2006). Most programmes are either not evaluated (Beech and Leather, 2006) or else subject to internal evaluations undertaken by the training provider themselves (eg Nunno et al, 2003), a common practice with clear ethical and validity implications. While some studies do report positive outcomes, many widely used training models either remain unsupported by valid evaluative research or are associated with various negative outcomes (eg Titus, 1989; Baker and Bissmere, 2000; Waclawski et al, 2004). This paradox has only recently been recognised, but is perhaps reflected in the call of a recent authoritative national report on residential child care for urgent evaluation of a widely used training model (Kilpatrick et al, 2008). This appears to contradict the Joint Review's (Smallridge and Williamson, 2008) call for the introduction of the theoretical element of this same model into Young Offenders Institutions, which in turn is in conflict with the companion report on restraint in Secure Children's Homes (Hart, 2008), which concluded that the restraint methods used in this approach were 'universally disliked'.

The National Health and Safety Executive review in the UK National Health Service concluded that traditional skills-based conflict management training often merely serves to increase participant anxiety and a sense of isolation, increasing suspicions of the employing agencies' motivation (Zarola and Leather, 2006). McDonnell's (this volume) review of the extant literature reached similar conclusions, suggesting that the huge worldwide training industry seldom achieves reductions in assault rates.

Skills-based conflict management training effectively individualises the problem of aggression management (Johnstone, 1988), deflecting attention from the organisational factors which promote violence. Hence, unless training operates from a whole-organisation approach (Paterson and Leadbetter, 2009), as recommended by bodies such as the Health and Safety Executive and World Health Organisation (Sethi et al, 2004), it may well produce counter-productive results, especially where it is expected to operate as a stand-alone, panacea solution.

As Baker and Bissimere (op cit) conclude, although necessary, training is an insufficient stand-alone response to challenging behaviour. Further research is necessary to progress beyond the potentially dangerous and simplistic claims of the training industry. It is probable that skills training acts like a lens, magnifying the cultural characteristics of services. In fundamentally sound services it improves the quality of life of those they serve and reduces the need for restrictive interventions. However, in flawed or corrupted service cultures, violence and aggression training may also raise expectations, reinforce blame agendas and provide staff with carte blanche to abuse service users using 'legitimate', albeit highly unsafe, restraint methods.

Restraint is therapeutic

The term 'therapeutic' implies positive change. Logically, restraint can be experienced as rewarding (in which case the restrained person is likely to seek more restraint via engaging in more challenging behaviour) (eg Jones and Timbers, 2003), or aversive (ie punishing). This begs the question, 'How then can restraint be therapeutic?'

Many commentators find the concept of 'therapeutic restraint' to be a deeply offensive euphemism with the potential to justify dysfunctional and/or abusive staff interventions, especially when training includes unsafe and/or fragile restraint techniques. Violence also begets violence:

> *'Using violence on these children (offenders) – most of whom are*
> *vulnerable, with these complex problems – simply confirms their*
> *offending behaviour and does nothing to tackle underlying issues.'*
> Lord Carlile of Berridge QC, 2007 (p 23)

The literature also confirms that restraint is commonly used for trivial, punitive and coercive purposes, with resulting trauma and the undermining of professional relationships with service users (Sundram et al, 1994; Sequeira and Halstead, 2001; Morgan, 2004; Hawkins et al, 2005). Hence the rhetoric of influential sections of the training industry regarding the therapeutic, non-violent or non-aversive nature of their products must be viewed with extreme caution. As Mohr et al (1998) conclude, although not universal, the increasingly dominant view is that most restraint approaches are ineffectual, lead to superficial compliance only and promote anxiety in service users, with the paradoxical effect of encouraging further misbehaviour through negative reinforcement.

Restraint can be safely implemented by all staff

Perhaps, where staff are fit, motivated and professional, it can. This is, however, not the staff profile that exists in many services. Emphasising the need for reflective practitioners, the report of the Royal College of Psychiatrists (RCP), British Psychological Society (BPS) and Royal College of Speech and Language Therapists (RCSLT) (op cit) concludes that the most complex and dangerous behaviours are often supported by the least trained and lowest paid staff group in which competency or task-centred (ie S/NVQ), rather than analytical, training is the dominant model:

> 'Within staff teams there is little expertise. Most staff are untrained, staff turnover is high, and what training people have received is likely to have been restricted to reactive management methods rather than proper preventive and ecological strategies. Once challenging behaviour escalates to a frequent, severe problem the staff may not be able to cope.'
>
> RCP/BPS/RCSLT (op cit, p 15)

Similarly, in children's services:

> 'Children's Homes do not have well qualified staff. Sometimes staff don't know how to handle it and they react physically.'
>
> Chakrabarti (in Johnstone, 2003, p 5)

As Grimley and Morris (2000) report, staff fitness also varies enormously and, in many services, is likely to veer towards the lower end of the continuum. Equally, the age profile in many human services suggests an older, largely female workforce (Hunter et al, 2004; Children's Workforce Development Council, 2008).

Short training courses achieve competence

Many training models employ a short course format, using a standardised generic script, unsupported by valid research, which may have limited relevance for specific service contexts. Effectiveness may falsely assume pre-existing staff skills. Many courses are of very brief duration. Although commercially attractive, such brevity is counter-indicated by the literature on skill development and retention (see Bell and Stark, 1998; Stothard and Nicholson, 2001; Bleetman and Boatman, 2001), and may effectively promote and collude with organisational box-ticking in relation to health and safety requirements. Physical skill acquisition requires over-learning through constant repetition. If many training providers are to be believed, restraint training is the only physical activity exempt from the investment of time required by all other areas of physical competence. This quick-fix approach is rejected by other high-risk professional groups (eg police, military, fire and ambulance services, etc), where a huge time investment is made in the rehearsal of simulated operational situations.

Where the short course format is employed in cascade training, through scripted train-the-trainers programmes, it is likely to promote the narrow individualising, reductionist perspective described above. The negative impact of such training programmes requires urgent consideration.

Restraint reduction strategies

Managing challenging behaviour is not amenable to simplistic managerial approaches alone. This is not least because of its potential to generate primitive fight-or-flight responses in staff (ie fear, anger, avoidance, freezing, etc), who are often operating in the context of poorly resourced organisational blame cultures, with inadequate leadership, little training and minimal wages. In recognising these dynamics, Bloom (2006), in her 'trauma-informed' approach, asserts that organisations act, not like machines, but like people. When placed under stress by challenging behaviour, they develop dysfunctional coping responses in which staff behaviour increasingly mirrors that of challenging service users through the dynamic of 'parallel processes'. These responses commonly include: rigid and ineffective thinking, problem-solving and communication patterns, and the imposition of simplistic, punitive solutions. These compromise the organisation's ability to learn from experience or to develop effective adaptive responses to the problem. Consequently, rigid group solidarity or 'group think' develops, which maintains the 'collective disturbance' and punitive service culture. Unsurprisingly, these dynamics probably increase the appeal of heavily marketed, simplistic training packages which fail to impact on practice or values, and whose restraint methods often include unsafe and potentially punitive restraint methods, the appeal of which resonates with corrupted service values and increases the potential for the abuse of both staff and service users by legitimating responses which are in themselves potentially dangerous and/or abusive. The cure then becomes worse than the disease.

Skills training cannot somehow compensate for fundamental structural inadequacies at a national and service level (see *Figure 1*, Leadbetter 2003), and can be totally counterproductive when used as a panacea or a substitute rather than as a supplement to agency action. The moral may be that we need to fix the foundations before we fix the roof. Safe practice requires a multi-dimensional agency approach aimed at producing a safe practice jigsaw, while the omission of any piece obscures the overall vision. Agency practices combine to prevent the known dynamics of dysfunctional services and corrupted cultures of care (Wardhuagh and Wilding, 1993). They must pro-actively address the three modalities (thought/feeling/action) to ensure a client-centred regime. A client-centred value base requires the empowerment and involvement of staff, who must be both supported and held accountable in order to maintain morale and prevent the development of negative and, inevitably, punitive personal attitudes and service cultures. Positive morale, attitudes and service cultures are a fundamental underpinning and pre-requisite of effective action. As Bloom (2006) suggests, the development of approaches that understand and address the dynamics of organisational stress is the key to becoming a safe, resilient 'learning organisation' (Argyris and Schon, 1978)

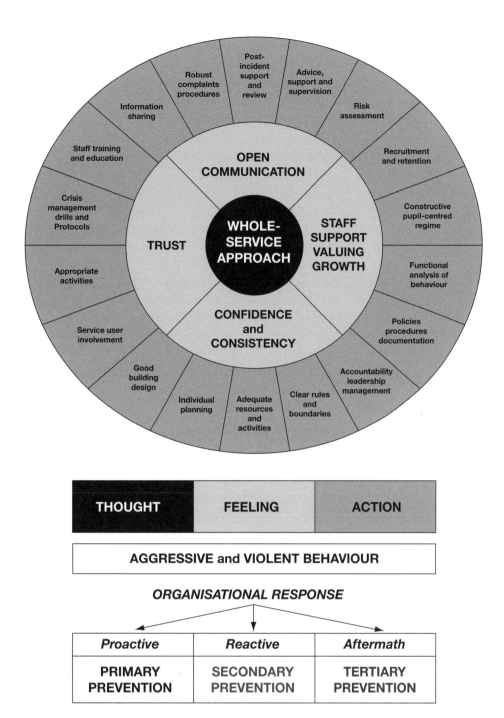

Figure 1: Challenging behavour: a total organisational response.

A constant theme in abuse inquiries is the clear link between staff morale, powerlessness and critical incident levels. In their analysis of the 'Pindown' regime, Wardhaugh and Wilding (1993) suggest that:

'If power corrupts, so too does powerlessness. Whilst staff have near absolute power over many clients, they are in many other respects powerless. They are taken for granted by the organisation. Seldom regarded as its heroes, given little support, not consulted about the organisation of their work.' (p 12)

Effective restraint reduction is unlikely to be accomplished by simple dictate or policy alone. Reflecting broader cognitive behaviourist models, effective action must offer direction and support on three interlinked levels:

1. *Thought* – Developing knowledge, explicit practice models, behavioural psychology, agency vision, mission statements, appropriate values at the level of the individual and the service culture, etc

2. *Feeling* – Maintaining staff and team morale, promoting the open discussion of negative emotional responses, counter-transference, post-incident trauma, sense of powerlessness, etc

3. *Action* – Clear protocols, policies etc on required action

Unlike in the UK, the discourse in the USA has placed greater emphasis on strategic restraint reduction, with a growing literature of positive case studies. USA initiatives are again a response to tragedy and consequent media publicity. The USA General Accounting Office (1999) estimates that up to 150 restraint-related deaths occur each year in human services. In both the UK and USA, the media proved to be a major catalyst for subsequent, albeit limited, social policy action. In the UK, the BBC programme *McIntyre Under Cover* (1999) provided crucial impetus which led to the development of the BILD Code of Practice and physical intervention accreditation scheme and the joint Departments of Health and Education and Skills policy statement. In the USA, the spark was provided by the publication of a database of 142 restraint-related deaths by the *Hartford Courant* newspaper (Weiss,1998), leading to restraint reduction projects in both child care (CWLA, 2004) and mental health (Hucksthorn, 2005).

United Kingdom government responses across jurisdictions have varied. The Scottish Government has published exemplary guidance for child care (Scottish Institute for Residential Child Care, Scottish Executive, Social Work Inspection Agency 2005). Section 10 of this guidance specifies unsafe restraint methods, but regrettably is unsupported at present by any enforcement mechanism. Worryingly, but perhaps unsurprisingly, therefore, subsequent audit by the Scottish Commission for the Regulation of Care (2008) found 52 per cent of Scottish child care services in non-conformance with this guidance.

The Welsh Assembly appears to have vacillated between an initial ban on prone restraints. (2005), a reversal in response to lobbying from prone using training providers, reconfirmation (Hutt, 2006) and further subsequent apparent attempt at reversal (Jewel and Kennedy, 2008).

The UK Government overall has defended current practice and expanded the circumstances of legitimate restraint use, at least in respect of education (Ministry of Children, Schools and Families, 2008) and secure children's services (Ministry of Justice, 2007). This potential expansion in restraint usage as a result of these recent statements continues to be the focus of high-level legal challenges to the UK Government's position.

As described above, the US Government has progressed in the opposite direction by funding restraint reduction initiatives in both the psychiatric and children's sectors. In response to the publication of the *Hartford Courant* database, Congress initiated an $8 million grant-aided study administered by the Child Welfare League of America involving a three-year, five-site study on restraint reduction, using pre- and post-training measures, thus making it the biggest such study to date. The only non-US domestic training provider, a team led by the author, achieved the lowest injury rates (CWLA, 2004a); the constructive collaboration with agency management was the crucial element in this process. This highlights the importance of leadership, the absence of which training alone cannot compensate for. Effective training requires a relationship in which agency management is actively involved in the training design and delivery process, and where training programmes are informed by, and serve to promote, a positive agency culture, ethos and policy framework. As emergent research demonstrates (and contrary to popular beliefs, expectations, and marketing claims), positive performance outcomes seem unlikely to be achieved through generic, off-the-shelf, skills-based restraint and conflict management training programmes, which neither influence, nor are influenced by, agency culture. Although common, such expectations are part of the current problem.

The final report (CWLA, 2004) identified the following as crucial factors:

- Strong leadership

- A person-centred organisational culture

- Clear policies and procedures

- Regular training

- Relationship-based treatment milieu

- Tracking restraints through data

The CWLA process also acted as a positive catalyst for a range of supportive initiatives, including international conferences and publications on best practice (CWLA, 2004b; Bullard et al, 2003; Nunno et al, 2008)

In USA mental health services, the National Technical Assistance Centre produced a Six Core Strategy Planning Tool (Hucksthorn, 2005) which facilities are required to implement. This addresses: leadership; use of data; workforce development; risk assessment; consumer involvement; and de-briefing. Hucksthorn (2007) reports an overall reduction of restraint and seclusion hours of 79 per cent within the eight mental health facilities submitting data further to the use of this tool.

Various other studies report the success of holistic restraint reduction strategies based on similar principles. Thompson et al (2008) report significant reductions in the use of restraints, assaults, and property damage, including an 80.2 per cent reduction in the mean frequency of restraint use in a USA youth treatment group home. Carter et al (2008) describe a similar strategy in a Canadian children's mental health service, cutting restraint use by half. In an initiative in a USA public special educational and behavioural difficulties day school, Ryan et al (2008) achieved a 39.4 per cent reduction in seclusion and 17.6 per cent less restraints post-training. Unusually and commendably, they also acknowledge the limitations of the study in confirming the efficacy of de-escalation training, given the inability to control for other explanatory variables. Similar conclusions are outlined in Suess' (2008) description of practice in a USA disability rehabilitation agency. These studies build on an existing literature and confirm that, regardless of setting, restrictive measures, as well as actual challenging behaviours, can be reduced by coherent, broadly based organisational strategies.

There are also a number of familiar organisational resistances to restraint reduction:

- *'We need restraint to avoid anarchy.'*
- *'We support unusually challenging service users.'*
- *'You liberals have not worked in this setting.'*
- *'Staff and managers are too busy – we are overworked as it is.'*
- *'We could never change staff attitudes.'*

The above excuses form a familiar mantra recited in support of organisational inaction. Although occasionally necessary, high levels of restraint are not a badge of honour. Quite the reverse. Given the breadth and depth of available evidence on restraint reduction (sadly almost exclusively from the USA), the continuing high use of restrictive measures in human services and, indeed, failure to develop an implement a coherent restraint reduction strategy, must now be recognised for what it most clearly is – a key indicator of ineffective management and dysfunctional services.

The Colton Audit Tool

'Our job is not to fix people, but to design effective environments'
Rob Horner in RCP/BPS/ RCSLT (op cit, p 1)

The highly constructive audit tool developed by Dr. David Colton provides a road map for restraint reduction (Colton, 2004). Based on an analysis of more than eighty reference sources, it identifies the essential themes required for effective restraint reduction with operationally defined outcome scales to rate progress on each element. The key dimensions are:

I. Leadership
Leadership must involve the provision of a clear agency vision of required approaches to behavioural management, and an explicit practice model with an unequivocal commitment to restraint reduction as a formal service aim. However, to uphold the wider duty of care and ensure that staff do not avoid using restraint in legitimate situations, management must also commit to supporting staff who work within agency policy.

2. Orientation and training

Crisis management is often the only training many staff receive. It invariably relies on a range of pre-existing skills. Training must be coherent, consistent and broadly based. It is a key aspect of inducting new staff into the culture, philosophy and policy structures of the agency.

3. Staffing

Adequate and properly skilled staffing is a requirement of safe practice. Within baseline levels, safety can be enhanced by the tactical deployment of staff resources to cover known setting conditions and trigger points in agency routines, such as transitions, change of shift, evenings, etc.

4. Environmental factors

These impact heavily on safe practice, both in terms of the general quality of life and the more specific demands of behavioural management. Factors such as noise, sight lines, ventilation, temperature, privacy, etc must be considered.

5. Programmatic structure

This involves the activities, routines, rituals and rules of the service. Successful regimes tend to be strength-based, encouraging personal responsibility rather than a reliance on external staff control.

6. Timely and responsive treatment planning

Effective treatment or care plans are potentially most effective when they are individualised and enlist the service user and other stakeholders as active partners in the treatment process. Review, revision, consultation and prompt responses to change in client circumstances are essential.

7. Processing after the event (debriefing)

Post-incident debriefing is a widely used but often poorly understood process. Post-hoc analysis of a restraint event potentially meets a range of needs:

- Restoration of relationships

- Promotion of alternative service user coping skills

- Staff support and trauma reduction

- Agency learning

Too often, staff experience debriefing as a search for blame (ie 'What did you do wrong then?'). Casual discussion, rather than a skilled formalised process, is often the norm, and debriefing may in any case merit a low priority due to time pressures. Conclusions around gaps in the required 'safe system of work' (Health and Safety at Work Act, 1974; The Management of Health and Safety at Work Regulations, 1999) should be identified. De-briefing should follow a managerial, rather than a psychological, debriefing model (such as critical incident stress debriefing) which is increasingly contra-indicated by emergent research and guidance (eg HSE, 1998; Richards, 2003; Rose et al, 2004).

8. Communication and consumer involvement

Lack of transparency and isolation from the wider community are recurring features of corrupted care. Consultation on behavioural management and required control measures must be undertaken with the service users, their families and representatives and other stakeholders both prior to, and after, a restraint or seclusion event.

Systems evaluation and quality improvement

Human behaviour is complex and often unpredictable. In services supporting individuals with complex needs, mistakes are almost inevitable. While undesirable, these are arguably excusable; failure to learn from them is not, however. Complex organisations and blame cultures often constantly repeat the same mistakes, perhaps due to the unspoken staff belief that, 'If I do what we always do, I won't get into trouble'. Blame, the automatic assumption of fault, discourages learning. Ideally, services need to aspire to the status of learning organisations, in which mistakes are examined systematically and accountability exercised on a criteria-based, no-blame basis, using post-incident de-briefing and/or the more sophisticated process of Root Cause Analysis (Joint Commission on Accreditation of Healthcare, 2005).

Data on intervention patterns must also be used to understand trends, gaps and patterns. Conclusions then close the feedback loop by updating care plans, risk assessments and underlying policies and procedures, which, in turn, ensure that the agencies' wider goals are met.

Conclusions

> *'And why beholdest thou the mote that is in thy brother's eye, but considerest not the beam that is in thine own eye?'*
>
> Matthew (Ch. VII, v 3)

The current crisis and debate on restraint use presents a window of opportunity to redress the balance of rights. Which of the contending stakeholder groups exercise greater political influence will determine the outcome. Although most vulnerable to restraint abuse, people with intellectual disabilities and young people in the care and juvenile justice system enter this debate from a position of disadvantage. Although the Government's acceptance of the recommendations of the Joint Review in respect of restraint reduction strategies and a mandatory restraint training accreditation scheme is to be welcomed, many other aspects of recent official reports contain the seeds of contradiction and seem at odds with both the existing knowledge base and judicial judgements. Their brief coverage and apparent lack of insight around the relationship between restraint misuse and organisational culture is certainly worrying, and may suggest they have missed the point. Whether these reports will advance good practice remains to be seen, but it is often better to travel hopefully than to arrive.

A clear evidence base demonstrates that restraint reduction is perfectly possible. We have, as they say, the technology, but do we have the will? Reducing restraint requires a paradigm shift which recognises that much challenging behaviour arises from shortcomings in service quality rather than from the pathology of service users. However, such a shift in thinking carries clear political risks. For politicians, public and media alike, the abuse of favoured groups (eg nurses, social care workers, teachers etc) by ungrateful, deviant, disfavoured groups (ie violent service users) is a popular and useful stereotype.

Presently, 'reductionism' rules. Positive change requires a holistic approach. Such a paradigm shift will, however, expose the structural inadequacies of current service provision, which is an unattractive option for politicians, given the need to maintain a public perception of the adequacy of public services. Behind the rhetoric of the wonderful welfare state, evidence suggests that the current moral panic and resulting emphasis on crisis management and physical intervention stems directly from basic service level structural inadequacies and a failure to employ a trauma-informed approach. This is a dynamic which a recession may well exacerbate. At present, a false paradigm predominates. The role of sections of the training industry in its promotion and maintenance must now be considered. While most services may be able to effectively warehouse and meet the basic needs of non-challenging service users, evidence suggests that, in the face of behavioural challenges, many services are neither sophisticated nor resilient. Their consequent dysfunctional responses result in a game of 'pass the parcel' until the challenging individual ends up in a service where their behaviour is controlled by reliance on highly restrictive practices. The systematic exploration of the reasons behind the behaviour, and the interaction between individual pathology and the specifics of agency practice, remains a tragic and consistent omission.

Albeit an incorrect perception, the honest answer to the question of why physical restraint continues to be overused in human services is likely to be, because in political terms, it is still seen as the easier option.

Now back to dreamland!

References

Allen, D (2001) *Training Carers in Physical Interventions: Towards Evidence Based Practice.* Kidderminster: BILD Publications.

Allan, B (1998) *Holding Back, Restraint Rarely and Safely.* Bristol: Lucky Duck Publishing.

Argyris, C and Schön, D (1978) *Organisational learning: A theory of action perspective.* Reading, Mass: Addison Wesley.

Baker, P A and Bissmire, D (2000) A Pilot Study of the Use of Physical Intervention in the Crisis Management of People with Intellectual Disability who present Challenging Behaviour. *Journal of Applied Research in Intellectual Disabilities,* 13, 1, 38–45.

Beech, B and Leather, P (2006) Workplace violence in the health care sector: A review of staff training and integration of training evaluation models. *Aggression and Violent Behavior,* 11, 27–43.

Bell, L and Stark, C (1998) *Measuring Competence in Physical Restraint Skills in Residential Child Care*: Edinburgh: Scottish Office Central Research Unit.

Bleetman, A and Boatman, P (2001) *An Overview of Control and Restraint Issues for the Health Service*. London: Department of Health.

Bloom, S (2006) *Organisational Stress as a Barrier to Trauma. Sensitive Change and System Transformation,* Adapted from: *Living Sanctuary; Complex Antidotes to Organisational Stress in a Changing World*. Available from www.sanctuaryweb.com (accessed 20 April 2009).

Brady, B and Owen, J (2007) The Abused: Scandal of assaults on children in custody. *The Independent*, 3 December 2007.

BILD (2006) *Code of Practice for the Use of Physical Interventions* (Second edition). Kidderminster: BILD Publications.

Bullard, L, Fulmore, D and Johnstone, K (2003) *Reducing the Use of Restraint and Seclusion, Promising Practices and Successful Strategies*. Washington: Child Welfare League of America Press.

Cambridge, P (2002) The Risks of Getting it Wrong; Systems Failure and the Impact of Abuse. In D Allen (Ed) *Ethical Approaches to Physical Interventions. Responding to challenging behaviour in people with intellectual disabilities*. Kidderminster: BILD Publications.

Carlile, J (2006) Is this Ever Right? *Community Care*, 23 August 2007.

Carlile, J (2006) *An Independent Inquiry into the use of Physical Restraint, Solitary Confinement and Forcible Strip Searching of Children in Prisons, Secure Training Centers and Local Authority Secure Children's Homes*. London: The Howard League for Penal Reform.

Carter, J, Jones, J and Stevens, K (2008) Beyond a Crisis Management Program: How We Educed Our Restraints by Half in One Year. In M Nunno, L B Bullard and D M Day (Eds) *For our own safety: Examining the safety of high-risk interventions for children and young people*. Washington, DC: Child Welfare League of America.

Child Welfare League of America (2004a) *Achieving Better Outcomes for Children and Families. Reducing Restraint and Seclusion*. Washington, DC: Child Welfare League of America.

Child Welfare League of America (2004b) *Behaviour Management. Best Practice Guidelines*. Washington, DC: Child Welfare League of America.

Colton, D (2004) *Checklist for Reducing your Organisations readiness for Reducing Seclusion and Restraint*. Staunton, VA: Commonwealth Center for Children and Adolescence.

Crichton, J (1997) The Response of Nursing Staff to Psychiatric Inpatient Misdemeanor. *The Journal of Forensic Psychiatry*, 8, 1, 36–71.

Crichton, J H M (1999) Staff response to disturbed behaviour in group homes for adults with a learning disability. *Criminal Behaviour and Mental Health*, 9, 215–25.

Children's Workforce Development Council (2008) *The State of the Children's Social Care Workforce, A statistical overview of the workforce providing children and families social care in England*. London: CWDC.

Department of Children, Schools and Families (2008) *The Use of Force to Control or Restrain Pupils. Non Statutory Guidance*. London: DCSF.

Deveau, R and McGill, P (2007) *As the Last Resort: Reducing the Use of Restrictive Physical Interventions*. Canterbury: Tizard Centre, University of Kent.

Doward, J (2007) Children at Risk from Jail Restraint. *The Observer*, 8 September 2007.

European Court of Human Rights, 4 December 1995, *Ribitsch v Austria*, (A/336).

Fisher, J A (2003) Curtailing the use of restraint in psychiatric settings. *Journal of Humanistic Psychology*, 43, 2, 69–95.

Forquer, S, Earle, K, Way, B, and Banks, S (1996) Predictors of the Use of Restraint. and Seclusion in Public Psychiatric Hospitals. *Administration and Policy in Mental Health and Mental Health Services Research*, 23, 6, 527–532.

General Accounting Office of the United States (1999) *Report to Congressional Requesters: Mental health: Improper Restraint or Seclusion Places People at Risk*. Washington, DC: United States General Accounting Office.

Goffman, E (1974) *Frame Analysis: An Essay on the Organization of Experience*, New York: Harper and Row.

Gournay, K (2000) *The Recognition, Prevention and Therapeutic Management of Violence in Mental Health Care: A Consultation Document*. London: United Kingdom Central Council for Nursing and Midwifery.

Grimley, S and Morris, P (2001) The Training of NHS Staff in Non-Mental Health Settings in the Recognition, Prevention and Management of Violence and Aggression and Conflict Management. In A Bleetman and P Boatman (Eds) *An Overview of Control and Restraint Issues for the Health Service*. London: Department of Health.

Hart, D (2008) *Restrictive Physical Intervention in Secure Children's Homes, Department for Children Schools and Families*. London: National Children's Bureau.

Hastings, R P and Remington, B (1994) Staff behaviour and its implications for people with learning disabilities and challenging behaviors. *British Journal of Clinical Psychology*, 33, 423–438.

Hawkins, S Allen, D and Jenkins, R (2005) The Use of Physical Interventions with People with Intellectual Disabilities and Challenging Behaviour. The Experiences of Service Users and Staff Members. *Journal of Applied Research in Intellectual Disabilities*, 18, 19–34.

Health and Safety at Work Act (1974). London: HMSO.

Press release E244:98. Health and Safety Executive (1998).

Heider, F (1958) *The Psychology of Interpersonal Relations*. New York: Wiley.

The Supreme Court of Judicature, Court of Appeal (Civil Division), on appeal from the Queens Bench Division, Divisional Court, Lord Justice Maurice Kay and Mr Justice Burton, CO/6174/2007, 28 July 2008.

HMSO (1997) *Children's Safeguards Review (The Kent Report)*. Edinburgh: Social Work Services Inspectorate for Scotland.

Hucksthorn, K (2005). *Six Core Strategies for Reducing Seclusion and Restraint Use*. Alexandria, VA: National Technical Assistance Center.

Hucksthorn, K (2007) *Changing Cultures of Care in Mental Health Settings Preventing the Use of Seclusion and Restraint: US Leadership Strategies for Transforming Care*. Presentation to the 5th European Congress On Violence in Psychiatry. Amsterdam.

Hunter, L, Hosie, A, Davidson, J, and Kendrick, A (2004) *Residential Child Care Qualifications Audit*. Glasgow: Scottish Institute for Residential Child Care.

Hutt, J (2006) Minister for Assembly Business, Equalities and Children. Welsh Assembly Letter. *Letter to D Lloyd, AM*.

Jewel, T and Kennedy, R (2008) *Safe Management of Mental Health in Patients*. Cardiff: Welsh Assembly Government.

Johnstone, S (1988) Guidelines for Social Workers coping with Violent Clients, *British Journal of Social Work*, 18, 377–90.

Johnstone, I (2003) Care home staff accused of lying to cover up fights with children. *Scotland on Sunday, 16 February*.

Joint Commission for Health Care (2005) *Root Cause Analysis in Health Care: Tools And Techniques*. Joint Commission for Health Care, Washington, DC.

Jones, R J and Timbers, G D (2003) Minimizing the Need for Physical Restraint and Seclusion in Residential Youth Care through Skill-Based Treatment Programming. *Families in Society: the Journal of Contemporary Human Services*, 84, 1, 21–29.

Kilpatrick, R, Berridge, D, Sinclair, R, Larkin, E, Lucas, P, Kelly, B and Geraghty, T (2008) *Working with challenging and disruptive situations in residential child care. Sharing Effective Practice. Children and Family Services Knowledge Review No 22*. London: Social Care Institute of Excellence.

Kuhn, T S (1962) *The Structure of Scientific Revolutions*. Chicago: University of Chicago Press.

Lee, S, Wright, S, Sayer, J, Parr, A M, Gray, R and Gournay, K (2001) Physical restraint training for nurses in English and Welsh intensive care and regional secure units. *Journal of Mental Health*, 10, pp 51–62.

Leadbetter, D (2003a) *CALM Associates Training Manual*. Menstrie: CALM Training Services.

Leadbetter, D (2003b) Good Practice in Physical Interventions. In D Allen (Ed) *Ethical Approaches to Physical Interventions. Responding to Challenging Behaviour in People with Intellectual Disabilities*. Kidderminster: BILD Publications.

Leadbetter, D, Paterson, B, Miller, G and Crichton, J (2005) *From moral panic to moral action*. Paper presented at Cornell University/Stirling University conference on high risk physical interventions, New York.

Leadbetter, D (2007) Millfields Charter. Finding the Middle Ground. *Learning Disability Practice*, 10, 3, 34–37.

Leadbetter, D and Paterson, B (2009) Towards Restraint Free Care. In R Hughes (Ed) *A Balance of Care: Practice and policy perspectives on reducing restraint in health and social care*. London: Kings College.

Lee, S, Wright, S, Sayer, J, Parr, A, Gray, R and Gournay, K (2001) Physical restraint training for nurses in English and Welsh psychiatric intensive care and regional secure units, *Journal of Mental Health*, 10, 2, 151–162.

Management of Health and Safety at Work Regulations (1999). London: HMSO.

McDonnell, A, Sturmey, P and Butt, S (2005) *Training in Physical Interventions; A Review of the Literature*. Unpublished report.

McDonnell, A (2007) Millfields Charter. Why I am in favour. *Learning Disability Practice*, 10, 3, 26–29.

Ministry of Justice (2007) *Statutory Instruments 2007 N01709.Secure Training Centres, England and Wales. The Secure Training Centre (Amendment) Rules*. London: Ministry of Justice.

Mohr, W K, Mahon, M M and Noone, M J (1998) A restraint on restraint. The need to reconsider the use of restrictive interventions. *Archive of Psychiatric Nursing*, 12, 2, 95–106.

Morgan, R (2004) *Children's Views on Restraint*. Newcastle Upon Tyne: Commission for Social Care Inspection.

M A Nunno, L B Bullard and D M Day (Eds) (2008). *For our own safety: Examining the safety of high-risk interventions for children and young people*. Washington, DC: Child Welfare League of America.

Nunno, M A, Holden, M J and Leidy, B (2003) Evaluating and Monitoring the Impact of a Crisis Intervention System on a Residential Child Care Facility. *Children and Youth Services Review*, 25, 295–315.

Paterson, B (2007) Millfields Charter. Drawing the wrong conclusions. *Learning Disability Practice*, 10, 3, 30–33.

Paterson, B and Duxbury, J (2007) Restraint and the Question of Validity. *Nursing Ethics* 207, 14, 4, 535–545.

Paterson, B and Miller, G (2006) *Promoting Safe and Therapeutic Services, National Health Service Security Management Service. Trainers Handbook*. London: Security Management Services.

Paterson, B, Leadbetter, D, Crichton, J and Miller, G (2008) Adopting a Public Health Model to Reduce Violence and Restraints In Children's Residential Care Facilities. In Nunno, M, Day, D M and Bullard, L (Eds.) *For our own safety: Examining the safety of high-risk interventions for children and young people*. Washington, DC: Child Welfare League of America.

Richards, J (2003) *Management of Workplace Violence Victims*. Geneva: International Labour Office, International Council of Nurses, World Health Organisation, Public Services International.

Ritchie, S (1985) *Report to the Secretary of State for Social Services concerning the death of Mr. Michael Martin*. London: Special Hospitals Service Authority.

Rose, S, Bisson, J and Wessely, S (2004) Psychological debriefing for preventing post traumatic stress disorder (PTSD). [Systematic Review] Cochrane Depression, Anxiety and Neurosis Group *Cochrane Database of Systematic Reviews*, 2.

Royal College of Psychiatrists (1998) *The Management of Violence in Clinical Settings: An Evidence Based Guideline*. London: Gaskell.

Royal College of Psychiatrists (2005) *Managing Imminent Violence in Learning Disability Settings*. London: Royal College of Psychiatrists.

Royal College of Psychiatrists, British Psychological Society and Royal College of Speech and Language Therapists (2008) *Challenging Behaviour: A Unified Approach. Clinical and service guidelines for supporting people with learning disabilities who are at risk of receiving abusive or restrictive practices*. London: Royal College of Psychiatrists.

Ryan, J B, Peterson, R L M, Teteault, G and van der Hagen, E (2008) Reducing the Use of Seclusion and Restraint in a Day School Program. In M Nunno, D M Day and L Bullard (Eds) *For our own safety: Examining the safety of high-risk interventions for children and young people*. Washington, DC: Child Welfare League of America.

Sailas, E and Fenton, M (1999) Seclusion and Restraint as a Method of Treatment for People with Serious Mental Illness. *The Cochrane Library*. Issue 3 Oxford: Update Software (Cochrane Library number CD001 163).

Scottish Institute for Residential Child Care, Scottish Executive, and Social Work Inspection Agency (2005) *Holding Safely – A Guide for Residential Child Care Practitioners and Managers about Physically Restraining Young People*. SIRCC: Glasgow.

Scottish Commission for the Regulation of Care (2008) *Protecting Children and Young People in Residential Care. A review by the Care Commission of Practice in Residential Care for Young People Concerning Protecting Children, Planning for Their Care and Using Physical Restraint.* Edinburgh: The Care Commission.

Sethi, D, Marais, S, Seedat, M, Nurse, J and Butchart, A (2004) *Handbook for the Documentation of Interpersonal Violence Prevention Programmes.* Geneva: Department of Injuries and Violence Prevention, World Health Organization.

Sequeira, H and Halstead, S (2001) 'Is it meant to hurt, is it? Management of violence in women with developmental disabilities. *Violence Against Women,* 7, 4, 462–476.

Smallridge, P and Williamson, A (2008) *Independent Review of Restraint in Juvenile Secure Settings.* London: Ministry of Justice, Department for Children, Schools and Families.

Standing Nursing and Midwifery Committee (1999) *Mental Health Nursing: Addressing Acute Concerns.* London: SNMAC.

Stothard, C and Nicholson, R (2001) *Skill Acquisition and Retention in Training.* Land Department of Defense, Defense, Science and Technology Organisation. DSTO Support to the Army Ammunition Study Operations Division Electronics and Surveillance Research Laboratory DSTO-CR-0218.

Suess, G (2008) Lessons from 30 Plus Years of No Physical Intervention. In M Nunno, D M Day and L Bullard (Eds) *For our own safety: Examining the safety of high-risk interventions for children and young people.* Washington, DC: Child Welfare League of America.

Sundram, C, Stack, E W and Benjamin, W P (1994) *Restraint and Seclusion Practices within New York State Psychiatric Facilities.* Schenectady, NY: New York State Commission on Quality of care for the Mentally Disabled.

Stubbs, B, Knight, C and Yorston, G (2008) Physical interventions for managing aggression in mental health: Should Physiotherapists be Involved? *International Journal of Therapy and Rehabilitation,* 15, 1, 8–12.

Stubbs, B, Leadbetter, D, Paterson, B, Yorston, G, Knight, C and Davis, S (2009) Physical intervention: a review of the literature on its use, staff and patient views, and the impact of training *Journal of Psychiatric and Mental Health Nursing,* 16, 99–105.

Thomson, R W, Huefner, J C, Volmer, D M G, Davis, J L and Daly, D (2008) A Case Study of an Organisational Intervention to Reduce Physical Interventions. Creating Effective, Harm Free Environments. In M Nunno, D M Day and L Bullard (Eds) *For our own safety: Examining the safety of high-risk interventions for children and young people.* Washington, DC: Child Welfare League of America.

Titus, R (1989) Therapeutic Crisis Intervention Training at Kinark Child and Family Services: Assessing its Impact. *Journal of Child and Youth Care,* 4, 61–71.

Tumeinski, M (2008) Personal correspondence.

Waclawski, E, Bell, L and Leyden, J (2004) Impact of Training in the Management of Aggression on the Incident Rates and Perceptions of Staff. *Occupational And Environmental Medicine,* 61, 11–20.

Wardhaugh, J and Wilding, P (1993) Towards an explanation of the corruption of care. *Critical Social Care,* 37,13, 4–31.

Weiss, E M (1998) Deadly Restraint. *Hartford Courant,* October 1998, pp 11–15.

Welsh Assembly Government (2005) *Framework for Restrictive Physical Intervention, Policy and Practice*. Cardiff: Welsh Assembly Government.

Zarola, A and Leather, P (2006) *Violence and Aggression Management for Trainers and Managers: A National Evaluation of the Training Provision in Health Care Settings. Research Report 440*. Nottingham: University of Nottingham/Health and Safety Executive.

Index

abuse, and physical restraint, 6, 117
accreditation, and requirements for effective
    programmes, 29
    see also Physical Interventions Accreditation
    Scheme
Adams, D, 57, 58, 59, 60, 63
aggressive behaviour, and positive programming
    and anger, 173–4
    and barriers to implementation of, 185; external
        variables, 186; overcoming, 186–7; service
        user variables, 185–6
    and functional assessment, 174; ability to
        engage in treatment, 177; aims of, 174;
        assessing internal processes, 176; case study,
        'Josephine', 175; case study, 'Loui', 176;
        communication skills, 174; coping skills, 175;
        intellectual skills, 174; measures of anger and
        aggression, 177–8; motivation for treatment,
        177; nature of anger problem, 177; role of,
        175
    and functional communication training, 178;
        approach of, 179; case study, 'Josephine',
        180; effectiveness of, 179; limitations of, 180
    and functionally equivalent skills, 178
    and functionally related skills, 181
    and rule-governed behaviours, 181
    and social skills, 181
    and theoretical basis of approach, 173–4
    and underpinning principle of, 187
    see also cognitive behavioural therapy (CBT)
Allan, B, 197
Allen, D, 56, 57, 58, 59, 60, 61, 63, 65, 113, 143,
    148, 156
allergies, and challenging behaviour, 164
Alliance to Prevent Restraint, Aversive
    Interventions and Seclusion (APRAIS),
    112–13, 117
anger, and aggressive behaviour, 173–4
    see also aggressive behaviour; cognitive
    behavioural therapy (CBT)
antecedent interventions, and challenging
    behaviour, 156
    and demand-related behaviours, 160–2; task
        choice, 162

and environmental enrichment, 162–3
and functional assessment, 156, 157
and health and antecedent conditions, 163;
    allergies, 164; dysmenorrhoea, 164; epilepsy,
    165; gastrointestinal disorders, 164; mental
    illness, 165–6; otitis media, 165; pre-
    menstrual syndrome, 164; sleep, 163
and implementation challenge, 166
and increased emphasis on, 158
and manipulation of settings, 156
and non-contingent reinforcement, 159–60;
    skills teaching, 159–60
and positive behavioural support, 166
and psychotropic drugs, 166
and removing/altering antecedent conditions,
    158–9; neutralising routines, 158
and types of antecedents: discriminative stimuli
    (SDs), 157; motivating operations (MOs),
    157
and understanding the individual, 156
antipsychotic medications, and rapid
    tranquilisation, 100–1, 106
Ashworth Special Hospital, 196
as-required medication, 95–6, 98–9
Association for Real Change (ARC), 96
Attention Deficit Hyperactivity Disorder, 166
autism, and seclusion, 118–19
aversive procedures
    and characteristics of, 112–13
    and examples of, 113

Bailey, J, 179
Baker, P A, 156
Bambara, L M, 147
basket holds, and restraint-related deaths, 133
Battaglia, J, 103
Becker, A, 164
behaviour, and training effectiveness, 3–4, 5
behaviour change
    and positive behavioural support (PBS), 171
    and strategies for, 155
behaviour management strategies, 171
    and consequence-based interventions, 157–8
    and limitations of, 143

Bennett, David, 127, 130, 133
benzodiazepine, 103
 and rapid tranquilisation, 100–1
benztropine, 101
Bick, P A, 104
Bieniek, S, 103
Black, L, 184
Blackwood, Orville, 129
Bloom, S, 202
Bohmer, C J, 164
Bond, W, 105
Braithwaite, K L, 179
breakaways, 18
British Institute of Learning Disabilities (BILD)
 and assessment of individual techniques of
  physical intervention, 35
 and Code of Practice for the Use of Physical
  Interventions (2006), 30; pain, 6
 and Code of Practice for Trainers in the Use of
  Physical Interventions (2001), 28–9
 and *Physical Interventions – A Policy
  Framework*, 27–8
 and Principles for Practice on use of mechanical
  restraints, 82–3
 and professional development, 32
 and role of, 27
 see also Physical Interventions Accreditation
  Scheme (PIAS)
British National Formulary (BNF), 97, 99, 101
British Psychological Society, 155, 201
 Clinical Practice Guidelines, 62
British Training and Education Council (BTEC),
 150

carbamazepine, 104
Care Quality Commission, 89
Carlile of Berridge, Lord, 200
Carr, E G, 152, 164
Carter, J, 205
Caruso, M, 78
Chadwick, P, 184
Challenging Behaviour Foundation (CBF), 56
Children Act (1989), 61, 120
Child Welfare League of America, 205
chlorpromazine, 100
Chouinard, G, 104
civil rights, and physical restraint, 195
clonazepam, 104
clozapine, 101, 106
Cochrane database, 7
cognitive behavioural therapy (CBT)
 and anger and aggression, 181–2
 and assessment of individuals, 176; ability to
  engage in treatment, 177; motivation for
  treatment, 177; nature of anger problem, 177
 and cognitive deficits approach to anger
  treatment, 182; case study of self-
  management, 'Loui', 183–4; evidence base
  for, 182–3; relaxation, 182, 183–4; self-
  instructional training, 182, 183; self-

management, 182; social problem-solving,
 182, 183
 and cognitive distortions approach to anger
  treatment, 184; evidence base for, 184–5
 see also positive programming
Colton Audit Tool, and restraint reduction, 206–8
 and communication, 208
 and consumer involvement, 208
 and environmental factors, 207
 and leadership, 206
 and orientation and training, 207
 and post-incident debriefing, 207
 and programmatic structure, 207
 and staffing, 207
 and treatment planning, 207
Colton, D, 206
Commission for Social Care Inspection, 97
 and mechanical restraint, 80
communication difficulties, and challenging
 behaviour, 173
 see also functional communication training
  (FCT)
confidence, and training effectiveness, 18
consequence-based interventions, 157–8
constipation, 164
context, and training effectiveness, 5
control and restraint system, 6, 196–7
coping skills, and positive programming, 172, 175
Cornwall Partnership NHS Trust, 20, 77, 114,
 115, 123
Council of Europe, and mechanical restraint, 81
Counter-Intuitive Strategies, 155
Craig, Michael, 130, 132, 133

Dagnan, D, 184
deaths, restraint-related, 6, 63, 195
 and basket holds, 133
 and case analysis, 128–35
 and implications for practice and policy, 135–6
 and intellectual disability, 135, 136–7
 and lack of research into, 127
 and mechanical restraint, 77, 131–2
 and medication, 135
 and need for systematic analysis, 137
 and pre-existing medical conditions, 134–5
 and prone restraint, 132–3
 and recovery position, 133
 and respiration, 133–4
 and seated restraint, 132, 133
 and staff misconceptions, 134
 and supine restraint, 133
 and survey of, 127–8; inclusion criteria, 128;
  individual cases, 129–31
 and United States, 204
demand avoidance, and reinforcement of
 challenging behaviour, 156
demand-related behaviour
 and antecedent interventions, 160–2; task
  choice, 162
Department for Education and Employment, 29

Department for Education and Skills
    and Guidance for Restrictive Physical
        Interventions, 120
    and time out, 116
Department of Health, 29
    and Guidance for Restrictive Physical
        Interventions, 120
    and mechanical restraint, 81–2
    and time out, 116
depression, 165
Desrochers, M N, 173
diazepam, 100
Dicesare, A, 166
Donnellan, A M, 148, 155, 171–2
Dorevitch, A, 104–5
Dozier, C L, 157
droperidol, 104
Duker, P, 83–4
Duncan, D, 173
Durand, M V, 163
dysmenorrhoea, and challenging behaviour, 164

effectiveness of training, see training effectiveness
e-learning, and training, 151
Embregts, P J C M, 182–3
Emerson, E, 84, 114, 118, 148, 165
environmental enrichment, and antecedent
        interventions, 162–3
epilepsy, and challenging behaviour, 165
establishing operations, and training effectiveness,
        5
European Court of Human Rights, 195
expert, and questionable value of concept, 37, 127
extinction, 158

Fairley, Zoe, 130
Falconer, David, 129
family carers, 61–2
    and access to training in physical intervention,
        60
    and barriers to training provision, 60, 61–2;
        concerns over incorrect application and
        misuse, 61; concerns over vicarious liability,
        61; lack of knowledge about family needs,
        69–70; lack of legislative drivers, 60–1; lack
        of recognition of need for, 61; perceived
        conflict with child legislation, 61
    and challenging behaviour experienced by, 55–6
    and delivering training to, 65–9; case reports
        on, 66–8; compliance with good practice, 66;
        legislative
    and policy requirements, 69; Positive
        Behavioural Management (PBM), 68–9; pre-
        consideration checklist, 66–7
    and impact of challenging behaviour: emotional
        impact, 56; exclusion from services, 58;
        physical injury, 56–7; placement of children
        outside family, 58; restricted opportunities,
        58; stress, 56, 70
    and limited services for, 55

and need for training in physical interventions,
        62
    and proactive approaches to challenging
        behaviour, 62, 70
    and reactive behaviour management approaches
        by, 58–60
    and reasons for training in physical
        interventions, 69; carers desire for, 64–5;
        maintaining family placement of children, 64;
        reducing injury risk, 62–3; reducing risk of
        incorrect application and misuse, 63–4
Farnham, F R, 134
Federal Drug Administration Agency (USA), 131
feedback, and training effectiveness, 4, 5
Fisher, J A, 198
flumazenil, 101
flunitrazepam, 104–5
Frank, J G, 137
functional assessments, 156, 157
    and positive programming, 174; ability to
        engage in treatment, 177; aims of, 174;
        assessing internal processes, 176; case study,
        'Josephine', 175; case study, 'Loui', 176;
        communication skills, 174; coping skills, 175;
        intellectual skills, 174; measures of anger and
        aggression, 177–8; motivation for treatment,
        177; nature of anger problem, 177; role in,
        175
functional communication training (FCT), 161,
        178
    and approach of, 179
    and case study, 'Josephine', 180
    and effectiveness of, 179
    and limitations of, 180

Garza-Trevino, E S, 104
gastroesophageal reflux disease (GERD), 164
gastrointestinal disorders, and challenging
        behaviour, 164
Goffman, Irvine, 198
Goldwater, Michael, 130
Gordon, H, 77
Gournay, K, 199
Green, T, 58, 64, 66–8
Grimley, S, 201
Guidance for Restrictive Physical Interventions
        (DfES/DoH, 2002), 29, 120

Hadwin, Samuel, 196
haloperidol, 100, 103, 104, 105, 106
Halstead, S, 114
Hannah, A L, 104
Harris, J, 85–6
Hartford Courant newspaper, 204, 205
health, and challenging behaviour, 163
    allergies, 164
    dysmenorrhoea, 164
    epilepsy, 165
    gastrointestinal disorders, 164
    mental illness, 165–6

otitis media, 165
    pre-menstrual syndrome, 164
    sleep, 163
Health and Safety Executive, 200
Healthcare Commission National Audit of
    Violence (2007), and seclusion, 114, 115
Heider, F, 198
Hodgkins, Geoffrey, 131
Holland, Kurt, 130
Horner, R H, 158, 206
Hucksthorn, K, 205
Human Rights Act (1998), 120, 195

Imposed Mechanical Restraint Inventory (IMRI),
    83–4
injuries
    and control and restraint system, 197
    and family carers, 56–7, 62–3
    and training courses, 6
Irvine, P, 131
Iwata, B A, 157

Jackson, Janice, 130
Jones, R S, 176
Jordan, Andrew, 131
Juster Purchase Probability Scale, and risk
    assessment tool, 39

Kazdin, A E, 148
Kennedy, C H, 164
Kennedy, H G, 134
Kuhn, Thomas, 196

Lancioni, G E, 182–3
Langthorne, P, 166
Latham, Freda, 77, 129, 131
La Vigna, G W, 155, 171–2
Laws, J, 173
Learning Disability Award Framework (LDAF),
    96
Lindsay, W R, 173, 184
lorazepam, 100, 103, 104, 106
Lovegrove, Derek, 131, 133
Lovell, Michael, 130
low arousal approaches, 158
Lowe, K, 56
Lyon, C M, 118, 119

McDonnell, A, 68, 197
McGill, P, 62, 162
McIntyre Under Cover (tv programme), 204
Makaton, 175, 180
manding, and functional communication training
    (FCT), 178, 179, 180
Mannion, L, 103
Marsh, Bryan, 128, 129
Martin, Michael, 128, 129
Martin, Shaun, 129, 132
Mason, T, 114, 118
Masters, K, 122

mechanical restraint
    and application of: good practice guidelines, 86–8;
        good vs bad practice, 82
    and definition of, 79–83
    and inappropriate use of, 77–8
    as last resort, 77
    and measurement of restrictiveness, 83–4
    and monitoring of, 88–9
    and need for debate on use of, 88–9
    and prevalence of, 84–5
    and reliance on, 77
    and restraint-related deaths, 77, 131–2
    and self-injurious behaviour (SIB), 77
    and side-effects of, 85–6
media, and social policy change, 204
medication, and management of imminent
    violence, 95–6
    and administration of, 96–8; consent, 96;
        dosage, 97; method, 97, 105–6; procedure,
        97; record keeping, 97; right medication, 96;
        timing, 97
    and advantages of, 106–7
    and as-required medication, 95–6, 98–9
    and good practice guidelines, 95
    and need for clear policy on, 105, 107
    as part of care plan, 105, 107
    and rapid tranquilisation, 95; evidence base for
        effectiveness of, 103–5; follow-up and review,
        102; guidelines for use of, 99–100; means of
        administration, 105–6; medications for,
        100–1; protocol for administration, 101;
        protocol for monitoring, 102; training
        requirements, 102–3
Medline, 7
Meehan, T, 122
Mencken, H L, 133
Mental Capacity Act, 88
    Deprivation of Liberty Safeguards, 120–1
Mental Health Act, and seclusion, 112, 119–20
Mental Health Act Commission
    and exclusionary practices, 111
    and mechanical restraint, 88–9
Mental Health Foundation, 55, 58
mental illness, and challenging behaviour,
    165–6
Mental Welfare Commission for Scotland
    (MWCS), and mechanical restraint, 80
methylphenidate, 166
Meyer, K A, 164
midazolam, 103, 105
Miles, S H, 131
Millfield Charter, 195
Miltenberger, R G, 160–2
Mirenda, P, 179
Mohr, B D, 134, 201
Mohr, W K, 134
Morrison, A, 131
Morris, P, 201
Murphy, G, 78, 84, 85
Myatt, Gareth, 132, 133, 195

and organisational case study in training, 149–51
and outcomes of, 148–9
and potential applications of, 147
and proactive strategies, 171
and reactive and proactive strategies, 155
and skills teaching, 159
and social validity, 148, 149
and toolkit of, 147–8
positive programming
and barriers to, 185; external variables, 186; overcoming, 186–7; service user variables, 185–6
and coping skills, 172
and definition of, 171–2
and functional assessment, 174; ability to engage in treatment, 177; aims of, 174; assessing internal processes, 176; case study, 'Josephine', 175; case study, 'Loui', 176; communication skills, 174; coping skills, 175; intellectual skills, 174; measures of anger and aggression, 177–8; motivation for treatment, 177; nature of anger problem, 177; role of, 175
and functional communication training (FCT), 178; approach of, 179; case study, 'Josephine', 180; effectiveness of, 179; limitations of, 180
and functionally equivalent skills, 172, 178
and functionally related skills, 172, 181
and general skill development, 172
and reducing/eliminating challenging behaviours, 172–3
and rule-governed behaviours, 181
and social skills, 181
and theoretical basis of, 173–4
and underpinning principle of, 187
pre-menstrual syndrome (PMS), and challenging behaviour, 164
preventing challenging behaviour, 152
and neglect of, 144
and positive behavioural support (PBS), 146–9; characteristics of, 146–7; development of, 146; organisational case study in training, 149–51; outcomes, 148–9; potential applications of, 147; social validity, 148, 149; toolkit of, 147–8
and systemic approaches to, 144–6; macro-organisational factors, 145; micro-organisational factors, 145–6; socio-cultural factors, 145
primary prevention strategies, and positive behavioural support (PBS), 171
problem-solving, and cognitive behavioural therapy, 182, 183
procyclidine, 101
professional development, and British Institute of Learning Disabilities, 32
Profile of Anger Coping Skills (PACS), 178
promethazine, 103

prone restraint holds, 20
and anxiety over, 128
and restraint-related deaths, 132–3
and restrictions on use of, 136
and service users views of, 50
Provocation Inventory (PI), 177
psychotropic drugs, and behavioural toxicity, 166
punishment
and criticism of use of, 158
and physical restraint, 5

Qureshi, H, 56, 57, 58–9

Rangecroft, M E, 114
rapid tranquilisation, 95
and advantages of, 106–7
and evidence base for effectiveness of, 103–5
and follow-up and review, 102
and guidelines for use of, 99–100
and means of administration, 105–6
and medications for, 100–1
and protocol for administration (NICE, 2005), 101
and protocol for monitoring (NICE, 2005), 102
and training requirements, 102–3
reactive behaviour management
and family carers, 58–60
and role of, 155
real-time training, 5
recovery position, and restraint-related deaths, 133
reinforcement
and challenging behaviour, 156
and consequence-based interventions, 157–8
and environmental enrichment, 162–3
and non-contingent reinforcement, 159–60; skills teaching, 159–60
Reiss, S, 165
relaxation, and cognitive behavioural therapy, 182, 183–4
restraint reduction
and Colton Audit Tool, 206–8; communication, 208; consumer involvement, 208; environmental factors, 207; leadership, 206; orientation and training, 207; post-incident debriefing, 207; programmatic structure, 207; staffing, 207; treatment planning, 207
and feasibility of, 209
and future direction of, 208
and motivation for, 193, 209
and organisational resistance to, 206
and strategies for, 202–6; three-level approach, 204
and systems evaluation, 208
and United States, 204, 205–6
Richdale, A L, 179
risk assessment tool, 40–3
and assessment of, 50–2
and assessment of techniques: by panel members, 45–6; by service users, 48–50; web-based study, 47–8

and family carers, 60; barriers to access to, 60–2; delivering training to, 65–9; reasons for providing, 62–5
and impact of, 65
and myth of improved safety, 199–200
and *Physical Interventions – A Policy Framework*, 27–8
and positive behavioural support (PBS), 149–51
and rapid tranquilisation, 102–3
see also training effectiveness
training effectiveness, 3, 35–6
and avoidance of training, 5
and confidence, 18
and context of teaching, 5
and deaths, 6
and establishing operations, 5
and evaluation, 20–1; data collection, 17; inadequacy of, 37; problems with, 17; requirements for, 17
and feedback, 4, 5
and generalisation of skills, 4, 19
and injuries, 6
and literature review, 7; content of training courses, 13–17; method, 7; outcomes of training, 7–13
and organisational factors, 5, 19–20
and pre- and post-training staff observation, 19
and research limitations, 20
and skill use and retention, 18
and social validity, 18
and staff behaviour, 3–4, 5
and study design, 19

and training environment, 19
Tumeinski, M, 194
Turnbull, A P, 56
turnover (staff), and training effectiveness, 5

United Nations Committee on the Rights of the Child, 194
United States
and restraint reduction, 204, 205–6
and use of time out, 116–18

Vollmer, T R, 162
Vygotsky, L S, 182

Ward Anger Ratings Scale, 178
Wardhaugh, J, 203
Welsh Assembly, 204
and physical intervention, 80
Wilding, P, 203
Williams, Gary John, 131
Willis, T, 155, 171–2
Willner, P, 177, 185
Wink News, 116
Wolkowitz, O M, 103
World Health Organisation, 200
Wray, J, 58, 64, 66–8

Youth Justice Board for England and Wales (YJB), 38, 47, 195

zuclopenthixol acetate, 100, 103